Universities in Crisis

Also Available from Bloomsbury

Academics' International Teaching Journeys,
edited by Anesa Hosein, Namrata Rao, Chloe Shu-Hua Yeh and Ian M. Kinchin
Early Career Teachers in Higher Education,
edited by Jody Crutchley, Zaki Nahaboo and Namrata Rao
Class, Race, Disability and Mental Health in Higher Education, *Mike Seal*
Utopian Universities, *edited by Miles Taylor and Jill Pellew*
Changing Higher Education for a Changing World,
edited by Claire Callender, William Locke and Simon Marginson
Dominant Discourses in Higher Education,
Ian M. Kinchin and Karen Gravett
Pursuing Teaching Excellence in Higher Education,
Margaret Wood and Feng Su
Locating Social Justice in Higher Education Research,
edited by Jan McArthur and Paul Ashwin
Subjectivity and Social Change in Higher Education,
Liezl Dick and Marguerite Müller
Decolonizing University Teaching and Learning, *D. Tran*
Social Theory and the Politics of Higher Education,
edited by Mark Murphy, Ciaran Burke, Cristina Costa and Rille Raaper

Universities in Crisis

Academic Professionalism in Uncertain Times

Edited by
Eric Lybeck and Catherine O'Connell

BLOOMSBURY ACADEMIC
LONDON · NEW YORK · OXFORD · NEW DELHI · SYDNEY

BLOOMSBURY ACADEMIC
Bloomsbury Publishing Plc
50 Bedford Square, London, WC1B 3DP, UK
1385 Broadway, New York, NY 10018, USA
29 Earlsfort Terrace, Dublin 2, Ireland

BLOOMSBURY, BLOOMSBURY ACADEMIC and the Diana logo are
trademarks of Bloomsbury Publishing Plc

First published in Great Britain 2023
Paperback edition published 2024

Copyright © Eric Lybeck and Catherine O'Connell and contributors, 2023

Eric Lybeck and Catherine O'Connell and contributors have asserted their right under the
Copyright, Designs and Patents Act, 1988, to be identified as Author of this work.

For legal purposes the Acknowledgements on pp. xi–xii constitute an
extension of this copyright page.

Cover design: Grace Ridge
Cover image © Piranka / Getty Images

All rights reserved. No part of this publication may be reproduced or
transmitted in any form or by any means, electronic or mechanical, including
photocopying, recording, or any information storage or retrieval system,
without prior permission in writing from the publishers.

Bloomsbury Publishing Plc does not have any control over, or responsibility for, any
third-party websites referred to or in this book. All internet addresses given in this
book were correct at the time of going to press. The author and publisher regret
any inconvenience caused if addresses have changed or sites have ceased
to exist, but can accept no responsibility for any such changes.

A catalogue record for this book is available from the British Library.

A catalog record for this book is available from the Library of Congress.

ISBN:	HB:	978-1-3502-4998-1
	PB:	978-1-3502-4999-8
	ePDF:	978-1-3502-5000-0
	eBook:	978-1-3502-5001-7

Typeset by Integra Software Services Pvt. Ltd.

To find out more about our authors and books visit www.bloomsbury.com
and sign up for our newsletters.

Contents

List of Figure vi
List of Tables vii
List of Contributors viii
Acknowledgements xi
List of Abbreviations xiii

1 Academics, Professionals and the University: Pathologies and Possibilities *Eric Lybeck and Catherine O'Connell* 1
2 The Very Idea of Academic Professionalism: At an End or Beginning Anew with an Eco-professionalism? *Ronald Barnett* 23
3 Selling Academe's Soul to the Devil? Performativity, Pressured Professionalism and the Rationalisation of Knowledge Production *Linda Evans* 41
4 Luck and Precarity: Contextualising Fixed-term Academics' Perceptions of Success and Failure *Vik Loveday* 73
5 Academic Professionalism in the Measured University *Cathal Ó Siochrú, Roland Bloch, Catherine O'Connell and Jakob Hartl* 93
6 International Student Recruitment: Policy, Paradox and Practice *Sylvie Lomer* 117
7 University Management as Court Society: A Processual Analysis of the Rise of University Management *Eric Lybeck* 141
8 Re-imagining the Place of Professional Education in the University *Vivienne Baumfield* 157
9 The Power and Beauty of the Disciplinary Infrastructure of Our Culture *Julian Williams* 177
10 Epilogue: The New Class (Room) Struggle in the Neoliberal University *John Holmwood* 195

Index 206

Figure

9.1 How metacognitive reflection has a role in each of the levels
(from Williams and Roth, 2019: 31)   184

Tables

1.1 Two different forms of professionalism in knowledge work in Evetts, J. (2013) Professionalism: Value and ideology. *Current Sociology*, 61 (5–6): 778–96   10
6.1 Hypothetical example of a student's offers. Author's compilation   131

Contributors

Ronald Barnett is Emeritus Professor of Higher Education at University College London Institute of Education, UK, where he was a Dean and a Pro-Director. He was Chair of the Society for Research into Higher Education, was awarded the inaugural prize by the European Association for Educational Research for his 'outstanding contribution to Higher Education Research, Policy and Practice' and is President of the Philosophy and Theory of Higher Education Society. He has published 35+ books and hundreds of papers, and has given 150 keynote talks. He has been cited over 25,000 times and described as 'the master scholar of the university'.

Vivienne Baumfield is Professor of Professional Learning in the Graduate School of Education and co-leader of the Centre for Research in Professional Learning at the University of Exeter, UK. She is interested in the interaction of research, policy and practice when university-based researchers work with practitioners in the creation and translation of knowledge across contexts. This interest is linked to the wider issue of understanding the relationship between theory and practice in professional learning and is grounded in a perspective derived from pragmatism. Her teaching and research examine international perspectives on the professional development of teachers and the impact of school-university partnerships as communities of pedagogical inquiry.

Roland Bloch is Post-doctoral Researcher at the Center for School and Educational Research at Martin-Luther-University Halle-Wittenberg, Germany and board member of the German Society for Higher Education Research (GfHf). In his dissertation, he has analysed the Bologna reforms' effects on student practice. Lately, he has co-edited a volume on Universities and the Production of Elites. His current research focuses on the organizational transformation of universities in teaching, doctoral education and academic careers, as well as emerging stratifications in higher education.

Linda Evans is Professor of Education at the University of Manchester, UK, where she currently holds the role of the Faculty of Humanities' associate dean for academic and research staff development. She has previously worked at the Universities of Warwick and Leeds, and before becoming an academic was a primary school teacher. Broadly focused on working life in education contexts, her research incorporates foci on leadership, professional learning and development, professionalism, researcher development and research leadership. Located within the 'new wave' of critical leadership studies, her recent provocative work questions whether leadership is a myth that we have reified.

Jakob Hartl is a Research Fellow at the Research Institute Social Cohesion (FGZ-RISC) at Martin-Luther-University Halle-Wittenberg, Germany. His recent research into higher education covered the question of social stratification among further education students and students in HE in general, as well as academic career paths and the third mission of HE institutions. Besides HE research, he focuses on social inequality and cohesion, political sociology and collective memory studies.

John Holmwood is Emeritus Professor of Sociology at the University of Nottingham, UK, and Senior Researcher in the Centre for Science Technology and Society Studies at the Institute for Philosophy of the Czech Academy of Science, Czech Republic. He was co-founder of the *Campaign for the Public University*, editor of *A Manifesto for the Public University* (Bloomsbury 2011) and co-author (with Therese O'Toole) of *Countering Extremism in British Schools: The Truth about the Birmingham Trojan Horse Affair* (2018) and (with Gurminder K Bhambra) *Colonialism and Modern Social Theory* (2020).

Sylvie Lomer is Senior Lecturer in Policy and Practice at the University of Manchester, UK, where her research expertise focuses on international higher education. Her first book, *Recruiting International Students in Higher Education*, critically examined UK policy on international students. Follow-up work on blended learning pedagogies led to multiple funded projects on how deficit narratives of international students shape pedagogic practices through institutional internationalization/global engagement policy enactment. As a critical scholar of policy and practice, she is primarily a qualitative researcher, building leading expertise in documentary analysis. She teaches on the PG Certificate in Higher Education, the MA International Education, and the PhD student training programme.

Vik Loveday is Senior Lecturer in the Department of Sociology at Goldsmiths, University of London, UK, whose work is concerned with the analysis of contemporary UK universities, including issues related to governance, precarity and inequalities. Aside from work on Higher Education, Vik is also interested in cultural memory and identity, and is currently conducting research on perceptions of public art and architecture in 'post-communist' contexts.

Eric Lybeck is Presidential Fellow at the University of Manchester, UK, working in the interdisciplinary field of 'University Studies'. His research and practice draw on processual and civic approaches to social knowledge to make new connections between the disciplines of sociology, history and education. Lybeck's doctoral research at Cambridge explored the history of the social and legal sciences during the late nineteenth-century transfer of university models from Germany to America. He has since published two books related to the long-term development of higher education: *The University Revolution: Outline of a Processual Theory of Modern Higher Education* (2021) and *Nobert Elias and the Sociology of Education* (2019).

Catherine O'Connell was Senior Lecturer in Education at Liverpool Hope University, UK. She co-directed the Centre for Education and Policy Analysis (2014–21) with a focus on researcher development and the promotion of inclusive research practices. Her research explores counter-narratives which respond to dominant discourses associated with rankings and metrics. Current research examines issues and tensions associated with the fuller articulation of the social mission of universities and considers the conceptual tools and social practices that assist in enacting this mission. She now works on a freelance basis on academic projects and as a solution-focused therapist.

Cathal Ó Siochrú is Senior Lecturer in Education Studies at Liverpool Hope University, UK. He has helped to develop and teach courses which integrate Psychology into the study of education. His research area is the psychology of education and he specializes in the impact of student beliefs and perceptions on their studies. Other research interests include Personal Epistemological and Pedagogical beliefs, Action Research, Assessment Practices and Feedback and Collaborative learning. He is editor and co-author of the book *Psychology and the Study of Education: Critical Perspectives on Developing Theories*.

Julian Williams is Professor of Mathematics Education at the University of Manchester, UK, and has led the Critical Pedagogies (and Mathematics Education) research group for many years. He also convenes the Green Research in Education Group since it was founded three years ago.

Acknowledgements

A version of Chapter 4 was originally published by the author in the *British Journal of Sociology* as 'Luck, chance and happenstance? Perceptions of success and failure amongst fixed-terms academic staff in UK Higher Education', vol 69, Issue 3, pp. 758–75, 2018 and is published here with permission from Wiley. © London School of Economics and Political Science 2017 ISSN 0007-1315 print/1468-4446 online. Published by John Wiley & Sons Ltd, 9600 Garsington Road, Oxford OX4 2DQ, UK and 101 Station Landing, Suite 300, Medford, MA 02155, USA on behalf of the LSE. DOI: 10.1111/1468-4446.12307.

A version of Chapter 7 was originally published by the author in *Social Theory and the Politics of Higher Education: Critical Perspectives on Institutional Research*, M Murphy, C Burke, C Costa and R Raaper (eds) 2021 and is published here with permission from Bloomsbury Academic an imprint of Bloomsbury Publishing Plc.

The origins of this volume were two unintentionally almost concurrent conferences held by the co-editors in Manchester and Liverpool in April 2019.

Eric would accordingly like to thank the University of Manchester and the Leverhulme Trust for funding the event 'Academic, Professionals and Publics: Changes in the Ecologies of Knowledge Work'. Thanks also to presenters and audience members for incisive thinking on the day, before and since, including Andrew Abbott, Stuart Jones, Helen Carasso, Aaron Hanlon and more. Eric is further grateful to his family as we have moved four times since then and have also grown in size by one – so, I would especially like to thank and welcome Cecilia who so kindly shared her Merseyside strolls with me during her first six months when we were otherwise in full lockdown. My memory of these were of constant sunshine. Much of the thinking in this book took place over this period, though any errors or omission are surely not hers, but mine alone. I should also acknowledge how rewarding it has been to work with Catherine who has kept this project going and growing from day 1.

Catherine would like to thank Liverpool Hope University's Centre for Education and Policy Analysis for funding the 'Pathologies of Professionalism' Colloquium which provided an impetus for the book. By happenstance, in the same month, Eric Lybeck convened a conference sharing similar concerns and aspirations and we developed fruitful collaboration in hosting the two events and in producing this subsequent publication. It has been a pleasure working with Eric. I appreciate his warmth, humour and intellect and it was lovely to meet his family along the way. Thanks to the contributors for the collegial approach to shaping the book. Thanks to my family, as always, for their unwavering love and support.

Abbreviations

BERA	British Education Research Association
CARA	Council for at Risk Academics
DfE	Department for Education
EAP	English for Academic Purposes
EPD	Early Professional Development
EPEE	Empowering Partnerships: Enabling Engagement
GTCNI	General Teaching Council Northern Ireland
HE	Higher Education
HEI	Higher Education Institution
HEA	Higher Education Academy
HESA	Higher Education Statistics Agency
ITE	Initial Teacher Education
ITT	Initial Teacher Training
KEF	Knowledge Exchange Framework
KPI	Key Performance Indicators
PGCE	Postgraduate Certificate in Education
PGDE	Postgraduate Diploma in Education
PGT	Postgraduate Taught
PVC	Pro-Vice-Chancellor
QTS	Qualified Teacher Status
RAE	Research Assessment Exercise

REF	Research Excellence Framework
RSA	Royal Society for the Encouragement of Arts, Manufacture and Commerce
SG	Social Generativity
SGA	Socially Generative Action
STEMM	Science, Technology, Engineering, Mathematics and Medicine
SUPI	School University Partnership Initiative
TEF	Teaching Excellence Framework
TLRP	Teaching and Learning Research Programme
UCET	Universities' Council for the Education of Teachers
UCU	University College Union
USS	Universities Superannuation Scheme
UUK	Universities UK

Academics, Professionals and the University: Pathologies and Possibilities

Eric Lybeck and Catherine O'Connell

Introduction

To say 'universities are in crisis' is akin to observing the 'sky is blue'. The rhetoric of 'crisis' seems to follow higher education throughout its 800+ years of history like a lost puppy. Can one really describe an event as a 'crisis' if it exhibits this level of permanence? Is an institution whose 'normal' condition is 'crisis' not contradictory at best and hyperbolic at worst?

Of course, the etymological roots of 'crisis' are the same as 'critical' (Law, 2014) – so, perhaps we need to remain vigilant in determining what *specifically* is in crisis today, which might be different from yesterday and tomorrow. Furthermore, insofar as we are entering a new phase of a truly unprecedented expansion of credentials – a 200+ year 'university revolution' akin to the industrial and democratic revolutions (Lybeck, 2021) – we might not be hyperbolic in observing the very real cumulate, compounding and growing problems surrounding higher education. Without focusing on those critical elements of universities that are the outcomes, causes and preconditions for a wide range of internal and external social problems, we surely stand little chance of overcoming these.

But, this book is not another addition to that familiar genre of anti-'neoliberal' critiques that tread and re-tread the same observations without seeming to have any impact on the direction of travel. Indeed, our aim here is to move beyond mere criticism – towards a post-critical – and reconstructive engagement with academia as a profession. In this regard, while we are attentive to the external forces constraining higher education today, we see the future as largely still within the hands of those academics, professionals, students and stakeholders.

Collectively, we must recover our latent powers to turn away from permanent crisis, towards something resembling a sensible, sustainable and healthy arrangement of things.

We have experienced significant and intensifying challenges in the higher education environment, with sector expansion, public funding reduction, alternative forms of provision and new forms of accountability making new demands on academia (Holmwood, 2011). Nixon (2003) deploys the metaphor of the 'runaway world' to depict multiple crises in wider society which are impacting upon the sector: fiscal crises, fragmented civil society, relentless globalization, institutionalized individualism. A prevalent market logic which emphasizes the extrinsic value of higher education to consumers more than intrinsic value to society translates to increased precarity of employment and commodification of knowledge production. The 'real' economy becomes a growing factor in redefining the academic role, in fostering a climate of heightened scrutiny, decreased cohesion and worsening employee relations. These shaping forces constrain the capacity of universities to reach out to wider communities and, as with other professional domains, the paradoxical effects of enhanced public scrutiny and declining public trust are much in evidence (Fitzpatrick, 2019; O'Neill, 2002).

Academic dissatisfaction intensifies in response to the cumulative and emergent effects of these global trends (Kuznetsova and Kuznetsov, 2020). Amidst a bottleneck in PhD production, faith in the traditional academic career is in decline and there is an increasing disparity between external, codified career 'scripts' and the lived experience of professional life in academia (Whitchurch et al, 2021). Within this wider context academics are adjusting their expectations of, and approaches to, careers in HE (Marini et al, 2019). This book is intended as a source of orientation for those of us trying to navigate this increasingly complex and chaotic institutional context.

Analyses of the worsening conditions of higher education continue to proliferate in the higher education (HE) research literature, much of which is directed towards and acknowledged by policymakers as an agonized complaint from the academic workforce (Willets, 2017). For many isolated and confused academics, both young and old, male, female and non-binary, BAME and majority ethnic, veteran and early career, there comes a point at which we as individuals ask: why our institutions are organized around such irrational bases? However, by interpreting, analysing and reassessing the transformations of higher education in recent decades using the lens of professionalism we can begin to uncover our own agencies within these processes. We can not only explore those points where we submit to irrationalities, but those places where we directly reproduce and sustain them. Our analysis centres on how the academic profession sees itself and is seen by others and addresses the central question of what kind of academic professionalism can survive current conditions of change and precarity.

Changing Jurisdictions

Universities do not hold a pre-ordained position in the landscape of knowledge production. Historically they have been buffeted by competing jurisdictional claims on the legitimacy of their role in research and dissemination (Abbott, 1988, 2005; Lybeck, 2019). Perhaps, the current priority of place the academic profession has in today's landscape of higher learning is a temporary one (even if it has lasted a few hundred years). This central and unique position of academia within the wider system of professions is nonetheless highly contingent and held in relative stability through a balance of social tensions, jurisdiction, functions and authorities. We can observe the changing roles and functions around us as new jurisdictional claims are made on different facets of academic work, including new professional and semi-professional roles for a range of experts engaged in work related to universities, but not necessarily as 'academics' as such. The most obvious are the administrators and professional services personnel managing ever-more complex structures related to 'student experience', admissions, estates, information technology and so forth. This also includes the 'wonks', consultants, policy advisors and upper management developing 'strategy', 'process' and 'change' without either necessarily relying on new academic research (despite often having been academics in unrelated fields) or indeed conforming to regulated training typical of professions. Many of these figures rely on relatively thin business studies notions that seem to percolate and diffuse through the institution and sector without any particular centre or origin. In one sense, these technocratic buzzwords are distillations of a Foucauldian discourse of power, engulfing academic authority in the wake and riptide of 'managerial blah' (Moran, 2021; Morrish and Sauntson, 2019). On the other hand, the de-professionalization of higher education after decades of policy, discourse and audit creep has produced a condition of 'ajurisdiction' (Lybeck, 2019) – a vacuum where once stood the jurisdiction of academics in the past – a vacuum quickly filled by 'wonks', EdTech 'solutions' and permanent revolutions of 'change' from above via spreadsheet and strategic planning.

For one definition of universities began with the idea of universities as a *guild* – a professional association that has self-organized itself for hundreds of years in order to preserve the quality of degrees. Similar associations were established by students for similar purposes to ensure that knowledge was not simply an arbitrary matter of that which conformed with immediate secular powers, ideological whims or instrumental efficiency. Universities only make sense in a context wherein knowledge is recognized to be 'hard' – difficult to master, accumulate, organize and extend. In the modern era, beginning in Germany, the basis of university learning began to shift from religious purposes to more industrial and 'modern' ends – particularly the training of a rapidly expanding state civil service, and then a corporate managerial class in the United States and beyond. As Wellmon (2015) explains, the differentiation of knowledge and academic disciplines was a means of 'organizing enlightenment' by training graduates as bearers of deep and specialized expertise that would be collectively gathered at the level of the university as a whole.

In both the religious and more modern understanding of the university as a corporation of members, fellow, graduates, alumni, we can observe that the profession of academics was central if not, indeed, constitutive of the university as such. To borrow a slogan that emerged during the 2018 USS strike in Britain – quite literally: 'We are the University'. Universities are communities and corporations of people. It is only due to a sustained misrecognition that we think universities consist merely of places, buildings, logos, governing boards and managers. The corporate form is an emergent public trust to manage the relation between academics and students – with academics being professionally responsible for the management, extension and reproduction of advanced knowledge, including specialized knowledges within their respective fields (largely contained within the philosophical faculties of arts and sciences) as well as other differentiated professional and vocational courses, including Medicine, Law, Business, Theology, Accounting and so forth.

Obviously, such work requires resources and the university corporation has historically drawn on many external sources of income, including student fees, church and state moneys, philanthropy and so on – resulting in increasing levels of interpenetration with the outside world. As Neil Smelser (2013) argued, this expansion of functions resulted in a form of 'structural accretion' – more and more sub-structures and roles grew, resulting in more complexity, resulting in further needs for more and more administration and organization. This has produced a devil's bargain of a kind: while the origins of this system remain in supporting the work of students and academics to engage in higher learning, the complexity and proliferation of functions have elevated the role of particular kinds of knowledge – that is, particular kinds of professionals in the organization of universities.

Most substantially we can see the increase of certain forms of business and management penetrating the way universities are run. While we would not wish to discount the wide variety of useful knowledge business schools can and have produced – particularly in the fields of critical management studies, sustainability, complexity, innovation science and other forms of rigorous scholarship – we would suggest that the particular, often dated and discredited, forms of managerial science that have penetrated universities are quite literally ruining them.

In the field of university studies, this is not a particularly new argument. But, in the context of universities – complex and cutting edge, engaged in a plethora of activities that, when truly innovative and fulfilling of their stated purpose to advanced and sustain knowledge – is it not a bit absurd to think we or anyone can get a strategic overview of such activity and, in turn, to be able to 'steer' such activity without dramatically altering and distorting the 'business' of higher learning as such?

Using Andrew Abbott's terminology we can observe the changes in 'jurisdiction' within the university (Abbott, 1988; Lybeck, 2019). Whereas the 'university revolution' of the early nineteenth century involved a transfer of the responsibility for conserving knowledge from the priestly class and Theological discipline towards more 'modern' fields of study in Arts, Sciences and Social Sciences – i.e. the modern 'academic' profession as such – we can observe the past fifty or more years as a similarly slow jurisdictional takeover by those Kant called the 'Geschaftsleute' – or businessmen, whose embeddedness is worldly affairs makes them constitutionally unable to contribute positively to the professional work of academics. Ironically, these business graduates are products of the very institution they now colonize and transform in their own image. And, more tragically, the particular forms human resource management, diversity, inclusion and harassment, industrial relations, innovation and even accounting systems are wildly out of date.

While Google, Facebook and related technology companies we are expected to emulate build their schedules and campuses around dining together and playing ping pong during regular relaxation periods, academia is submitted to unrealistic 'Workload Allocation Models' and performance management metrics. Those who complain about sexual harassment or workloads leading to epidemic levels of mental health strains and burnout are subjected to intimidation and weaponized, Orwellian applications of 'dignity and respect' policies. Managerial cliques cordon themselves off from criticism, while creating arbitrary additional layers of management and 'accountability' between themselves and actual academic labour. Actual contact for students and staff via ground-level administration – secretarial support – which historically sustained (often uncredited) the professional labour of professors, journals and communities – is replaced with part-time para-administrators with no opportunity to gain tacit knowledges or participate in collegiality with colleagues and students. Common rooms have been replaced with Costas and Starbucks designed to extract money from employees who are encouraged to work in transparent and surveilled open-offices.

Indeed, as the authority centre of the university shifts from academics to professionals and managers, we see increasing investment in airy buildings and high-tech, but unventilated and reverberant rooms. Debts and refinancing, salary and pension cuts are sent to the sacrificial altar to ensure these loans and capital plans are sufficiently 'prudent'. We see the very architecture of the university comes to reflect the hollowing out of our professional authority. Just as we have been made into anonymous, auditable subjects for REF returns, so too are we made into walking talking embodiments of the photoshopped, smiling persons architects have added to their renderings of transparent glass buildings full of hot, yet apparently eco-friendly, air.

The Academic Profession?

We set out our interventions by treating the academic profession *as a profession*, with all the positive and negative connotations implied. For professions are – at root – public, civic communities and ethically responsible to society. Recall, we have historically been responsible for retaining and sustaining the quality of knowledge (via students' degrees). Can we legitimately defend the current arrangements as the best we can provide graduates and, by extension, all those organizations these schooled individuals inhabit? Or do we have a responsibility to criticize, then reconstruct those aspects of knowledge we find pathological? This includes of course the pathologies of professionalism and disciplinarity itself. Far too often academic professionals claim undue status and exhibit elitist, exclusionary absences of humility. Disciplines become what Norbert Elias called 'scientific establishments' with only tenuous relationships to reality as such. Professional protection is also regularly wielded to protect bad behaviour to intimidate and exclude. Our obsessions with niche specialized topics can result in navel-gazing and disengagement with the public. And so on. We would not suggest retention of these pathological qualities, but neither do we feel rejection of the category of 'professional' useful – not least within the context of jurisdictional takeovers by registrars, wonks and other professionals. Rather, we would encourage a reconstruction of what it means to be an academic in the twenty-first century.

There is ongoing debate on whether academia can be seen as a single profession as the conditions of academic labour become more fragmented (Kogan et al, 1994, Locke et al, 2016; Marini et al, 2019). Empirically, the academic role is more diverse and differentiated as an occupational group: with more than 50 per cent on teaching-only contracts, and increasing contractual precarity in the UK context, for example (Marini et al, 2019; Locke and Bennion, 2011; Locke et al, 2016). In a context of increased atomization of academic work, through unbundling and blending of academic roles (Kogan et al, 1994; Whitchurch, 2015) it may be appropriate to consider academia as a plurality of profession(s). Furthermore, to associate the term 'profession' with the academic role is anathema in some quarters, on conceptual, empirical and normative grounds. The academic role is seen not so much occupational category as valued self-identity (Billott, 2003; Stronach et al, 2002; Winter and O'Donohue, 2012) and the rhetorical and managerial connotations of the term can be seen as undesirable. Empirical studies show 'professional' to be an intrinsically ambivalent term associated with tendency towards closure and inward-looking self-interest (Evetts, 2013; Noordegraaf, 2007).

We propose it is fruitful to refer to the 'academic profession' for a number of reasons. Universities are key sites of professional education and therefore implicated in processes of professional formation. As discussed in subsequent chapters, the contexts, conditions and trajectories of professionalization vary within different disciplines. As with other professions, academic role(s) are subject to increasing accountability in form of metrics; multiple jurisdictions of measurement and shifts from professional to performative modes of accountability can have the perverse effect of eroding public confidence (O'Neill, 2002; Ranson, 2003). As noted, we are the university, and in reconstructing and empowering ourselves we do a considerable service to those knowledges and communities we care about and for – including, of course, students – but not exclusively those lucky enough to pay. Both to survive and to restore itself academia must become a fully public profession – engaged with and embedded in a much wider field of activity, locally, nationally and globally. We must re-imagine and reorganize our universities to accomplish these aims. And we must do this together with our neighbours, partners and those who have been historically excluded from what has been affirmed as valid 'knowledge'.

What are the possibilities for our profession in the twenty-first century and beyond? As we allow our profession to be influenced by narrow, limited and dated conceptions of academic practice and professional ethics what are we allowing to be done not simply to ourselves as knowledge workers, but to knowledge as such? Throughout the book we argue that academia can be seen as a profession in an inclusive sense. In the next section we consider whether academia can be seen as an occupational or organizational profession – a pivotal question which helps to clarify how the profession sees itself and to determine the direction of travel. We focus on contemporary debates surrounding the term 'professionalism' as a fruitful way of considering the dynamics of the profession, the trajectories of development and foregrounding important normative matters.

Trends and Counter-trends of Professionalization

Traditionally, the state has defined the locus of control and jurisdiction of professions. Through a framework of authority predicated on hierarchical control, universities were granted autonomy and legitimacy and controlled through standards and regulation (Whitley, 2011). Historically, through state-granted powers, academic institutions (as with other professions) controlled from 'within' through delegated authority (Evetts, 2013). Since the late twentieth century the growth of non-hierarchical practices of political coordination is attributed to a more globally networked economy and a pervasive ethos of new public management, which is characterized as a shift from 'government' to 'governance' (Gläser, 2010; Rizvi and Lingard, 2010). In many contemporary national contexts, the nexus of power and influence is diffuse, de-centred and applied at multiple levels. Therefore, power and control over professions are exercised at multiple levels and through means and methods of control which are applied at organizational level increasingly (Whitley, 2011).

A heightened state commitment to high-level knowledge production in the interests of business, innovation and international competition is much in evidence within the global knowledge economy (Universities UK, 2018). This commitment is reflected in national workforce strategies focused on upskilling in emerging and in-demand sectors, and prioritizing investment in high-skill and high-value roles (World Economic Forum, 2020). An increasing number of 'graduate professions' are delineated by tertiary educational routes, professional standards frameworks and accountability mechanisms. An enlarged professional cadre is associated with increasing standardization and bureaucratization of professional practices (Noordegraaf, 2007). This trend towards professionalization reflects a confluence of both aspirational discourses and 'successful ideology' (Evetts, 2013) which serves individual interests in status and reward and state concerns to foster commitment and compliance to lifelong learning practices (Fejes, 2010). At the same time, there are counter-forces to the trend towards professionalization. State policies of strengthening vocational educational and training routes and de-regulation of educational provider status, as seen in both the legal and academic professions, create a proliferation of alternative routes to achieve professional recognition and redefine the parameters of the professional community.

The classic professions, representing high-status, high-discretion, self-regulating communities, provide an enduring image and normative framework for the development of new professional niches. There has been a tendency in newly forming professions to mimic classic professions (Evetts, 2013) through occupational 'purification' whereby a profession seeks to close ranks in order to assert professional autonomy (Evetts, 2013; Noordegraaf, 2007). However, the conditions for 'pure professionalism' are eroding and the professional landscape is shaped by social changes, capitalist forces and consumerist orientations that constrain professional autonomy (Noordegraaf, 2007). There has been a widespread shift away from professional self-regulation towards more consumer-driven and marketized methods of control (Ranson, 2003).

Increasingly professionals are located within stronger organizational structures and subject to managerial modes of authority. Different methods of control are applied through organizational and occupational professional frameworks (see Table 1.1), differentiated in terms of control structure, mode of regulation and ethical framework. This can create a form of situated professionalism which reflects the attempt to reconcile organizational and occupational modes of control (Noordegraaf, 2007). Organizational control, where marketized logic prevails, can reflect implicit values of efficiency and effectiveness. In everyday discourses, professionalism is imbued with within inherent value but, as shown empirically, it can be an ambiguous enterprise which is prone to inward looking practices and defensive concerns (Marini et al, 2019). In this sense, professionalization can be seen as a non-normative response to external, market-driven forces to achieve occupational closure (Evetts, 2013). Yet this strategy can create plurality and generate multiple, competing value frameworks (Nixon, 2003).

Table 1.1 Two different forms of professionalism in knowledge work in Evetts, J. (2013) Professionalism: Value and ideology. *Current Sociology*, 61 (5–6): 778–96.

Occupational professionalism	Organizational professionalism
• Discourse constructed within professional groups	• Discourse of control used increasingly by managers in work organizations
• Collegial authority	• Rational-legal forms of authority
• Discretion and occupational control of the work	• Standardized procedures
• Practitioner trust by both clients and employers	• Hierarchical structures of authority and decision-making
• Controls operationalized by practitioners	• Managerialism
• Professional ethics monitored by institutions and associations	• Accountability and externalized forms of regulation, target-setting and performance review
• Located in Durkheim's model of occupations as moral communities	• Linked to Weberian models of organization

A significant strand of the research literature on professionalization explores the changing means and methods of professional control and the new professional groups that are associated with these control techniques (e.g. quality assurance managers). A focus on accountability frameworks can give insight into the professional domain and determine the forms of jurisdiction and extent of control from 'above' and 'within' the professional community (Wallenberg et al, 2019). These wider forces of professionalization and de-professionalization have prevailed on the academic community, and much of the literature can be read as a critique of a shift from occupational to organizational professionalism (see Table 1.1).

Comparative research on the state of the academic profession internationally provides insight on both the factors associated with worsening conditions and those factors which contribute to job satisfaction (Kuznetsova and Kuznetsov, 2020; Locke et al, 2016; Marini et al, 2019; Whitchurch et al, 2021). Empirical studies and institutional surveys highlight the importance of nuanced interpretation of wider policies which take account of institutional mission and values, meaningful engagement in decision-making processes, high-trust institutional relations and scope for individuals to negotiate career plans within institutional career frameworks (Kuznetsova and Kuznetsov, 2020; Locke and Bennion, 2011; Marini et al, 2019; Whitchurch, 2015). The portrayal of pressured professionals within wider literature is well documented within the higher education context (Evans, 2018). The pressure that is produced throughout the

HE system is reflected in contemporary fault lines in employee relations practices. Case analyses of trade union archives illustrate divergent logics and a deepening of camps at institutional level in how to interpret and enact wider policies: 'The aggregate tendency of universities' organizational practices is rooted not in the market pressures directly but in internal structures and procedures that interpret these pressures' (Kuznetsova and Kuznetsov, 2020: 2440).

Collegial and managerial modes of authority are typically juxtaposed and a focus on management-professional interactions tends to form a core interest in the research literature. Debate continues as to whether the concepts of management and collegiality are necessarily in binary opposition. Management, in the university context, can be framed as 'junior-senior' relations given that many are managers are (or have been) academics or occupy blended roles (Marini et al, 2019; Whitchurch, 2015). Several studies find instances of productive co-existence of managerial and collegial practices (Reale and Marini, 2017; Tight, 2014). Close-up empirical studies can demonstrate how organizations, subjected to the same external regulation, can deploy differing responses and, in some cases, reflect a shared, collective endeavour to '*repair outside regulation*' (Wallenburg et al, 2019: 640).

Scholarly attention to processes of professionalization and the concept of situated professionalism largely centres on the means of control rather than the ends. By contrast, the expansive concept of 'hybrid professionalism' can be used to restore a sense of collectivity, solidarity and wider purpose:

> Hybrid professionalism pursues the 'content of control' and relates professional work to changing societal circumstances in a broader sense: it is about controlling the meaning of control, organizing, and professionalism. Professionalism is used not so much to improve organizational contexts but to improve the idea of professionalism in changing organizational contexts.
>
> (Noordegraaf, 2007: 775)

Thus, differing conceptualizations of professionalism invite a fundamental question of whether academic professionalism is about retaining power within the professional community or about sharing it with others for the public good. Deem (2019) articulates the differing management strategies that can be directed towards these distinct goals and advocates a set of more holistic and authentic conceptions of professionalism oriented to the latter objective. Broadly we argue for the latter too: relinquishing some control as a way of maintaining the collective. From this stance, measurement and control methods are about showing professionalism to enact meaningful and legitimate work practices.

Post-critical Perspectives

It is tempting to blame abstract forces like 'neoliberalism', new modes of governance or particular managers and vice chancellors for the contemporary conditions in universities. In many instances, these are as much the outcome of pathological processes and unintended consequences as they are agents with any power or efficacy whatsoever. For some time, sociological analyses of changing conditions of higher education have focused on 'neoliberal governmentality', drawing on the ideas of Michel Foucault or Pierre Bourdieu. It is useful to go beyond these now-familiar analyses which tend to characterize academics as passive subjects, rendered auditable and self-disciplining in their conformity to external scrutiny, or as strategic actors, drawing on and cynically exploiting metrics to validate their professionalism as a form of capital exchangeable across different fields.

Several lines of scholarship advocate shifting the emphasis of research from structure to practices, to avoid a narrow focus on state actors and policies and to reflect the de-centred way in which governance regimes develop at multiple levels. Structural analyses of governance only partially account for varying effects at organizational level and the differing types of institutional work that go into both enacting and resisting external modes of control (Wallenburg et al, 2019). Gunter et al (2013) define distinct forms of policy research which can proceed on shared assumptions of the policy rationale (reflected in functional, 'gap filling' forms of research) or which challenge explicit policy assumptions (reflected in 'critical research' orientations). However, both approaches tend to research within, or in direct response to, the explicit policy. A socially critical position recognizes power as relational and gives more attention to emergent forces and unanticipated effects of policy.

In contemporary contexts of networked 'governance' it is useful to reconceptualize jurisdiction in ways which recognize emergent and unanticipated effects. Gläser (2010: 10) advocates the need to overcome a problem-solving bias in research which overemphasizes the explicit purposes for which a system was built and give more attention to 'resultant forces, synergies between structures and processes seemingly unrelated – more reflective, congruent with multi-level nature of problem'.

A post-critical mode of analysis may or may not require an explicit normative orientation predicated on a particular worldview of power and social order. Deetz (1996) contrasts differing research orientations: consensus research discourses are characterized by a tendency to focus on the relationship between research and existing social orders. Research associated with a dissensus orientation considers 'struggle, conflict and tensions to be the natural state' (1996: 197). The former tends to be theory-driven (macro-sociological) and focused on the forces of social reproduction. The latter view of social relations, more aligned with a post-critical perspective, offers a conception of power as de-centred, diffuse and productive. From this perspective, the problem is not group against group but rather suppression of parts of the human being and the presence of destructive control processes, problems which are located in the micro-practices of the work site itself (1996: 197). As such, a 'post-critical' orientation is oriented to actions that can be taken in the present through empowerment of individuals and communities rather than future emancipation (Hodgson et al, 2018).

Having spent much of the past few decades critiquing the myriad problems and crises plaguing higher education and, indeed, the world at large, post-critical approaches offer the promise of building on this work to nonetheless work towards something better (Anker and Felski, 2017; Felski, 2015). In order to become 'better' some normative assessment of what is 'good' should be in view. There are some possibilities we could draw upon within emerging research – in and beyond educational studies – that could direct our efforts towards new horizons of possibility. These might include new civic, convivialist and generative approaches that attempt to transcend and get beyond the crises of liberalism in particular, but also those limits of socialism and anarchism (Convivialist International, 2020; Lybeck, 2018; Neary, 2020).

The relatively unfamiliar theory of Social Generativity (SG) developed in Italy by Mauro Magatti and Chiara Giaccardi can be drawn upon to diagnose the specific pathologies facing universities today (Magatti, 2017). Social generativity is a 'paradigm for social change' that identifies what 'good', generative action consists of compared to the more individualistic, alienating and 'adolescent' culture of contemporary consumer societies. Based on empirical observation of 100 social and economic organizations these scholars identified three moves within socially generative action (SGA): (1) bringing something into the world, (2) taking care of it and (3) releasing it. There is thus some similarity between alternative paradigms of 'innovation', 'sustainability' and 'inclusivity', which are increasingly common in HE language. And yet, one can 'change' a technical process without improving it; 'sustain' an otherwise rotten or soulless urban environment; or 'include' historically disadvantaged individuals in an ever-accelerating and dissatisfying rat-race. In fact, these paradigms are fairly typical of postwar liberalism in that they lack normative content, avoiding articulation of a vision of good or bad civic processes, presuming instead that these will come from a procedural aggregation of individual preferences. Yet, as the swell of populist politics, acrimonious social media and untenable public and private finances suggests, a large proportion of individuals in contemporary society seem dissatisfied with the direction of travel. What we seem to be less clear on is where we would like to go instead.

Social generativity provides a means of transcending and synthesizing the three paradigms above, while moving beyond them. SGA does this across three dimensions: temporal, relational and contextual – thus creative actions can be assessed in terms of their durability, their exemplarity and the extent to which they 'authorize' others to join in these actions. Thus, unlike mere innovation – change for its own sake – SGA also creates conditions for others to be involved in creative processes, become activated by them and then spread these activities beyond their point of origin, thereby reinforcing, supporting and improving the wider social context and environment. In the wake of neoliberal changes to higher education, particularly the turn to a consumerist framing of what education is for, we can see three pathologies persist when measured against the SG normative standards. For SG notes the same dynamics present in the three 'moves' can become 'implosive' and degenerative – thus, creative action (1) can lead to egocentrism and narcissism; taking care (2) can lead to bureaucratization and control; and releasing (3) can lead to abandonment and neglect. Thus, the SG perspective moves beyond a mere critique of neoliberalism to specify precisely those features of contemporary academic life which are symptomatic of degenerative processes, thereby encouraging us to generate alternative practices to change course. These symptoms could be accordingly identified specifically as: (1) research superstars and ranking culture; (2) growth of unaccountable, centralized management; and (3) precarity – all of which should be strategically displaced and mitigated in future. SG gives us a sense of what that might look like – for example, we could decentralize our management structures and encourage more collegial and generative relations within and between departments. We can provide means of encouraging creativity and innovation in ways that do not result in narcissistic research superstars and a mass of precarious early career professionals willing to do anything to stay in the system. As the crisis of our profession continues, caught within the pincer of left and right populist and neoliberal challenges to our bases of power, authority and expertise, we must not only diagnose this problem, but look beyond these crises to a future where such pathologies are mitigated and vicious cycles have been reversed.

Chapter Contributions

Although national jurisdictions are becoming less salient in higher education governance, the nation state has been critical, historically, in granting legitimacy and delegated authority to universities. In the context of prevailing neoliberal critiques, the UK HE is regarded as being at sharp-end of a new mode of public sector governance with a high degree of output regulation, applied through performance-based research funding and fee-driven models for teaching. The effects of this mode of governance are reflected in devolved organizational control, greater autonomy at organizational level with leeway and discretion in recruitment, tenure decisions and promotion procedures and, consequently, greater influence in shaping career markets than in countries which are more externally driven by state regulation (Marini et al, 2019; Whitley, 2011). Recent international surveys reflect increased differentiation and diversification of employee contracts: with a growing proportion of academic staff on fixed term, teaching only contracts (Locke, 2014; Locke et al, 2016; Marini et al, 2019). For these reasons, debates about professionalism are particularly resonant in the UK context and will be of relevance to other national contexts where developments are proceeding on this trajectory. The themes and preoccupations in the book reflect widespread concerns which transcend the national context: precarity, metrics and measurement, public engagement, internationalization and increasing organizational control.

The subsequent chapters provide a glimpse into the contemporary terrain of knowledge production while avoiding a research-centric analysis. Writers illuminate the contemporary conditions of professional life in academia from different vantage points, in terms of age, career stage and type of institution. The chapters reflect various manifestations of the changing political and public climate, as well as the unease that surrounds contemporary debates and positions the academy in troubling ways. Each of the contributors focuses on the possibilities, in the near future, for advancing academic professionalism. Prioritizing empirical insight rather than sociological description (Holmwood, 2011), and through a focus on academic practices rather than functional boundaries, our contributors address the matter of professionalism conceptually and empirically through scholarship which offers explicit ethical orientations and psychological nuance. Collectively, authors offer insight into where the boundaries of professionalism might lie and what forms of theoretical and conceptual construction are necessary to respond to contemporary challenges.

Reflecting analytic priority on spaces for negotiating and advancing and advancing professionalism, the contributions align broadly with the concept of hybrid professionalism and apply post-critical orientations to offer possibilities for redefining professional purposes in ways 'commensurate with modern world' (Nixon, 2003).

In Chapter 2 Ron Barnett characterizes the pressured academic, located in conditions of 'super-complexity' and portrays the difficulty of determining which tasks hold value. Addressing this ethical question Barnett widens the theoretical lens with ecological crisis theory, in terms of interdependency and needing to situate within a greater sense of connectivity; and this has to inform our sense of ourselves and our profession generally.

The following four chapters turn the gaze inwards to the internal modes of interaction which contribute to the fabric of contemporary professional life from different organizational vantage points and from the sharp end of precarity, marketization, measurement and consumer discourses. Linda Evans provides a vivid account of pressured professionals through empirical research with professors in different disciplines. She illustrates how 'demanded' professionalism manifests as expectations of an occupational group, and which may, to varying degrees, shape the group's 'enacted' professionalism. There are normative ideas around publication practices within STEM disciplines, for example, which create adverse pressures in the sphere of knowledge production. The empirical research reflects the pressure to be 'all singing, all dancing' academic and the effects and offers insights on policies and practices which can mitigate these effects.

In the context of increased precarity and differentiation on career contracts, Vik Loveday explores the narratives of early career academics. The research provides rich psychological insights into personal sense-making of career circumstances and outcomes and portraying a widespread sense of being 'out of control' and a tendency both to individualize failure and distance 'success'. The narratives portray a sense of disconnectedness from conceptions of what it is to be a 'proper academic'. Loveday considers the implications of these narratives in the wider academic workforce in foreclosing the possibilities of solidarity and directs critique towards inauthentic and individualist discourses which widely prevail and proposes pushing back through counter-discourses to puncture the neoliberal logic of enterprise.

A crisis discourse tends to surround the use of metrics within HE. In comparative research on academic responses to teaching and research metrics in England and Germany Cathal O'Siochru et al consider whether state involvement in this mode of evaluation makes organizational policies more or less important in terms of how metrics interact with academic identity. Their empirical analysis highlights factors that can influence these effects and organizational practices that can expand or limit democratic participation, maintain professional standards and enable or limit professional autonomy.

Drawing on analyses of national-level policies, data sets, institutional-level strategies, national-level branding and local administrative practices, Sylvie Lomer illuminates the industrialization and commodification of the international HE market, portraying a 'solution that leads to new problems'. The analysis portrays vividly the clashing logics of professional communities within the organization. Lomer highlights the lack of professional and critical engagement with pedagogic implications and advocates for more deliberation on the pedagogic rationale in the academic sphere and professional practices to mitigate these issues. She offers comment on the possibilities for integrating professional spheres of deliberation and realigning logics which take more ethical account of widening participation and equity.

The latter chapters of the book explore the potential roles and interactions of academic professionals in the wider context and offer more expansive definitions on the public role and functions needed to support professional renewal. Eric Lybeck traces the history of jurisdictional change within one fictionalised university as management took over the traditional rights of academics over several decades. He draws historical parallels in the prevailing conditions which contributed to the French Revolution and the large-scale collective USS strike action of UK academics in/since 2018.

Vivienne Baumfield re-imagines the place of professional education in the University. The question of what academic professionalism might look like in terms of teaching, research and outreach into the community is addressed by examining the work of those academics with responsibility for educating professionals. In so doing, trends in the construction of what it means to be an academic and the implications of shifting perspectives on professionalism can be articulated. Taking this as the focus enables the taking of a 'long view' of the purpose of higher education and its role in the establishing of professional jurisdictions. The 'quest for legitimacy' portrayed in the analysis throws into sharp contrast the elements of what counts in terms of becoming established within academia and how these can shift over time. The analysis draws attention to the epistemic hierarchies of academic work within HE. To address these tensions, Baumfield re-asserts the value of a public intellectual conception of academic professionalism in establishing authority and earning public trust and elaborates on the form this ideal might take.

Julian Williams considers the diverse and sometimes contradictory activities, disciplines, interests, institutions and functions that constitute the academy in today's social and political economic context. These contradictions suggest many possible trajectories. He explores how the ethical relation between professional/client is constructed and could be constructed and articulates a conception of professionalism as: finding ways for the profession to 'see' itself, the collectivity of the profession, working with communities for the public good. He articulates unifying concepts which have traction in the contemporary context. To achieve this, he argues for the transcending of disciplinary boundaries and for academic professionals to be 'knowingly undisciplined' – reflecting on the contribution and limits of each discipline to the object of study.

In his 2011 Bloomsbury publication *Manifesto for the public university* John Holmwood reflected on pathologies of higher education systems increasingly subject to marketized logics. More recently,[1] in response to the global situation created by the pandemic, he has re-asserted the urgent need to reframe the public purpose of higher education. In the epilogue he provides a penetrating historical analysis of the social and political conditions of public higher education in a neoliberal market context. He offers a commentary on the lines of action that may be fruitful in collective efforts to improve the 'health' of the HE sector internationally at this pivotal time and concludes with a galvanizing call for collective action to mitigate the 'instrumentalization of knowledge' and 'erosion of democracy'.

This book is only a starting point for a process of co-production. Indeed, it is even more preliminary than that. For in large part, we present here a range of expert analysis across several dimensions and areas of academic work but do not claim it to be exhaustive. We hope that the book raises a number of questions that invite the reader to think on, in terms of their own developing professional practice, and about the future of Higher Education more generally.

Note

1 https://discoversociety.org/2020/03/24/uk-universities-and-covid-19-time-for-cooperation-not-competition/

References

Abbott, A. (1988) *The system of professions: Essay on the division of expert labour*. Chicago: University of Chicago Press.

Abbott, A. (2005) Linked ecologies: States and universities as environments for professions*. *Sociological Theory*, 23(3): 245–74. DOI: 10.1111/j.0735-2751.2005.00253.x.

Anker, E. S. and Felski, R. (2017) *Critique and postcritique*. Durham, NC: Duke University Press.

Billot, J. (2003) The imagined and the real: Identifying the tensions for academic identity. *Higher Education Research and Development*, 29(6). DOI: 10.1080/07294360.2010.487201.

Convivialist International (2020) The second convivialist manifesto: Towards a post-neoliberal world. *Civic Sociology*, 1(1): 12721. DOI: 10.1525/001c.12721.

Deem, R. (2019) The academic profession: Changing conditions of employment and the darker side of professionalism in higher education. Keynote lecture. *Pathologies of Professionalism in Higher Education Colloquium*, Liverpool Hope University (April, 2019, Liverpool).

Deetz, S. (1996) Describing difference in approaches to organisation science: Rethinking Burrell and Morgan and their legacy. *Organization Science*, 7(2): 191–207.

Evans, L. (2018) *Professors as academic leaders: Expectations, enacted professionalism and evolving roles*. London: Bloomsbury Academic.

Evetts, J. (2013) Professionalism: Value and ideology. *Current Sociology*, 61(5–6): 778–96.

Fejes, A. (2010) Discourses on employability: Constituting the responsible citizen. *Studies in Continuing Education*, 32(2): 89–102.

Felski, R. (2015) *The limits of critique*. Chicago: University of Chicago Press.

Fitzpatrick, K. (2019) *Generous thinking. A radical approach to saving the university*. Baltimore, MD: Johns Hopkins University Press.

Gläser, J. (2010) From governance to authority relations. In R. Whitley, J. Gläser and L. Engwall (eds.) *Reconfiguring knowledge production. Changing authority relationships in the sciences and their consequences for intellectual innovation*, S. 357–69. Oxford and New York: Oxford University Press.

Gunter, H., Hall, D. and Bragg, J. (2013) Distributed leadership: A study in knowledge production. *Educational Management Administration & Leadership*, 41(5): 555–80. https://doi.org/10.1177/1741143213488586.

Hodgson, N., Vlieghe, J. and Zamojski, P. (2018) *Manifesto for a post-critical pedagogy*. Earth, Milky Way: Punctum Books.

Holmwood, J. (2011) *A manifesto for the public university*. London: Bloomsbury Academic.

Kogan, M., Moses, I. and El-Khawas, E. (1994) *Staffing higher education: Meeting new challenges*. London: Jessica Kingsley.

Kuznetsova, O. and Kuznetsov, A. (2020) And then there were none: What a UCU archive tells us about employee relations in marketising universities. *Studies in Higher Education*, 45(12): 2439–50. DOI: 10.1080/03075079.2019.1615045.

Law, A. (2014) *Social theory for today: Making sense of social worlds*. London: Sage.

Locke, W. (2014). *Shifting academic careers: Implications for enhancing professionalism in teaching and supporting learning*. Higher Education Academy. https://www.heacademy.ac.uk/system/files/resources/shifting_academic_careers_final.pdf (accessed on 2 March 2020).

Locke, W. and Bennion, A. (2011) The United Kingdom: Academic retreat or professional renewal? In W. Locke, W. Cummings and D. Fisher (eds.) *Changing governance and management in higher education. The changing academy – The changing academic profession in international comparative perspective*, Vol. 2. Dordrecht: Springer.

Locke, W., Whitchurch, C., Smith, H. J. and Mazenod, A. (2016). *Shifting landscapes: Meeting the staff development needs of the changing academic workforce*. https://discovery.ucl.ac.uk/id/eprint/1474087/ (accessed on 2 March 2020).

Lybeck, E. (2019) Ajurisdiction. *Theory and Society*, 48(1): 167–91. DOI: 10.1007/s11186-018-09337-x.

Lybeck, E. (2021) *The university revolution: Outline of a processual theory of modern higher education*. London: Routledge.

Lybeck, E. and The Editorial Board (2018) Extended aims and scope: The vision for civic sociology. *Civic sociology*. Berkeley, California: University of California Press.

Magatti, M. (2017) *Social generativity: A relational paradigm for social change*. Milton Park, UK: Taylor & Francis Group.

Marini, G., Locke, W. and Whitchurch, C. (2019) Centre for Global Higher Education working paper series *The future higher education workforce in locally and globally engaged higher education institutions: a review of literature on the topic of 'the academic workforce'*. Working paper no. 43.

Moran, J. (2021) The scourge of managerial blah. *Times Higher Education (THE)*, 19 August.

Morrish, L. and Sauntson, H. (2019) *Academic irregularities: Language and neoliberalism in higher education*. Milton Park, UK: Routledge.

Neary, M. (2020) Civic university or university of the earth? A call for intellectual insurgency. *Civic Sociology*, 1(1): 14518. DOI: 10.1525/001c.14518.

Nixon, J. (2003) Professional renewal as a condition of institutional change: Rethinking academic work. *International Studies in Sociology of Education*, 13(1): 3–16. DOI: 10.1080/09620210300200100.

Noordegraaf, M. (2007) From 'pure' to 'hybrid' professionalism: Present-day professionalism in ambiguous public domains. *Administration and Society*, 39(6): 761–85.

O'Neill, O. (2002) *A question of trust: The BBC Reith Lectures 2002*. Cambridge: Cambridge University Press.

Ranson, S. (2003) Public accountability in the age of neo-liberal governance. *Journal of Education Policy*, 18(5): 459–80.

Reale, E. and Marini, G. (2017) The transformative power of evaluation on university governance. In J. Enders, B. Lepori and I. Bleiklie (eds.) *Managing universities policy and organizational change from a Western European comparative perspective*, pp. 107–37. Cham, Switzerland: Springer.

Rizvi, F. and Lingard, B. (2010). *Globalizing education policy*. London: Routledge, pp. 116–39.

Smelser, N. J. (2013) *Dynamics of the contemporary university: Growth, accretion, and conflict*. Berkeley, CA: University of California Press.

Stronach, I., Corbin, B., McNamara, O., Stark, S. and Warne, T. (2002) Towards an uncertain politics of professionalism: Teacher and nurse identities in flux. *Journal of Education Policy*, 17: 109–38.

Tight, M. (2014) Collegiality and managerialism: A false dichotomy? Evidence from the higher education literature. *Tertiary Education and Management*, 20(4): 294–306.

Universities, U. K. (2018) Solving future skills challenges. https://dera.ioe.ac.uk/32069/1/solving-future-skills-challenges.pdf (downloaded 30 October 2021).

Wallenburg, I., Quartz, J. and Bal, R. (2019) Making hospitals governable: Performativity and institutional work in ranking practices. *Administration & Society*, 51(4): 637–63.

Wellmon, C. (2015) *Organizing enlightenment: Information overload and the invention of the modern research university*. Baltimore, MD: Johns Hopkins University Press.

Whitchurch, C. (2015) The rise of the third space professionals: Paradoxes and dilemmas. In U. Teichler and W. Cummings (eds.) *Forming, recruiting and managing the academic profession. The changing academy – the changing academic profession in international comparative perspective*, Vol. 14. Cham: Springer. https://doi.org/10.1007/978-3-319-16080-1_5.

Whitchurch, C., Locke, W. and Marini, G. (2021) Challenging career models in higher education: The influence of internal career scripts and the rise of the 'concertina' career. *Higher Education*. DOI: 10.1007/s10734-021-00724-5.

Willets, D. (2017) *A university education*. Oxford: Oxford University Press.

Whitley, R. (2011) Changing governance and authority relations in the public sciences. *Minerva*, 49(4): S. 359–85. DOI: 10.1007/s11024-011-9182-2.

Winter, R. P. and O'Donohue, W. (2012) Academic identity tensions in the public university: Which values really matter? *Journal of Higher Education Policy and Management*, 34(6): 565–73.

World Economic Forum (2020) *The Future of Jobs Report 2020*. https://www3.weforum.org/docs/WEF_Future_of_Jobs_2020.pdf downloaded 30 October 2020.

2

The Very Idea of Academic Professionalism: At an End or Beginning Anew with an Eco-professionalism?

Ronald Barnett

Introduction

Professionalism, both as idea and as a set of practices, is in difficulty – is actually facing *several* difficulties – and this observation holds for the idea of academic professionalism, and even more so. Indeed, it can plausibly be argued that the idea of professionalism has been severely undermined such that it can do no useful work. The difficulties that it is facing are such that professionalism – as idea and as practice – is close to being ended. Identifying some of these difficulties befalling professionalism, both in general and for academic professionalism in particular, form, therefore, part of the tasks of this chapter. But simply to stop at the elucidation of its challenges and difficulties would be to sell short the matter of professionalism in the twenty-first century. The more important matter, therefore, is whether a way of reconstituting professionalism can be glimpsed. This is what I shall be proposing.

The argument here will be as follows. In principle, the idea of academic professionalism has mileage to it. However, given their material and epistemic circumstances, academic members of universities are facing severe challenges to any professionalism that they might display. As a result, at best, it may seem as if academics can exhibit merely a stunted professionalism. The academic has been rendered into a rule-follower rather than a rule-maker, being steered by institutional, societal and global structures. In this sense, we see a falling short of an optimal professionalism acted out with autonomy and agency. However, surprisingly, if what it is to be a professional is now situated among the many ecosystems in which it is placed, and thereby accruing a *radical relationality*, a new kind of professional agency may be glimpsed. Such a sighting may offer a way towards some minimal and sustainable state of academic professionalism.

Structure and Agency – Revisited

For around thirty years or more, there have been two contrasting stories about academic professionalism. On the one hand, academics are depicted as increasingly subject to large forces over which they have little or no control; forces of state regulation and audit; of marketization (not least as states steer professions in the public sector into quasi-market situations) and, in turn, changed professional-client relationships in which professionals become more accountable to clients; and, in many professions, heightened managerial disciplines and control. At one time, what it was to be a professional was to have ownership over, and autonomy in, the means of (one's) own productions. Now, on this reading, what it is to be a professional is to demonstrate one's compliance with the accountability structures being imposed upon one. This situation befell academic life long ago, a situation that A. H. Halsey (1992) described as academic 'proletarianization', a situation that has become ever-more intense. 'Excellence' becomes a sign precisely of the skill with which one performs under such conditions imposed upon the academic life.

On the other hand, a quite separate story has been emerging, albeit more recently – a story that has two parts to it. It is noted that the world is presenting increasingly with mega-problems, of global warming and ecological crises, racism, gender inequities, post-colonialism, matters of identity, profound and growing socio-economic inequalities, concerns over human rights, and of the recognition of strangers and difference. In this context, being a professional now becomes a matter – in part – of heeding 'the other', the other understood as multitudinous claims of the world. My sense is that this matter – the implications of the call of the other (including the call of Nature but well beyond) for what it is to be a professional in the twenty-first century – has yet to be properly elucidated.

It may be felt that all this was worked through more than a generation ago in the theory of double-loop learning and its implied implications for professional life (Argyris and Schon, 1974). After all, double-loop learning was understood precisely as that learning that sprung from critical reflection on the systems at work. It was a form of learning that enabled the systems to perform better. However, it did not allow for rejection of the systems as such. The goal was that of helping the system to be more effective. On this theory, the professional was rendered into being a super-technician, adept at effecting quite major changes to a system but lacking the wherewithal fundamentally to critique a system with an alternative value background that might yield a quite different vision of it – OR even to reject it entirely. The present age calls for a radically different sense of professionalism, one that is able to imagine and to bring forward new possibilities, but worked through against a sense of the total context in which one is working.

There are, therefore, two grand theories of professionalism in the twenty-first century, one rather dismal, of the professional put upon by large forces in the world and diminished in the process; and the other as having space and responsibility to help in bringing forward a new world. As intimated, both of these readings are applicable to the academic as a professional.

Across the world, as systems of higher education have evolved within nations and been subject to state steering (even in marketized systems), academics have become subject to large and conflicting structures of markets, audit, ranking, regulation and managerial control. These structures have become onerous. Moreover, the academic community, to a large extent, not only falls in with the demands of these structures but produces its own. Disciplines assert their interests as they compete against each other, academic journals establish tight protocols, and epistemic communities spring up and quickly establish their own rules of entry (in their discursive ploys). This panoply of bureaucratic and epistemic structures delimits the room for academic manoeuvre which, on some readings, is having perverse effects. Even as outputs and efficiency rise – the numbers of students taught and the papers published – so the levels of creativity fall (Murphy, 2018).

This is a situation in which institutions of higher education exhibit a heightened intensity *and* a lowering of their energy levels. The structures are so numerous that they exhaust the air. Universities are becoming airless places – on this set of dismal interpretations at least – and slide into a state of near-stasis, in which the energy level of academic life as a system continues steadily to fall (Stiegler, 2014a).

However, a quite different – even opposite – reading of academic professionalism is emerging, although not yet recognized as such. Universities are increasingly being urged to situate themselves in the space of large ideas and movements, of ecology, justice, decoloniality, equity, community, global citizenship, the public good and wellbeing. These are large callings. They call academics out of themselves radically to extend their disciplinary and pedagogical identities. They are truly callings. Fame and fortune do not readily attach to those who take them up. These large ideas – which amount to the re-emergence of 'grand narratives' (Lyotard, 1984) – exert their influence, even their charms, without promise of reward. And through extending themselves to take up any of these callings – and others like them – academics becomes professionals anew.

A justification of that latter claim can go in this way. Part of the meaning of being a professional is that one gives one's allegiance to the severe demands ('standards') that are inherent in worthwhile collective epistemically oriented practices. One surrenders oneself to the ardours of a profession. They lie outside of one, constituting a habitus, a way of life. Moreover, to submit to such a calling requires insight: a profession contains a more or less integrated framework of beliefs. So it is with any of those callings just picked out. *Ecology* becomes a calling in virtue of it being underwritten by beliefs in the inherent value of natural systems, their impairment by human beings and possibilities of human remedy. *Justice* becomes a calling in virtue of understandings of societal orderings that play out with degrees of fairness, and of justifiable life changes. *Decoloniality* becomes a calling in virtue of understandings of domination by a race or ethnic group over another, of past wrongs still perpetuated in the present. Each of these callings has its legitimation in both facts and values, in both an allegiance to a set of facts about the world and to a set of values (that matters are worth pursuing and that impoverished situations may be remedied, at least to some degree).

Crucial is it that academics as professionals, in the sense now being suggested, are assumed to have a degree of liberty sufficient to enable them to take on the mantel of any of the new callings coming their way. It makes no sense to assail professionals with multiple tropes – of sustainability, justice, ecology, wellbeing and so on – if those professionals enjoy no liberty in which, and with which, to respond. Indeed, to continue to deploy the concepts of profession and professional is to grant a measure of space to those who bear that imprimatur. To be a professional is to heed these great callings from the world and form judgements as to where, how and to what extent some kind of action-in-response might be possible.

The categories of profession and professional, therefore, are betwixt and between: accounts both of structure *and* of agency can readily be produced to depict the situation. (Talk of the possibilities for interaction between structure and agency only compounds the complexity of the matter.) And so it is for academics but their situation is even more problematic.

Academic Professionalism – Hanging by a Thread

We may remind ourselves of those perennial issues about academics as professionals. Whereas long-standing elite professions – medicine and law – possess (i) a code of ethics (such that gross departures from it may lead to being struck off a professional register), (ii) a systematic training process, (iii) a definite knowledge base and (iv) a clear sense of the professional-client relationship and service thereto, all four are but weakly present for academics. It would be understandable if few academics use the terms profession and professional to locate their work-place identity.

But, as suggested, the very idea of professionalism is in great difficulty nowadays. Indeed, surely the word itself is passing out of general use, a situation that is both explicable and has some justification on its side. The concept of professionalism is almost metaphysical for it contains non-worldly and non-material connotations of spirit, of a calling, of a universal ethics, of timelessness and of living in a realm above and beyond. All these five aspects are problematic in an age which is material, here-and-now, situated, and immediate. To be a professional is to declare allegiance to domains of otherness, beyond the self, beyond the visible. It is to subject oneself to a code of life, of being, of a beyond. It is to surrender oneself to standards and disciplines outside of oneself. It is, in a way, to lose one's identity, to become an-other. All this runs against the temper of the age, which demands presence, immediacy, transparency, a cashing-out in measurable metrics and an affirmation of one's identity. This is an age in which the concept of professionalism becomes outré, unfathomable, peculiar.

And so the concepts of profession and professionalism fade into disuse. This account is the *explicable* side of the thesis suggested at the start of the last paragraph. But what of the *justificatory* side of the observation that the word 'professionalism' is passing out of general use?

The justification is double-headed and rests on a distinction between complexity and supercomplexity (Barnett, 2000). *Complexity* is an umbrella term for the manifold of real and open systems in which professional life is implicated. Consider a doctor. A doctor is a node in a welter of systems and structures of finance, medicine, drugs, patients, health system, pharmaceutical corporations, digital systems and audits. This welter of systems plays out in intricate and convoluted patterns that are always in motion. To put it formally in the theory of early critical realism, here we are in the presence of an open setting, in which systems inter-mingle and so generate unpredictable *emergent* phenomena (Bhaskar, 2008: 113–17).

At any one moment, the doctor may have too many patients to see, new drugs to understand (not to mention the incalculable effects of their interactions in a single patient), changing technologies (which are liable to change the doctor-patient relationship), new audit processes and requirements, and altering patterns of funding. And in this intermingling of systems and processes, new – unforeseen and *unpredictable* – patterns of disease may erupt. This kind of situation we may summarize as 'complexity'. The term bears witness to the ever-more complicated pattern of real structures which bear upon professional life, such that the doctor can be forgiven for feeling that her room for manoeuvre is all the time diminishing, faced as she is with unpredictability and uncertainty. It is hardly surprising that, under this pressure of a complex of forces (which is real and not imagined), doctors take early retirement and even commit suicide.

However, this is far from the end of our doctor's travails. Daily, the doctor is confronted with the question 'Who am I?' or even 'What am I'. What it is to be a doctor is contested and hotly so. To what or to whom does our doctor bear allegiance? Her profession? The patient? Her own health? The media? The epistemic standards of justified knowing and acting (where early action may save lives or injure them further)? The performance indicators in the audit regime to which the doctor is subject? The world (as clamours grow for the equitable distribution of scarce health and medical resources)? To those who can afford her services or to those who cannot do so? There are no answers to any of these questions that bear anything like a consensus.

It may be said that, a la Foucault (1980: 113) the doctor lives amid competing 'discursive regimes'. That is so, but it is totally inadequate in doing justice to the situation, which is at once one of competing values, identities, space-time complexes, hopes, faiths and self-understandings. It is a situation of multiplicities heaped upon multiplicities, with 'lines of flight' (Deleuze and Guattari, 2008/1980; Guattari, 2016) criss-crossing dynamically across several planes of the Real, of ideas, of imaginings and of value. All is in motion, with no point of stability in sight.

And if this is so for the professional in the health service, so it is for academics. In the realm of the Real, a large number of systems impinge, severely reducing an academic's autonomy. The state, audit, money, institutional competition (fuelled by world rankings), students-now-turned-collectively-into-customers, knowledge systems, and the polity (locally, nationally and even cross-nationally) interweave, and play the academic like a shuttlecock. Here the academic is subject to the forces of *complexity*. But the academic is subject also to the forces of *supercomplexity*. What is it to be an academic in the twenty-first century? Do not many on the academic staff of universities shun the very term 'academic', preferring to see themselves as co-learner, facilitator, guide, mentor, coordinator of learning experiences or even (for those who know their Heidegger (2004/1954: 15) as 'letting (the students) learn' or even as 'co-researcher'? In short, supercomplexity poses the question as to what it is to be an academic, and it may be considered, on reflection, that the category of 'academic' cannot hold anything but murky water.

It follows, from all these considerations, that the idea of academic professionalism is in trouble – both as idea and in the realm of the Real of the world – and it is not immediately obvious where any strong support for it may lie. Its most obvious interpretation is that minimally, it has to consist of the powers to handle both the complexity and the supercomplexity attendant on being an academic, but that is to say rather little. Academic professionalism seems to be hanging by a thread.

The Thread Becomes Thinner Still

Can anyone profess anything these days? To profess means to say something with conviction, to be sure of one's grounds, to declare that one has authority for and in one's pronouncements. One speaks out, because one believes one has a sure grasp of a matter. Is this not madness to believe that one has certainty in a sea of uncertainty?

Is there not an arrogance here? In making such tacit claims for oneself, one sets oneself off from the world. The professional, therefore, is liable to succumb to a kind of Cartesian delusion, in which she or he separates herself from the world in order to make pronouncements about it. The world exalted professionals, telling them that they were separate from the world both in their being and in their epistemic judgements. This professionalism called upon professionals to believe that they can stand apart from the world, *and* that they can form an objective – or at least a disinterested – account of their client's situation. This is both the ontological and the epistemological apartness from the world that Descartes (1966) tacitly implied was his, in his statement that 'Cogito, ergo sum' (I think, therefore I am). In saying this, Descartes believed one could go it alone and adopt the stance of a pure observer (Gellner, 1992). This is a double hubris now embodied in the modern concept of 'professional' that the professional is able to secure an independence from the world *and* is able to proffer secure readings of the world.

This is doubly an example of the *dualism* in human life that Roy Bhaskar, in a later stage of his philosophy of critical realism, came to warn against, especially in his turn to a philosophy of meta-reality (Bhaskar, 2002) where being is not separate from the world (in a state of duality), but is in the world and the world is in being. Admittedly, for Bhaskar (2002: 11), 'in the world as presently constituted', it was 'impossible to avoid oppositional duality', but still 'our becoming non-dual beings in a world of duality' remains a coherent ideal. This, then, is the beguiling hope, that if the idea of professionalism is to be saved – and the idea of academic professionalism in particular is to be saved – non-dual forms of being and knowing must be found.

But we have to be ready to go beyond Bhaskar in one sense, and to say something about non-duality in a way not found in critical realism. For Bhaskar, non-duality is intimately connected with 'reciprocity' and 'co-presence', understood as properties of all being. We need, though, to press this set of insights.

We are repeatedly being reminded that the world is interconnected. As well as that term – 'interconnectivity' – other concepts have emerged that tread in the same water, for example, entanglement, assemblage, rhizome, relationality and ecosystem. Each of these concepts contains their own nuances and, indeed, their own locations, having variously emerged in philosophy, social theory and ecological theory, and, even there, their own specific locations. 'Entanglement', for example, has its origin in quantum mechanics (Barad, 2007). I want to pick up just one of these, that of ecosystem.

An ecosystem is a system with certain properties, including those of (i) possessing some kind unity, such that there are strong and organic connections among its entities; (ii) tendencies of autopoiesis, that is towards its own reproduction; (iii) being impaired, falling below its optimal state; (iv) being of inherent value; (v) its impairment being in part due to human action; but (vi) to some extent, at least, that impairment being remedial, again by human action (Barnett, 2018).

I suggest that there are no less than eight ecosystems that possess all six characteristics and that especially bear upon academic life, those of knowledge, learning, culture, social institutions, the polity, persons, the economy and the natural environment (Barnett, 2021). The order is important: the economy and the natural environment are in the list, as they have to be, but they are not privileged among the (eight) ecosystems. Indeed, successful action to repair the natural environment calls for action in all the other seven ecosystems. So, not only is there connectivity within each of the eight ecosystems but there is connectivity across those ecosystems.

We are beginning, I think, to gain a fuller insight into what academic professionalism can and should mean in the twenty-first century, if the term is to have substance. *The academic profession is entangled with all eight ecosystems, logically and practically.* The academic life cannot be properly understood, then, unless we bring in, in turn, considerations of (i) *knowledge systems* (its lack of balance across the disciplines, its unevenness across the world); (ii) *learning* (of societal learning systems and the woeful levels of adult illiteracy and the mal-understandings of key issues across society, quite apart from the social injustices attendant on access to higher education); (iii) *social institutions* (of the connections or lack thereof with the wider society, with the civic realm); (iv) *culture* (of the formation and distortions in cultural processes and the impairments in the lifeworld); (v) the *economy* (of the unbalanced nature of an economy, failing to do due justice to the public realm and its dependence on science and technology); (vi) the *natural environment* (its crises and the ways that universities have been complicit in the formation of those crises); (vii) *persons* (their identities and state of wellbeing or otherwise); and (viii) the *polity* (its understanding of and policies towards higher education); **and** of the entanglements of these ecosystems with each other.

Sighting Academic Professionalism

It follows that now, academic professionalism – in the first place – has to connote an awareness and an understanding of each of these eight ecosystems and that there are connectivities between each ecosystem and the academic life. There is nothing very peculiar or outré about this idea. All good professionals understand much of this intuitively. They have not only an awareness of but a concern about facets of their environment, the social institutions, the culture, the economy, knowledge systems, societal learning systems and so forth. But now, from here on, professionalism has to connote an explicit and intentional concern to act out professionalism in a more deliberate concern for each of those ecosystems. And this holds for academics as professionals, namely that to be professional entails trying to understand something of the complex of ecosystems that bear upon an academic situation and to act in that understanding.

Of course, the academic situation is particular to each academic. There are, as it were, differences in the ontological situations in which academics find themselves. Academic situations vary across disciplines, institutions, cultures, economies and so forth. Moreover, each academic will form their own individual appreciation of their ecological situation: quite legitimately, each academic will have great or lesser interest in particular ecosystems, and their efforts will take on different profiles. One academic might be interested in the knowledge and learning systems and seek, say, to give talk to school pupils or to local societies to improve societal understandings of important but complex issues. Another academic might be interested in how human rights play out across social institutions, and put in effort in that way. Yet another might have an interest in addressing imbalances in the economy as an ecosystem and seek to put their expertise at the service of non-governmental organizations even free of charge. And another might be concerned about malformations, as it was seen, in the polity, and put effort into heightening the democratic character of elections and the political process. And yet another may become not just active in ecological groups but seek to bring their knowledge expertise to bear in the process.

Academic professionalism, then, would consist of academics, whether singly or in groups, actively coming to an increasingly sophisticated understanding of the total eco-environment in which they are situated. There is, of course, a danger of being paralysed into inaction, as the unfathomable complexities and dynamic entanglements of that environment are sensed and where insights unfold, within the eight ecosystems of professional life. Professional agency can be severely compromised, as intuitions turn into more substantive insights into the character and the impairments of each ecosystem. But, as indicated, while some buckle under the strain, and take early retirement or an even more melodramatic leave of this world, yet others flourish. Indeed, an awareness of the impairments in one or other of the ecosystems may spur an individual into even greater sense of self and widen the canvas of possibilities spreading out.

Indeed, the academic world is now increasingly opening the way for such insights, as it becomes ever-more embroiled with the wider world; indeed, with the Earth. Academics are seeing possibilities for political action, for communication with society, for addressing the malfunctioning of Nature, for rebalancing the inequities of epistemic injustice, for widening the space of reasoning in the world, for encouraging a revaluing of public institutions as part of the economy or for encouraging students' life*wide* learning (Jackson, 2020: 95) in society alongside their formal programmes of study.

Sustaining such an eco-professionalism, of deliberately taking on an agentic profile in one or more of the ecosystems attendant on professional life, will be far from easy. On any front, there will be resistance and even outright conflict. The virtues of persistence and courage will be called for.

This sense of academic professionalism, it will be evident, will be not value-impregnated but value-*saturated*. It calls for value choices and value breadth and, quite often, value-resistance; that is to say, a resistance to the values – of instrumentalism, of competition, of individualism or whatever it may be – that are dominant in a particular setting within an ecosystem. I suggested earlier that one element of the idea of an ecosystem is that of *impairment* and that another element is that any such impairment is in large part the result of human action. The societal learning ecosystem is disfigured as learning is unequally distributed and is skewed in favour of a performance mode of being; Nature is impaired as a result of human technologies; culture is impaired as a result of collective meanings that value extractive and showy operations; and so on. It follows that any attempt on the part of academics as professionals – in the *eco-professional* sense being contended for here – is liable to face resistance if not downright hostility.

The Academic as Whistle-blower

Let us flesh out these schematic remarks by imagining an academic who assumes the role of a whistle-blower. Perhaps she or he has noticed something amiss with the assessment standards as they are being applied in practice in a university; or it comes to light that the university is investing in fossil fuels and so running counter to its policies; or it becomes evident that individuals are being steered into leaving the university as a result of a highly dubious 'performance management' regime; or evidence accrues to the effect that the senior management team has been complicit in working with the state to identify activist students protesting about state actions; or becomes suspicious that a research team in the university has been fabricating data or their interpretation in a globally competitive situation (perhaps the renewal of the research centre's grant is up for review); or comes to consider, within our academic's field of expertise, that the state has adopted policies that are injurious to a particular aspect of the natural environment. Our whistle-blower, having become aware of any such situation, becomes troubled, and feels that there are some large issues at stake and senses that some action is called for.

We should note that the examples just given – which have been plucked randomly and many others could equally have been chosen – vary considerably. In the academic world, whistle-blowing has many registers. It may arise over concerns with actions or policies of the state, or of an institution's management or, indeed, of actions of one's peers in the academic world. Given this consideration, professionalism takes on a particular fuzziness. It can refer (i) to concerns over a falling away from tacit standards of academic professionalism – the data are being deliberately skewed for a favourable result; the students are being treated unduly leniently for fear of losing their fee income – OR it can refer to (ii) actions or policies adopted with the imprimatur of the university or by an entity in the wider society, including the state. It may be tempting to reserve the idea of professionalism to the first category of mal-actions, those that are immediately academic; but that would be short-sighted.

I have been trying to advance a *relational* account of academic professionalism, my claim being the idea is in difficulty and can only be saved by situating academics and academic life as intermingling with and spread across large ecosystems (and eight have been identified). It follows that the concerns of our would-be whistle-blower that fall under category (ii) – of problematic happenings beyond the academic community per se – are not *outwith* academic professionalism but fall four-square *within* academic professionalism.

The matter of responsibility arises here, and with some insistence. This relational – and as I am terming it, this ecological – conception of professionalism brings much wider horizons to professionalism that hitherto understood. I am depicting professional life as encircled by a number of ecosystems, and I have suggested that a feature of all ecosystems is that they are each impaired, in part as a result of human ideas and actions over time – even over centuries. In this understanding of professionalism, the professional is enjoined to be responsible not only to the immediate context – the clients, the organization that supplies the professional setting and the profession itself – but now also to those societal and global ecosystems and their impairments. Here, we may notice, lies a new meaning of the calling – or vocation – of professionalism. The professional is called forth to attend to the ecosystems of her/his professional life and their shortcomings. The professional is called upon to act, to express their agency so far as practicable.

There is seemingly arcane point to make here. The 'ism' in professional*ism* now also takes on new meaning. Often, that suffix 'ism' denotes a phenomenon or practice taken to undue degree and carries negative overtones. 'Neoliberalism', 'managerialism', 'academicism' and 'capitalism' each has this character. There is an implicit charge of an excess that overflows, and suppresses that on which it falls (*c.* Zizek, 2016: 326). 'Professionalism' also carries hints of this sort for it can betoken an unduly inward practice: a narrowness of approach and of being, unable to see the wood for the trees, unable to put the practice into a wider perspective. However, the professionalism that I am trying to espouse here turns that sense of the idea inside-out. This professionalism, instead of being focused inwards, concerned just with its own rules, procedures, standards and etiquette, is now turned outwards. Actually, one seeks a new term – a term minus the 'ism', which is too freighted with inwardness: it now becomes a profession*ale*se.

Another way of capturing this outwardness lies in the idea of the main part of the term, that of professing. The professional professes. (The professor professes.) The professional is able to pronoun with authority on matters within her purview. Originally, that authority derived its legitimacy from the professional's dual grasp of a body of knowledge and a set of cognate skills that had their expression *in situ*, in certain kinds of collective practice. (Overtime, the valuing of the professional life came to be weighted more on the skills component and less on the knowledge component. As Lyotard (1984: 51) remarked of the 'professionalist student': 'The question … is no longer "Is it true?" but "What use is it?"'.) Now, though, the professing that is being called for in the twenty-first century is that of professing-in-the-world rather than behind the closed doors of the consulting room or the lecture-hall – of the professional being now able and willing to venture out across the hazinesss of the ecosystems of the world, to speak and to engage within the bounds of her or his epistemic authority.

Characterizing the Ecological Professional

A number of large concepts spring forward as ways of characterizing the kind of professional that I have been trying to depict. I would pick out those of responsibility, virtues, criticality and imagination.

Responsibility is part of the professional's positionality *tout court*, but here it takes on particular resonance. Here, as indicated, this ecological professional is called out of her or himself to attend to the whole world in a way. This professional is attuned to the world, in all its eco-manifestations, is alert to its impairments and, within his or her compass, attends to those impairments – hence extraordinary phenomena such as *Medicins sans Frontiers* and CARA (Council for At-Risk Academics), where professionals (in the milieu of the academic world) not just have a care for the world but feel a responsibility to act out that responsibility, even at some risk. This is a responsibility to the other, but the other may be any entity in the world that is in peril (it might be in the professional's immediate locality or in another continent) and where the professional has resources that can be brought to bear on the matter.

Ordinarily, the professional's life is a life of *virtues* (plural), of care, carefulness, application, vigilance, clarity, precision, courage, persistence and so on. The professionalism of which I speak here necessarily entails all of the virtues of professionalism ordinarily conceived but now those virtues are carried out and across (the ecosystems of) the world. And this professionalism thereby becomes especially onerous, for in sustaining these virtues in the wider world, across many domains (of societal learning, of the polity, of Nature, of the economy, of culture or wherever it may be), the professional is now exposed and her/his actions generate much risk (to self, to the setting, to the many now involved, to the institutions wherein the action takes place). After all, there is venturing here of many kinds – personal, epistemic, social, physical – and the risk is compounded.

Criticality, too, takes on a heightened significance here, for now the professional is called upon to critique the world! It is not sufficient to be active in the world for now our professional has to have both the capacity and the will to be able to stand off from it – while being immersed in it – and to critique it. Critique is much more than critical thinking for it betokens the capacity to spontaneously to envisage that the world could be quite other than it is and to be able to conjure such an alternative world, bringing to bear large concepts – of justice, democracy, freedom, fairness, the public sphere and so forth. Critique is the capacity to see through existing frames of understandings (Barnett, 1997).

Academics might persuade themselves that critique is their stock-in-trade – that, there, at least they naturally possess in strength one element of the kind of professionalism for which I am contending. That belief, however, has to be put under scrutiny, i.e. the academic world is rife with its own *taken-for-granted* frameworks, of disciplines and their inter-relationships, of what it is to be an academic, of what it is to be a student, of what it is to teach and of what it is to be a university. To draw upon Charles Taylor's (2007) particular use of the term, the academic world has its being amid and with its own 'imaginaries', namely value and epistemic frameworks that structure that world and that resist change.

The case can plausibly be made that the university is an institutional space in which ideologies swirl in and out. Scholasticism (Bourdieu, 2000) attempts to hold its place alongside managerialism (again, the 'isms' are telling); and now, even ecology is turning into ecologism, a taken-for-granted *Weltanschuung* in and of the university in the twenty-first century (Charbonneau, 2018). There is an issue, therefore, as to how air is to be brought into the university such that all its frameworks, all its discursive regimes, might be kept under critical review (*c.* Irigaray, 1999).

Imagination – our fourth and last concept in characterizing the ecological professional – is a necessary means by which the frameworks of academic life might be critiqued. Unfortunately, as Nietzsche (2003) observed over one hundred years ago, universities lack imagination, lack spirit, lack daring: they have become 'forcing-houses for this ... spiritual instinct atrophy'. As large and complex institutions, they exhibit a measure of rigidity. The number of academic papers increases exponentially but the level of genuine creativity decreases. The intensity of human positive energy in our universities dwindles; it falls into a state of entropy. Can it be reversed – as Stiegler (2014b) put it – into a state of 'negentropy'?

Why is the level of imagination so poor in our universities, and at every level – in pedagogies, the shaping of curricula, research and scholarship and university leadership and the shaping of university missions? It is striking that many innovations – in technology, in biomedicine, in philosophy, in political ideas – have been seen outside universities. New kinds of 'university' are being set up outside the conventional university structures (Shore and Wright, 2019). Universities are not the kind of social institution that encourage imaginative ideas. This should hardly be surprising. In institutions that are near-saturated with audit, performance management, surveillance instruments, algorithms for monitoring actions and outputs, and ever-more precarious work contracts, one tends to play safe – to lessen the level of risk. The senior management team's meetings revolve around its risk assessments of its practices and possible projects. This risk-averseness affects academic life too, for the price of rejection by a journal can be high; and so one plays safe, remaining within the frameworks of one's epistemic community. Academic imagination falters, for it is tacitly discouraged.

Vigilance has to be maintained over this state of affairs, this diminution of the value given to the imagination. This may be one reason – perhaps the only reason – to give one cheer to entrepreneurialism for perhaps it prompts the use of the imagination (Shumar and Robinson, 2018).

Conclusions

The idea of professionalism is in trouble and on several fronts. The autonomy that it rests on is no longer available; its epistemic authority is contested; the social hierarchy that it buttresses is critiqued; the separation from clients that it trades on is repudiated; the values that it stands for seem for many to be those of a bygone age; the interest that it has in its own sustainability is considered to be unjustifiable professional self-interest. But these critiques, severe as they are, only scratch the surface of the travails of professionalism. The larger critiques now would see professionalism as sets of unredeemable claims in a fluid, entangled and conflicted world, in which the professional field has lost its borders, and now finds itself jostled by multifarious zones – of the polity, culture, economy, society, Nature, (societal) learning, knowledge and persons.

The sense can legitimately form that the idea of professionalism has been completely hollowed out; it is empty of meaning and substance and can perform no useful work. Indeed, it may be sensed that it is even a malevolent concept, pretending to an authority and an independence that it does not and cannot sustain. But the shutters should not come down precipitately, for this heightened sense of the multiple relationality attendant on professional life opens possibilities for a new conceptualization of professionalism.

Now, academic professionalism can become itself anew. Originally, academics as professionals professed. They may not have been backed by royal charter but professors professed; or at least should have done so. However, the pools of autonomy that academics enjoyed have been first withdrawn, by state decree, and then ontologically as the assemblage of the university found itself entangled with the ecozones of the world; and eight in particular have been picked out here. Now, if hesitantly, the academic can profess her or his wares in and across a multitude of eco-zones, and many academics are doing just that, venturing out to assist the world and to speak for others (including the glaciers and the whales) in all kinds of ways.

This professionalism will always be a struggle; sometimes, it will run into the buffers and falter. After all, often the cards are stacked against it; large forces will oppose and even deny the possibility of such academic activism. This agency is never going easily to be won. Pessimism is not unwarranted in the circumstances. But one has to go on, for what is the alternative?

References

Argyris, C. and Schon, D. A. (1974) *Theory in practice: Increasing professional effectiveness.* San Francisco: Jossey-Bass.

Barad, K. (2007) *Meeting the universe halfway: Quantum mechanics and the entanglement of matter and meaning.* Durham, NC, and London: Duke University.

Barnett, R. (1997) *Higher education: A critical business.* Buckingham: Open University Press and Society for Research into Higher Education.

Barnett, R. (2000) *Realizing the university in an age of supercomplexity*. Buckingham: Open University Press/Society for Research into Higher Education.

Barnett, R. (2018) *The ecological university: A feasible Utopia*. London and New York: Routledge.

Barnett, R. (2021) *The philosophy of higher education: A critical introduction*. London and New York: Routledge.

Bhaskar, R. (2002) *Reflections on meta-reality: Transcendence, emancipation and everyday life*. Thousand Oaks, CA, and London: Sage.

Bhaskar, R. (2008) *A realist theory of science*. London and New York: Verso.

Bourdieu, P. (2000) *Pascalian meditations*. Cambridge: Polity.

Charbonneau, B. (2018) *The green light: A self-critique of the ecological movement*. London and New York: Bloomsbury.

Deleuze, G. and Guattari, F. (2008/1980) *A thousand plateaus: Capitalism and schizophrenia*. London and New York: Continuum.

Descartes, R. (1966) *Essential works*. New York: Bantam.

Foucault, M. (1980) *Power/knowledge: Selected interviews and other writings, 1972–1977*. New York and London: Harvester Wheatsheaf.

Gellner, E. (1992) *Reason and culture*. Oxford, UK, and Cambridge, MA: Blackwell.

Guattari, F. (2016) *Lines of flight: For another world of possibilities*. London and New York: Bloomsbury.

Halsey, A. H. (1992) *Decline of donnish dominion: The British academic professions in the twentieth century*. Oxford: Clarendon Press.

Heidegger, M. (2004/1954) *What is called thinking?* New York: HarperCollins.

Irigaray, L. (1999) *The forgetting of air in Martin Heidegger*. Austin, TX: University of Texas.

Jackson, N. (2020) Ecologies for learning and practice in higher education ecosystems. In R. Barnett and N. Jackson (eds.) *Ecologies for learning and practice: Emerging ideas, sightings and possibilities*, pp. 81–96. London and New York: Routledge.

Lyotard, J. (1984) *The postmodern condition: A report on knowledge*. Manchester: University of Manchester.

Murphy, P. (2018) The platform university: The destruction and resurrection of universities in the auto-industrial age. In R. Barnett and M. A. Peters (eds.) *The idea of the university, Volume 2: Contemporary perspectives*, pp. 483–500. New York: Peter Lang.

Nietzsche, F. (2003) *Twilight of the gods and the Anti-Christ*. London: Penguin.

Shore, C. and Wright, S. (2019) Introduction. In S. Wright and C. Shore (eds.) *Death of the public university? Uncertain futures for higher education in the knowledge economy*, pp. 1–28. New York and Oxford: Berghahn.

Shumar, W. and Robinson, S. (2018) Universities as social drivers: Entrepreneurial interventions for a better futurre. In S. E. E. Bengtsen and R. Barnett (eds.) *The thinking university: A philosophical examination of thought and higher education*, pp. 31–45. Cham: Springer.

Stiegler, B. (2014a) *The re-enchantment of the world: The value of spirit against industrial populism*. London and New York: Bloomsbury.

Stiegler, B. (2014b) *For a new critique of political economy*. Cambridge, UK, and Malden, MA: Polity.

Taylor, C. (2007) *Modern social imaginaries*. Durham, NC, and London: Duke University.

Zizek, S. (2016) *Disparities*. London and New York: Bloomsbury.

3

Selling Academe's Soul to the Devil? Performativity, Pressured Professionalism and the Rationalisation of Knowledge Production

Linda Evans

Universities are knowledge brokers. They are 'the cutting edge institutions of the knowledge economy' (1997: 14), whose 'stock in trade is knowledge' (Barnett, 1997: 166), and who are 'more than ever at the heart of the system of knowledge production' (Godin and Gingras, 2000: 277). Articulated more than two decades ago, these perspectives have lost none of their currency; it remains consensually recognised (see for example Castro-Ceacero and Ion, 2018; Soysal and Baltaru, 2021; Stevens and Börjesson, 2021) that knowledge – its production and its dissemination – is essentially universities' *raison d'être*; as Gunn and Mintrom (2022: 67) observe, '[u]niversities are now expected to serve the knowledge economy as a principal contribution'.

For knowledge production, universities rely upon their key knowledge-producing agents: research-active academics whose attitudes to their work underpin their willingness and capacity to participate in what Lucas (2006) calls 'the research game in academic life'. To succeed in this 'game', the university as workplace must therefore be not only research-active- and knowledge-generation-conducive, but also (academic) workforce-supportive and -motivating. Yet the well-rehearsed discourse on the neoliberal university's impact on academic working life – a theme that runs through this book – has exposed a tension between these organisational and strategic priorities: essentially, people-centred priorities such as wellbeing-at-work agendas are in many respects at odds with performativity-focused strategies and policies. Against this backdrop, this chapter examines the implications for knowledge production of the fall-out of such tension: 'pressured professionalism'.

The notion of pressured academic professionalism emerged from my research into academic working life, carried out between 2011 and 2015. The chapter draws upon two of my projects whose findings exposed contentious issues relating to universities' knowledge production amid pressured academic cultures. To prelude examination of such issues, I begin by outlining the key features of, and the conceptualisations generated by, twenty-first-century research into professionalism.

Professionalism in the Twenty-first Century: Contexts and Concepts

In the sociology of professions – which, Švarc (2016: 393) notes, 'has undergone radical changes from the golden age in the 1950s and 1960s', and whose decline 'is marked by some scholars as the end of professions and the death of professionalism' – the focus has shifted from the trait-based approaches that dominated twentieth-century scholarship. Scanlon (2011: 27) identifies this shift as marking 'what might be called the advent of differently constructed new professionals'. It is increasingly recognised that issues such as professional status and who should have it are no longer important. Julia Evetts (2013: 780), for example, points out that '[t]o most researchers in the field it no longer seems important to draw a hard and fast line between professions and occupations but, instead, to regard both as similar social forms which share many common characteristics'. The consequence of this shift of priorities, she argues, is that we need 'to look again at the theories and concepts used to explain and interpret this category of occupational work' (p. 779).

Many post-millennium analyses (e.g. Barnett, 2011; Evetts, 2013; Karseth and Nerland, 2007; Noordegraaf, 2007; Scott, 2009; Švarc, 2016) redefine and/or reposition professionalism within a framework determined by the context of twenty-first-century working (and related social) life. Precisely how this context is interpreted and depicted varies in the detail. Barnett (2011) highlights its 'networked complexity', characterised by:

> a set of infinities ... of expanding accountability demands, resource challenges, global horizons of standards and developing techniques, shifting knowledges, and changing client relationships. There is no end to these changes; rather, they accumulate and expand, entering new regions of uncertainty.
>
> (p. 31)

He likens it (the context) to thin ice upon which today's – what he variously labels the 'modern', 'networked' or 'ecological' – professional must skate, trying to keep ahead of its cracking behind her; Noordegraaf (2007: 770) describes it as 'fuzzy' and 'loosely ordered', and Švarc (2016: 393) as 'radically changing circumstances'. The underlying issue in these depictions is the uncertainty within which modern-day professionals operate, and which demands a new conception of professionalism; as Noordegraaf (2007: 771) notes, '[a]mbiguous occupational domains call for an ambivalent understanding of present-day professionalism'. Explaining their interpretation of knowledge-based professionalism, Karseth and Nerland (2007: 337) refer to 'new organizational patterns' and the blurring of 'traditional distinctions' that require professionals to 'navigate in these shifting landscapes and to negotiate between different concerns'.

Reflecting such perspectival shift, my own interpretation of professionalism (Evans, 2013, 2018) is that 'profession' should no longer be – and, indeed, in everyday parlance often no longer is – a label applied only to a few elite groups; we may now apply it fairly indiscriminately across the workforce's diverse, role-differentiated, groups, making it the terminological norm, rather than the exception. It is against the backdrop of this evolution that I explain professionalism, as I conceive of it, as quite simply a description of people's 'mode of being' in relation to their work, irrespective of whether that translates into practice that is distinct and praiseworthy or practice that is despicable. Involving qualitatively neutral practice, to me, professionalism is not – as the wo/man in the street would probably have it – a merit-laden concept. A consequence of its qualitative neutrality is that the term '*un*professional' becomes both meaningless and redundant. The implication of this conceptualisation is that professionalism does not imply status that one is likely to pursue or aspire to; it simply denotes how people 'are', at work – an interpretation that probably overlaps with what is meant and understood by 'practice'; but which, by presenting professionalism as encompassing not only practice but also what underpins and influences it, avoids synonymising the two terms. As I interpret it, professionalism relates to and conveys: what practitioners do, how and why they do it, what they know and understand, where and how they acquire their knowledge and understanding and what (kinds of) attitudes they hold. Explaining them in detail elsewhere (e.g. Evans, 2011, 2018; Evans and Cosnefroy, 2013), I identify these as the key elements or dimensions of professionalism as a concept: what I call its componential structure, or, to use Kolsaker's (2008) term, its 'constitution'.

'Demanded' and 'Enacted' Professionalism

I also distinguish between four perspectival versions of professionalism that may be applied to the professionalism of any given occupational group (see Evans, 2018), and which reflect its (the specific professionalism's) substance – how 'real' it is: professionalism that is *demanded* (or *requested*); professionalism that is *prescribed*; professionalism that is *deduced or assumed*; and *enacted* professionalism. Of these four, two in particular – demanded professionalism and enacted professionalism – apply to the professionalism evidenced in data generated by two of the research projects whose findings inform my discussion here (see Evans, 2018: 40–3, for explanation of all four perspectival versions of professionalism).

Demanded Professionalism

Demanded professionalism denotes that which one or more constituency/ies – or even individual(s) – implicitly or explicitly demands or asks of another. Representing service level stipulations, guidelines or agreements, demanded professionalism may manifest itself in the form of professional standards, codes of practice, or ethical guidelines, or through more explicit rules and regulations that convey the nature of how one is expected to behave, think or feel in the context of carrying out one's work. Yet, as I illustrate below in discussing the pressured professionalism reported by many of my research participants, demanded professionalism may also be conveyed more subtly and implicitly through expectations that are held of a particular occupational group or workforce. Indeed, whilst its potency is likely to be greater where it is backed up by the kind of authority that an employer or manager may wield, the 'demanding' of the 'shape' (as I refer to it elsewhere (Evans, 2011)) of this or that professionalism may also be conveyed by anyone impacted by, or with an interest in, how an occupational group carries out its work – including the general public, clients, and work colleagues (junior or senior to the practitioner(s) or occupational group in question).

Enacted Professionalism

The simplest and most straightforward of my four perspectival versions of professionalism, as its name implies, denotes professionalism that is enacted: that is, professional practice and its bases *as observed, perceived and interpreted* (by any observer – from outside or within the relevant occupational group, including those doing the 'enacting').

How Real? From Insubstantiality to Reification

A key point is that, of all four perspectival versions of professionalism, only enacted professionalism may be considered to represent 'reality' – albeit a phenomenologically defined reality. So, no matter what 'shape' or nature of professionalism is 'demanded' by employers or colleagues, or 'prescribed' or 'deduced' or 'assumed' by analysts and commentators, it is 'enacted' professionalism that represents the only meaningful conception of professionalism – that which practitioners/professionals are actually seen to be 'doing'. Unless and until they are translated into 'enacted' professionalism, the other three versions remain nothing more than visions, representing insubstantiality ranging from articulated ideology to wishful thinking.

As I imply above, expectations can be, and often are, a key element of such translation. For many of the academics who participated in my research, expectations of them reflected the performativity-focused culture that characterises the twenty-first-century neoliberal university (or, as it tends to be labelled in the United States, the 'corporate' or 'managerial' university (Marine and Martínez Alemán, 2018)), and which spawned what, after Noordegraaf (2007), I call 'pressured professionalism'. Below, I outline details of the studies whose findings, in exposing pressured professionalism and illustrating how it may manifest itself, form the basis of this chapter.

Two Research Projects on Academic Life

The chapter draws upon selected findings from two research projects that focused on specific aspects of academic life: *Professorial academic leadership in turbulent times: the professoriate's perspective* and *Academic journal editors' professionalism: perceptions of power, proficiency and personal agendas*. Throughout, for brevity, I refer to these respectively as the *professorial academic leadership study* and the *journal editors study*. With limited space to devote to them, and since they are detailed more expansively elsewhere (Evans, 2018: 81–3), here I present only an outline of the *professorial academic leadership study*'s design and method.

Professorial Academic Leadership in Turbulent Times: The Professoriate's Perspective

Funded by the UK-based Leadership Foundation for Higher Education, over the course of one year (2012–13) the *professorial academic leadership study* gathered data from UK-based university professors. It addressed five research questions relating to professors' conceptualisations of, perspectives on, and experiences of enacting professorial academic leadership: that is, academic leadership provided *by* (rather than to) professors. The participants were those whom I call 'professors without portfolios', for, in the UK, as illustrated by Bolden and colleagues (2012), the term 'academic leadership' tends to denote not specific managerial role incumbency, but more nebulously defined and often unofficial, sometimes *ad hoc*, leadership that may take the form of, *inter alia*, collegial advice and support, mentoring, or role modelling. Such informal leadership was the study's focus.

For the benefit of readers located outside the UK, it is important to clarify too that the term 'professor' has quite a different meaning in the UK and many other European countries (as well as, for the most part, in Australasia and South Africa) from how it is applied in North America and much of Asia. In the UK the title is conferred only on a minority (currently around a tenth) of university academics – distinguished predominantly on the basis of research, but sometimes teaching, excellence – who equate to the North American full professor. 'Professor' and its etymological derivatives 'professorial' and 'professoriate' refer only to those at the pinnacle of the UK academic staff hierarchy; these terms are not used generically to refer to all academic staff, and my use of them throughout this chapter is consistent with their current usage in the UK, denoting this minority group: academics appointed to the most senior academic grade.

Data were collected first by online questionnaire (most of whose twenty main items required respondents to indicate their opinions by selecting from a set of response options) from a sample of potential questionnaire respondents selected (in a non-systematic manner, explained in more detail in Evans, 2018) from a population of academics who, on their university webpages, presented themselves as professors. The questionnaire yielded 1,268 largely complete responses from professors who, collectively, represented affiliation with at least 64 UK higher education institutions. Pre-1992 institutions were represented by 84.8 per cent of respondents, and post-92 universities[1] by 15.2 per cent of respondents. Reflecting broadly the gender imbalance represented in the UK professoriate,[2] 71.1 per cent of respondents identified themselves as male and 27.3 per cent as female, while 1.6 per cent failed to indicate their gender.

From among the 394 questionnaire respondents who indicated willingness to participate in a follow-up interview, 42 were selected with the aim of representing a wide range, as implied by questionnaire responses, of attitudes, perceptions and perspectives relating to the study's focus. In allowing professors to speak –

candidly, as most did – for an hour or more about their experiences and their attitudes to their work, these loosely structured interviews yielded data on many aspects of and perspectives on 'doing professorship' in the twenty-first-century UK university.

Academic Journal Editors' Professionalism: Perceptions of Power, Proficiency and Personal Agendas

Carried out over one year (2013–14), the *academic journal editors study* was intended to examine and analyse a key agential dimension of the academic knowledge economy: academic journal editors' professionalism. Applying my original conceptualisation of professionalism (Evans, 2008, 2013, 2015, 2018) that, as I explain above, interprets it not as the term is used in the vernacular, to denote a merit-laden concept, but simply as encompassing people's 'mode of being' in their work, the research was focused particularly on the extent to which journal editors are perceived as wielding power within their academic communities, the nature and extent of any such power and its consequences on those most likely to be affected by it: academic journal authors.

Funded by the UK's Society for Research into Higher Education, the study sought the perspectives of two constituencies: journal editors and authors – with the latter representing seven broad disciplinary groups that corresponded with the foci of the UK's seven research councils. Of the editors, all except two held salaried posts as academics in UK universities, and had taken on journal editing as an 'extra' to their jobs. The remaining two were what I call 'professional' journal editors; they held full-time salaried positions, in one case as an editor-in-chief and in the other case as a section editor, of a prestigious, high impact factor, STEMM (science, technology, engineering, mathematics and medicine) journal.

The *academic journal editors study* objectives were to: examine the nature of journal editors' professionalism (as the term is conceptualised above); identify within that professionalism the potential for exercising power (directly or indirectly); identify and examine specific examples of perceptions of actual (as opposed to potential) editorial power – revealing its nature; and examine the impact on individuals of editorial power. To meet these objectives, the research was directed towards addressing the following research questions:

- What is the nature of editorial practice?
- What are the bases of editors' decisions?

- What motivates people to become and remain journal editors and what influences (positively and negatively) their motivation, morale and satisfaction?
- What are the key current and future issues and challenges associated with editorial work?
- What perceptions of the journal editor role, responsibilities and professionalism – and of how these translate into power – are held by editors and authors (or aspiring authors)?
- What defines a proficient journal editor?

Data were gathered through an online questionnaire that yielded over 800 responses from authors, 32 per cent of whom characterised themselves as early career academics/researchers, 31.6 per cent as mid-career and 36.4 per cent as senior academics/researchers. Participant selection and recruitment were non-systematic, initially involving trawling universities' websites to identify academics whose profiles indicated that they had been published in academic journals or suggested that they were active researchers (and who therefore might be seeking publication). From those questionnaire respondents who volunteered to participate, interviewees were selected on the basis of their questionnaire responses, with the aim of representing a wide range of experiences of and attitudes towards being published. The potential editor participants were identified through a combination of non-systematic trawling of the websites of, first, academic journals representing a wide range of disciplines, to ascertain the names of UK-based editors, and, second, UK universities, for the names of academics who served as academic journal editors (this involved a keyword search: 'editor' was entered into the university website search box) and then inviting these academics' participation as interviewees.

Questionnaire-generated data collection constituted phase 1 of the study; phase 2 gathered data through loosely structured interviews with twenty editors and fifteen authors. Interviews with authors focused on, *inter alia*: their sources of job satisfaction and fulfilment; their attitudes to and perspectives on writing for publication; influences on their decisions relating to journal selection (for submissions); their experiences of the peer review process; their responses to rejection; and their perceptions of journal editors' power. Interviews with journal editors addressed issues such as their motivation to become editors; the processes they apply to their editorial work; the nature of their interactions with authors and editorial boards; and their perspectives on current and future issues and challenges associated with editorial work.

Data Analysis

In both research projects, analysis of quantitative questionnaire data was effected automatically by the online questionnaire system (*Bristol Online Surveys*, in both cases), which offered the facility to generate descriptive and inferential statistics. Qualitative data – from questionnaire responses (open-ended items) and from interviews – were analysed manually, through an incrementally reductive process through which were identified key issues and themes (relevant to the research objectives and questions) that illuminated people's attitudes, perspectives and experiences relating to the study's focus. In the case of the *professorial academic leadership study*, these issues and themes related to what it means to be a professor in the twenty-first century, and the challenges for professors of meeting people's expectations of them as academic leaders; in the case of the *academic journal editors* study, they related to academic journal editorship and/or of being or trying to be published in academic journals, attitudinal responses to these experiences, the bases of these responses, and the perceived effects on working life of, and the extent to which and the ways in which these may be considered to reflect power relations within, the business of getting published.

Collectively, the two projects yielded a wealth of rich data on twenty-first-century academic life in the UK, reflecting the perspectives of a broad spectrum of participants – professors, mid-career and early career academics – who all represented what (acknowledging Aronowitz and Giroux as the term-coiners) Castro-Ceacero and Ion (2018: 684) refer to as 'the concept of researchers as "knowledge workers"'. Data analysis revealed a pervasive finding that I foreshadow above: in the neoliberal university, academic working life reflects pressured professionalism.

Pressured Professionalism

I note elsewhere (Evans, 2017, 2018) that, whilst it is widely accepted in the UK that professors' main purpose is to provide academic leadership, definitional imprecision – lack of clarity about what such leadership 'looks like', and hence what professors should do in order to enact it – creates uncertainty about what is expected of these senior academics. For all that universities[3] in the UK seem to have appropriated the term to denote the overarching purpose of the professoriate, they provide little elucidation on precisely what such leadership entails; conveyed through vaguely expressed ideas and general hints, these features of it are implicit, rather than explicit. Asked whether he knew exactly what his university wants of its professors, one *professorial academic leadership study* participant, for example, an arts and humanities professor, responded, 'I don't think the *university* knows!' But such lack of clarity underpins confusion about where academic leadership's parameters lie: what counts as it, and what does not. For many of my professorial research participants, working out what – and, most importantly, *how much* – universities want from them as academic leaders seemed to involve interpretive guesswork.

The result of this confusion and uncertainty is that performance angst seems rife amongst the UK professoriate. My research revealed that, rather than risk tarnishing their reputations and denting their self-esteem, professors – a constituency that, representing academia's highest achievers, prides itself on its performance and is keen to meet people's expectations – often take on ever-more demanding workloads and expansive arrays of tasks, evidently hoping that these constitute satisfactory discharging of their academic leadership duties. The result is pressured professionalism.

The *professorial academic leadership study* generated detailed accounts of how pressured professionalism manifests itself in professors' day-to-day working lives. Employed in a pre-1992 university, education studies professor Alison (pseudonyms are used throughout) spoke of the constant pressure that she put herself under – not only to demonstrate her distinction as a scholar, but also to justify her senior status – by out-performing her junior colleagues in terms of academic publishing:

> I always do too much. But, I think ... I think I *am* always anxious about what, y'know, about ... like, have I done enough publications? ... I think I just – and I *have* actually done more publications than anybody else – and I think, as a result of that, I do ... over-achieve in the things that I'm supposed to do, but more because I keep thinking: oh, that's not enough, that's not enough.

Alison's self-imposed and self-acknowledged over-productiveness was evidently motivated by her seeking approbation from senior managers and from the university 'centre', as she readily admitted:

> I'm reviewed by a fellow chair and my head of department – and ... in the last [performance development review] they said, 'Oh you're doing really great'. Oh, yeah – and you still need to hear that! ... I'm constantly trying to push myself in all of this – and you can't do it all.

Computer sciences professor Simon similarly spoke of the importance of meeting his pre-1992 university's expectations in relation to producing research outputs that, in the UK's research excellence framework (REF),[4] would be graded at the highest level (which, at the time of writing, is 4*):

> Like any university [it] expects people to have good quality publications ... and y'know ... if you're a professor and you've not got, y'know, 4* publications, I mean, people would be looking at you and saying, well, y'know, 'Why is this guy a professor?' So, there's a certain element of pressure there – not direct, but, sort of, there's the perception that you obviously have to be doing things like that at a fairly high level. ... In terms of as a professor, there's an element of pressure, I suppose, in that you're expected to deliver perhaps things like, y'know, publications at a higher rate – and I don't necessarily mean numerically, but certainly in terms of quality.

It is important to emphasise that enacting pressured professionalism did not necessarily go hand-in-hand with dissatisfaction or low morale. Of those professors ($n=1,255$) who responded to a questionnaire item asking them to indicate their current morale level on an arbitrary 1–10 scale, fewer than 10 per cent (6.8 per cent) indicated the highest possible level (10), while just over 10 per cent (10.8 per cent) indicated very low morale levels (1–3), including thirty-four (2.7 per cent of the item's respondents) whose selection of the lowest number (1) implied that their morale was at rock-bottom. The largest proportion of respondents – almost a quarter – indicated a morale level of 8, with the next most frequently selected morale level indicators being 9 (selected by 16.9 per cent) and 7 (selected by 15.4 per cent). Well over half of the sample of full professors thus indicated relatively high to very high morale levels (gauged at 7 or higher). Indeed, for competitively focused, 'driven', individuals, pressured professionalism seems to have served as a conduit for them to perform, and, in performing, to achieve, and to 'self-actualize' – to use Maslow's (1954) term. For professors who considered themselves so overworked, however, or who faced so many demands on their time and attention that their capacity to self-actualise was eroded, the performativity-focused cultures that characterised their work contexts were perceived more negatively – in some cases, as toxic.

The narrative of STEMM professor Harry – who, in his thirties at the time of participating in the *professorial academic leadership study*, had relatively recently applied for and secured a named chair at his own pre-1992 university – was punctuated by remarks, such as 'you have to run to go backwards' and 'you're almost expected to do three full time jobs, and I don't feel I'm physically capable of sustaining that for the remaining thirty years of my career', that conveyed not only constant pressure to perform but also dissatisfaction with a workplace context that imposed such pressures. His current work situation, Harry divulged, was not his ideal one, which, he gauged, was likely to remain elusive:

> My expectation is that I'll never be able to reduce [my workload] to the level that ... would allow me to deliver fully on what I believe is expected of me on the research side, as well as the sort of, y'know, the sort of more, y'know, grown up expectations as a, sort of, reasonably experienced academic, in terms of actually guiding people, and so on. So, I think that's probably really my looking forward in terms of the ideals. I think there's too many things expected of me. I'm expected to lead in too many areas, and as I look around and I look for people who appear exceptionally successful, they only really do one thing. They ... put themselves in a position where they can really excel, and I think, to some extent, the way that we structure – and I don't think it's just *here* – kind of, we're not really able to excel in *anything*; we're, kind of, y'know ... we can only really deliver *mediocre* stuff because we simply don't have the capacity to deliver at the levels expected. And I feel the expectations at the very top of this university, where it's stated that professors should research more, teach more, do more administration, are unreasonable ... so it comes away a little bit from your ideal job.

Finkenstaedt (2011: 192) suggests that '[u]niversity teachers everywhere are quite prepared to work more hours than average civil servants. For full professors fifty hours per week during term time and a few hours less when classes are not in session is a realistic average for Europe'. Yet this suggestion underestimates the workloads that many of my professorial research participants reported having to carry; arts and humanities professor Elizabeth, for example, described the start of her day: 'the alarm goes off at 5.30 and I get out of bed as soon as I can. I try to be at my computer by 6.00', while STEMM professor Will mentioned having been working until midnight the evening preceding his research interview, and computer sciences professor Simon estimated his working week to take up eighty hours. For biological sciences professor Brian, work overload seems to have been the defining feature of his professorship. He reflected on his promotion with ambivalence, perceiving it to have brought additional pressure in the form of new expectations of him: '[Y]ou become a chair, and then ... the university has extra expectations of you ... of what they want out of *you* in return'. He spoke of 'the extra burdens' that his promotion had brought, and which had changed the nature of his work significantly, taking him away from research and turning him into an administrator – both of his own laboratory, and in relation to wider university citizenship-type responsibilities. His description of a typical day conveys the frenetic nature of 'pressured' professionalism as he perceived and enacted it:

> I just don't get into the lab. ... I mean, my working week is between fifty and sixty hours, and I don't work at weekends anymore because if I'm doing fifty to sixty hours during the week ... I don't see that I need to come in on a Saturday! Of course, with the internet, y'know, you're never free. I've taken to reading my email at quarter to seven in the morning just to clear the stuff that accumulates overnight ... er ... so, when I get to work, I then have a free hour before stuff starts coming in. And I'm just pulled in every which direction ... er ... and yesterday I spent a fruitless hour-and-a-half in a meeting about how we're going to deal with the UK border agency regulations for overseas students. And then it was straight from that and back to the lab here to host parents at open days, y'know. This afternoon I have *got* to go down to the teaching labs to fix two bits of equipment, which I need for my practical – which I run on Thursdays. But because the practical sessions are timetabled so badly ... in that we only have an afternoon to get the equipment ready, and the day then to run the practical, and that afternoon of the practical to put the equipment away again, everything's – there's just pressure on all sides ... all the time ... for doing things *now*! ... because we don't have time to do it *any other way*, and it's just *madness*! And so, what's happened in the last five years is ... the only time I step foot in there [points to the lab area] is to go to the loo or to go and get a cup of coffee. ... And, y'know ... even actually finding out exactly what my PhD students are doing ... I'm finding now that I spend less time sat over a ... bench with them, looking at [X][5] – which is what I *used* to do – because I just don't have the time. So, y'know, I end up having to get *them* to write the monthly reports, so I can, sort of, go through what they've done ... and find out that they've not done *this* control and not done *that* control ... and if I'd known about it ... y'know ... a month or a week ago ... or two weeks ago ... we could've just stopped all that.

For Brian, then, a key concern seems to have been trying to stay on top of the multitude of tasks that, with his promotion, had begun to land on his desk, and the numerous responsibilities that he found himself shouldering in his capacity as a professor who was both expected to run an efficient laboratory and undertake institutional citizenship. Brian's narrative resonates with the experiences, as he related them, of STEMM professor Will, who outlined how, with his morale at the time at rock-bottom (he estimated it as, on a scale of 1–10, having been at level 1), he had been so overwhelmed with work that detracted from the research he loved doing, that he had been on the verge of resigning from his pre-1992 university:

> I felt very overworked, with an average teaching load, more-than-average administration and tasks to do … reviews of this, that and the other, and writing reports, and so on … in the administrative sense, and bringing in a lot of research money which brought in research projects which needed leadership and sorting out. But that's not necessarily the same thing as actually looking down a microscope or doing the actual research – which is what I really want to do. So, even organising a bunch of post-docs to do their research is not the same thing as doing the … actually doing it. And I found I was getting … I had no time. And I felt I was … I was being pushed into a dead end, 'cos one of the big problems with academia and senior academics is that they can very easily morph into high level administrative positions, where you're administrating other people who are doing research. And I think that may suit some people, but it doesn't suit me. And I really felt a, kind of, genuine jealously of the post-docs around me who could breeze in and out when they wanted, and spend all their time, sort of, unveiling the secrets of nature, and I was finding it almost impossible to do that. So … the crisis, for me … really came when I … applied for a job somewhere else. And I was gonna go and take all my money and all my publications and my reputation and that. … And then – only *then*, when I was actually walking out of the door, they said, 'Hold on a minute – what do you actually want?' And I said, 'I want five years just to do research; it'll take two to clear the backlog, and then I can actually do something new and original, which is what I really want to do'. So, I'm in that process at the moment.

For many participants of the *professorial academic leadership study*, a key contributor to the pressure they reported seemed to be the diffuseness of the activities they found themselves taking on – the expansion of their repertoires – as they tried to prove themselves, to all interested constituencies, effective academic leaders and worthy of the title 'professor'. Unsure about what they may legitimately or justifiably say 'no' to, and what they ought to agree to, and finding themselves chasing unachievable targets and struggling to cope with a job whose boundaries were unclearly delineated, many seemed to be trying to be all things to all people, and some were evidently buckling under the pressure to do so. 'Profs have to be all-singing, all-dancing', wrote a questionnaire respondent. Another complained, 'I am less and less involved in doing things I'm good at and more and more tied up in admin work/bureaucracy, petty politics and HR activity', and another wrote, 'the job demands a level of multitasking that I can't do any more. I have no intention of being a passenger, and so I've applied for the soonest possible retirement'. A recurring complaint became something of a refrain in the research data: the job of being a professor can be so demanding as to be unmanageable. A questionnaire respondent wrote: 'I have felt well supported and well prepared, but expectations have grown, and I am expected to take on more and more', and another complained, 'the competing demands across the board create a feeling of inability to cope most of the time', while another commented, 'it [professorship] is an all-encompassing fluid role that has to be flexible. The problem is that it's just too big, and doing any of it requires compromises elsewhere'.

Yet, as I discuss below, such compromises and competing demands have a knock-on effect on the effectiveness, integrity and value of universities' overarching endeavour: knowledge production.

Compromise, Competitiveness and Corner-cutting: Pressured Professionalism's Impact on Knowledge Production

Illustrated in the quotes presented above, a key frustration expressed by professors who complained of being over-stretched was that they had insufficient time for their research – more specifically, insufficient opportunities to devote the sustained attention that was required for significant epistemic breakthroughs and output, and, as a result, were under-achieving on the knowledge-production front; to paraphrase interviewee Harry, they were having to settle for mediocrity, rather than excellence. Referring to the 'salami-slicing' of his mind that resulted from constant interruptions to his capacity to immerse himself fully in a research project, and of 'having to switch between different aspects [of his work]', Harry remarked,

> I'm caught with a very large teaching load, a very large administration load – because I'm expected to do a lot more sort of administration now – yet still somehow magically deliver all this research.

He continued:

> I get the most fun out of writing papers and completing papers. I enjoy that, and I find that very fulfilling. ... So, I get regular satisfaction out of that – and which is the bit that I've *not* managed to do.

In his demanding role as departmental research director and REF coordinator, education studies professor Eric similarly bemoaned having had no time for his own research:

> The REF is *so* all-consuming, and I have too many research students, that I have no time for my research. And you can live with that for a while – and you can even use previous stuff and reformulate it, for two or three articles, and then you can't. And then, if you haven't done the reading and you haven't done the research … and I'm just too tired to do it. And that's what stops.

Illustrated by such comments, a common theme to emerge as a prominent feature of pressured professionalism was the need for compromise: many professors found themselves having to make compromises to the ways in which they would ideally have liked to carry out their work.

Compromising Work Contexts

Elsewhere I argue (Evans, 2001, 2018) that job-related attitudes (specifically, morale, job satisfaction and motivation) are fundamentally influenced (albeit often unconsciously) by perceptions of the extent to which the contexts that shape what I refer to as people's 'job situations' are 'compromising' or 'uncompromising'; that is, the extent to which they essentially require people to compromise on the things that matter to them, such as their values, ideologies and current priorities. The more 'compromising' the work contexts, the more negatively they impact upon job-related attitudes; the more 'uncompromising' they are, the more positive the work-related attitudes that they foster. Conveying the notion of subtle gradations of 'compromisingness', rather than denoting a binary scale, 'compromising' and 'uncompromising' represent the two ends of a work context continuum (see Evans, 2018: 139–42, for an explanation of the term 'job situation' and more detail on the 'compromising-uncompromising' continuum). Finding much in their work contexts or situations that was at odds with their ideals, the evidently dissatisfied and/or frustrated professors quoted above were, at the time of participating in the *professorial academic leadership study*, located at various points towards the 'compromising' end of this continuum, distancing them from what, in explaining 'proximity theory' (Evans, 2018), I call their 'ideal job situations'.

In particular, many professors' compromising involved difficult choices to be made – about what to prioritise and what to skimp on, or what to relegate to a back-burner. Since it tends to be the most flexible and moveable component of their work, research was typically the activity that ended up being side-lined – a situation that provoked regret, for two reasons. First, as conveyed above in several of the professors' comments, the process of discovering new knowledge is for many research-focused academics a source of immense fulfilment that they are loath to forgo. Second, within the performativity cultures that pervaded their universities, many professors felt that falling short on research activity and output not only represented their under-performance but also diluted the scholarly and intellectual distinction that, as professors, they were expected to manifest. They experienced constant and pervasive frustration at being unable to realise their full intellectual potential.

'A competitive ethos has taken over in academia', observe Lund and Tierni (2019: 99), and while glimpses of it are evident in the comments of professors Alison and Simon, quoted above, the lure of a demanded professionalism that throws down the gauntlet, in the form of challenges to excel and achieve distinction, was exposed in the *academic journal editors study*, just as Lund and Tierni's case study of female academics at Finland's Aalto University revealed an appetite for taking up such challenges by playing 'the game'. Such game-playing was described by one of their early career research participants: 'I know what the game is and knowing that is as much as writing the work … you sort of become socialized to the American A journal culture, for better or for worse' (Lund and Tierni, 2019: 108). The *academic journal editors study* similarly found not only professors but also many early and mid-career academics to be embracing competitiveness. Angermuller (2017: 967) points out that academic researchers 'try to improve their positions in the hierarchical world of research by mobilizing formal and informal social categories'. My research revealed one of the most sought-after informal social categories to be that of author published in the highest-ranked journals.

In Pursuit of Holy Grails: The Quest for Distinction

'[R]esearchers, journals and universities alike owe a part of their reputation to their number of publications and citations, particularly in journals with "high impact"', observes Hernes (2021: 43) – and, indeed, from the *academic journal editors study*, obsession with securing publication in such journals emerged as a prominent feature of some academics' research activity. A lecturer[6] in economics, for example, remarked, 'I don't know if it's the same as in other disciplines, but actually, we [economists] … obsess over how journals rank qualitatively to one another'. He continued:

> You can ask pretty much anybody in economics, and they will say the same journals. So: *The American Economic Review*, *Econometrica*, *Quarterly Journal of Economics*, *Journal of the Political Economy*, and *Review of Economics*. They're

just referred to as 'the top five'. ... I mean ... most economists will spend their life trying to publish in one of these top five and not do it. There's actually a paper written on how much of your body would you be willing to sacrifice to publish in one of these, and I think it turns out most economists would sacrifice a *thumb* to publish in one of these journals! [slight laugh]. So, I mean, one publication in these journals can change the course of your career – especially early on – dramatically. I think ... I mean, it can change your earning potential ... definitely ensure you'll get promotion somewhere ... yeah, these are very, *very* important places to publish.

(*Interviewee, pre-1992 university*)

Such obsession emerged as pervasive in many STEMM fields, too, with publication in the journals *Nature*, *Science* and *Cell* having become mythologised as holy grails that many academics relentlessly pursued. Several *academic journal editors study* participants referred to career-long ambitions – usually ascribed to others (few admitted to such ambitions for themselves) – to secure such publication. The following illustrative comments were made by anonymous questionnaire respondents:

> Certain high impact journals have an enormous amount of power to impact research activity – a paper in *Nature* or *Science* came make or break someone's career, and so editors of these and other HI [high impact] journals have enormous amounts of power that directly impact the careers of young researchers.

> It could be argued that powerful journals (*Nature*, *Science*, *Cell*) now essentially 'make' funding decisions in that an applicant with publications there will tend to have a significant advantage when their grant or fellowship application is discussed at committee, and for job applications. ... In at least 2 cases in my own immediate area, the pressure to publish in such journals has led to fraud.

Consistent with the reference to fraud in the comment above, ethically dubious practices were identified by several senior STEMM academics as a toxic by-product not only of holy grail pursuit but also of other, related, features and/or causes of performativity-driven, pressured professionalism, including the rankings-focused climate that characterises the neoliberal HE sector, the competitiveness that such a climate fosters, and the impact of such competitiveness on academic careers, particularly of early career researchers. With what were perceived as negative effects, links – in some cases, direct, in other cases, indirect – were identified between such features of pressured professionalism and knowledge production. A biochemistry professor, for example, lamented the dilution of knowledge that he identified as stemming from academics' efforts to meet the top journals' requirements:

> [These journals are now] so demanding, both in terms of how sexy the project is, how broad-ranging the paper is, that you can't do what – I mean, I'm old fashioned; I quite believe in incremental, y'know, you show one thing, you publish it, because it's important for other people to know what you've done. You then use that, and you develop *other* stuff, and you publish it. And *now* you seem to pack what would've been six papers into one very brief paper – and with insufficient detail sometimes. And, of course, it means you can burn the careers of several PhD students and several post-docs if you use one paper ... whereas, previously, a PhD student might get *two* papers out of a PhD, of which they're the first-named author – which shows what their contribution was.

Moreover – and broadly reflecting the views of several interviewees – a senior physics professor who was approaching retirement argued that, mediated by institutional pressure, such journals were influencing the focus of knowledge that some STEMM academics choose to pursue:

> I take publication very seriously, and we always try to publish in the best journals that we can – although the type of work that we do unfortunately doesn't find its way into the journals that the university considers to have the best impact factor ... but there's only two of those, and that's *Nature* and *Science*. If you can't ... y'know, if you're doing something that *they* don't publish – you can't publish it. ... So, publication in good journals is very important to us. The interference with where we publish, and the pressure to publish in particular journals as opposed to others, because of some irrelevant numerology that ... the government or university administration is being convinced is somehow a quality measure – that's irritating.

Asked if there was explicit pressure at his university to publish only in certain journals, he replied:

> Yes. Ultimately it comes from the centre, yes. For example, if you *don't* publish in the right journals, your publications won't be included in the REF selection. If they're not included in the REF submission, then it's quite possible that you wouldn't get promoted. It's even possible that you might, at some future time when things are not going so well, be dismissed or made redundant. So, that doesn't bother *me* because it would take so long for them to do that with me that I should be gone anyway – but it's a real worry for my junior colleagues. Whereas, when I was in *their* position, the university was in some sense grateful *wherever* you published.

Most significantly, the interviewee continued, 'We hear a lot now about people retracting papers because they've fiddled the results, basically. And students – PhD students – they feel under pressure to do that. And that's terrible'.

It was a different physics academic who identified the epistemically delimiting effect of allowing the top journals to determine what knowledge was valuable:

> It means that ... certainly it makes it very difficult to do something genuinely new, or start a new area, or break into something where nobody else works. You won't get the work published, journal editors will think: no, this is not going to be of interest to our readers. So it is, I think, in the long term, it's going to be stifling for scientists.

Reminiscent of the earliest quantum physicists who, in the days before their field was both popular and considered epistemically justified, were forced to pursue their quantum work through covert moonlighting, as an add-on to their 'respectable' day-work, this interviewee's own response to what he called the 'stifling' of choice of research focus was to pursue two lines of scientific enquiry:

> At the moment I, essentially, I carry on, maybe, like I said, two lines of research. I do what I think is interesting and what I also think is genuinely novel – this is work that I find extremely hard to get published. And then I do other work which is popular, [which] you can get published reasonably well – easily – in high impact journals, because that keeps me going. I'm then, sort of, currying favour with the university and my peers in that way.

However, it was STEMM professor and academic journal editor Jonathan who offered a particularly insightful account of the potentially most epistemically corrosive effects of holy grail-pursuit. The account began with Jonathan's referring to 'a couple of incidences of fraud' involving data manipulation. The first case had been brought to his attention as editor-in-chief by a reviewer who recalled having reviewed a similar paper a few years earlier, by the same authors, but in which different data had been presented. Jonathan outlined his recollection of the events:

> So, we did a little bit of, kind of, forensic looking at those figures, and sure enough, it showed that a couple of the figures had been manipulated ... it was clear in the end. So, we wrote back to the authors for an explanation, and the authors explained that apparently ... as is normally the case, they blamed it on the post-docs who'd gone [i.e. left the institution] and ... and apologised terribly.

He then related the second case, which had occurred in a journal edited by a colleague with whom he frequently compares notes, since their two journals lie in closely related fields:

> He [the colleague] had a case of a paper that had been submitted to him which had a photo of [X^7], which he thought he, kind of, recognised. And, sure enough, he found it in another paper – except it was a bit different, because the legend in that said something completely different, and I think the thing was the other way around. So, we figured that one paper was claiming to be *one* thing, and then in *this* paper it was something different. So, he wrote to the author, and to all of the co-authors. What's interesting is that the *co-authors* all came back to him and said that they hadn't even known that this paper had been *submitted*; they'd had nothing to do with it, they'd never seen it!
>
> (Jonathan, STEMM journal editor)

Emerging from the *academic journal editors study* as relatively commonplace within some STEMM fields was the practice, alluded to in the quote above, of what, at best, could be labelled strategic co-authoring, and at worst as fraudulent authorship claims. An evidently symbiotic arrangement, this practice was explained by several research participants as usually involving the agreement of high-profile distinguished researchers, despite their having had no involvement in writing it, to be listed as co-authors of a paper, on the basis that such inclusion would not only increase those distinguished researchers' publications (and potentially citations) profiles, but also increase the *bone fide* authors' chances of having the paper accepted for publication. A medical sciences researcher employed at a research-intensive university spoke defiantly of his refusal to adopt such practice:

> The world of [names a specific field] research is relatively small still, and it's led by a group of people, a smallish group of people, and what people tend to do is put people's names on papers in order to get people's attention, and that's completely clear in the way you see the publications coming out.
>
> *Interviewer: You mean, these people are not actually authors?*
>
> They tend to be people of importance in the world of [specific field] who've been put on [the paper]. And, of course, when you put on, you know, 'contributions' ... 'contributed to the paper, to the manuscript', but you know in your heart that they probably haven't done very much for it ... but it's a very small world, and if you want something published in a high impact journal then you tend to accept the fact that this guy has to be a co-author. And I've always said, 'Well, unless you've had decent participation, you don't go on the paper'. But, y'know, maybe I'm too – maybe it's me that's at fault, and maybe I *should* be playing the game.

It's difficult to know, isn't it? But we've had a couple of decent articles that, clearly, had they been written by people in the field whose names were either more popular at the time, or more famous, would probably have had a higher chance of at least being submitted for review. Often these things don't even get reviewed if they don't have the right name, or you're not the right person.

The *academic journal editors study* could not, of course, gauge the extent and magnitude of such editorial practice: the prioritisation of distinguished researchers' papers over (and potentially to the exclusion of) unknown authors. But the study did uncover multiple *perceptions* on the part of medical researchers that strategic co-authorship was prevalent – including a journal editor who not only identified the practice as *de rigeur* in his field, but also admitted to being influenced by it:

> There's no point denying it, if I get a manuscript in and it's got three big names that I recognise, or I get a manuscript that's got no names I recognise ... already, there's a psychological effect of that. There *shouldn't* be – you try and counter it ... but there is. And people know that. So, if you're a junior member of staff and you're looking to get published, often you try and include your former mentor on the paper.

Through the compromising that it may impose on academics, then, pressured professionalism is not only highly susceptible to deteriorating into what, by eroding job fulfilment, may be considered *impoverished* professionalism, it also spawns corner-cutting – and, in extreme cases, cheating. When they are applied to research, however, corner-cutting and cheating have epistemic consequences.

Selling Academe's Soul to the Devil? The Risk of Epistemic Corruption's Becoming a By-product of Pressured Professionalism

Epistemic worthiness is important. It underpins the integrity of knowledge producing work and of those who engage in it, and it underpins the value of the knowledge we use – rely on – for societal growth. Described as a 'thorny philosophical issue' (Christias, 2015: 33), epistemic justification (or worthiness), as Šešelja and Straßer (2014: 3112) explain, fundamentally relates to the augmentation of knowledge and understanding:

> Epistemic justification is ... traditionally conceived of as providing standards for the acceptability of certain beliefs in the knowledge base or the cognitive system

of an intelligent agent. Applied to a scientific theory, it provides criteria for its inclusion and acceptance into the grand corpus of our scientific knowledge. It concerns the question as to whether we have good reasons to consider it as being (approximately) truthful, empirically adequate, etc.

To justify our reliance on specific knowledge, we must – to paraphrase Šešelja and Straßer – have good reason to be confident of its 'truthfulness', 'empirical adequacy' or worthiness. Yet the research findings presented above have uncovered a hole in what should be a watertight receptacle for gathering and safeguarding knowledge: university research. With the rationalisation of knowledge production, epistemic worthiness has evidently been side-lined – paid insufficient attention – not least in and by universities.

The Rationalisation of Knowledge Production

Faced with too many tasks to complete, many of the *professorial academic leadership study* participants had to take the difficult decision to cut back their research activity. But such reduction has the knock-on effect of putting limits on – rationalising – (potential) knowledge production, for knowledge that might have been generated by this or that research project risks being diminished or overlooked. Illustrating such a perspective is the narrative of Harry, who, quoted above, implies that he could achieve so much more on the research front if he were not required to metaphorically keep so many other balls in the air, forcing him towards – to use his term – mediocrity, rather than excellence: '[A]s I look around and I look for people who appear exceptionally successful, they only really do one thing'. In support of Harry's expressed sentiments, it is worth noting that a great many of those recognised as great thinkers and intellectual giants have been mono-focused, and needed peace and tranquillity – often isolation – to be creative. Isaac Newton, Cropper (2004) tells us, was self-centred and reclusive and, 'at least during his most creative years, was a secret introvert' (p. 21), and James Clerk Maxwell 'decided that he did not need an academic appointment, with all its accompanying duties for which he was not well suited, to continue his researches' (Cropper, 2004: 159), and so resigned his post at King's College London to continue his work in the peace and solitude of rural Scotland. Not for these luminaries the frenzied, multifarious existence that requires constant refocusing – if such had been their lot, society is likely to have missed out on their scientific legacies.

'Universities are pulled between producing stellar research and providing mass education, being global producers of knowledge and contributing to the advancement of national and regional economy', note Soysal and

Baltaru (2021: 313). 'How do these pressures play themselves out in the purpose and mandate of universities and institutional logics that prevail in higher education?', they ask. From the research findings presented above, we see how such pressures 'play themselves out' in the working lives of academics, for whom the implications of such out-playing are alluded to by Angermuller (2017: 968):

> The socially recognized labels, classifications and categories that constitute an academic subject position must not be misunderstood as a mere outside, as a marketing ploy that cynic actors create of themselves. These categories define the social existence of academics.

Consistent with what I call 'proximity theory' (Evans, 2018), what drives academics to enact pressured professionalism, then, is their pursuit of what I introduce above as 'uncompromising' work contexts that take them (these academics) closer to realising what they *currently* perceive to be their 'ideal' job situations, and which in turn are key components of their wider current idealized selves. This pursuit occurs within such a 'social existence' – to quote Angemuller (2017) once more – in which, '[e]ntangled in a web of relationships with many other researchers, researchers participate in discourses in which they build up and consolidate academic subject positions in the social world of research' (p. 965), allowing them to 'occupy academic subject positions which are valued in their communities' (p. 964). Angermuller (2017: 968) continues:

> [T]o pursue their careers, researchers try to consolidate and improve their positions in higher education institutions (by moving up the academic status ladder ...) *and* in scientific communities (by enhancing their reputation as recognized experts in a disciplinary field, ...). And they participate in many other, non-academic positioning games, which sometimes make a difference as well (e.g. recognition in the mass media). As a result of these positioning dynamics which involve many members in large communities, some come to be counted as established academic researchers (a process Bourdieu has called 'consecration' ...) while others are less recognized, stay in precarious jobs or finally drop out.
>
> (original emphasis)

Yet, as my research findings show, in encountering tensions and challenges that impede their progress along the 'pressured professionalism' road – a road that they choose because it points the way to their idealised 'consecrated' selves (to apply Angermuller's reference to Bourdieu's term) – many academics find themselves branching off onto side paths that they anticipate will get them to their destination quicker, or make for an easier journey, or that they reluctantly assess to be the only viable way through. But, where they traverse the 'Compromise', 'Corner-cutting', or wild and untamed 'Cheat' territories of the academic research landscape, these side paths, by inflicting untold damage onto its finely balanced eco-system, ravage the knowledge production environment that universities have undertaken to protect and cultivate. Viewed with hindsight, this reveals itself to have been a rash undertaking, for it requires unwavering commitment to the notion that universities – and the knowledge they produce – should be focused on, and serve, the public good. Yet on this issue universities have taken their eye off the ball, allowing themselves to be distracted by their eagerness to jump onto the neoliberal bandwagon. Then, once their knowledge and knowledge producers became commodified, they (universities) found themselves playing a whole new ball game – potentially with diabolical consequences.

A Faustian Transaction?

It is, of course, recognised that knowledge is always propositional: liable to being superseded or displaced, sometimes simply by future epistemic discoveries, sometimes as a result of what Kitcher (2000) calls scientific controversies. Such is the nature of scientific dynamism. But what the findings presented here expose is a more insidious form of evolution: one that risks degenerating into epistemic *corruption* – a notion that is described by Kidd et al (2021: 152) as:

> a form of damage done to people's epistemic character by their subjection to conditions or processes that erode epistemic virtues such as curiosity and thoughtfulness and facilitate the epistemic vices like dogmatism or closedmindedness.

Elaborating on this description, Kidd et al (2021: 154) continue:

> [W]e conceive of epistemic vices as traits of epistemic character that make us bad thinkers. Vices can do this in one or both of two ways. Effects-vices are traits that tend to cause a preponderance of bad epistemic effects: inattentiveness, for instance, means one will systematically fail to detect epistemically relevant features or a situation, in ways that impair one's ability to acquire knowledge and understanding. Motives-vices are traits that are vicious because they express or manifest bad epistemic motives or values, such as an indifference to truth, or a desire to interfere with the epistemic agency of others, a sort of epistemic malevolence.

A clear chain of consequence that is evident in the research findings presented above may be outlined as follows. The twenty-first-century university in the developed world, whose culture of performativity reflects neoliberal ideologies, spawns pressured academic professionalism. For some academics, this pressured professionalism serves as a self-actualising vehicle; for others, it serves as a straitjacket, forcing them to compromise on their values and priorities, including by constraining their participation in their most cherished activity: research. Knowledge production risks being adversely impacted in the latter cases by potentially expert knowledge producers having to ration their time on the pursuit, inevitably reducing the amount and/or quality of knowledge being generated. There is a risk of time-poverty-and-competing-demands-imposed inattentiveness, whose consequences may be what Kidd and colleagues refer to above as failure to detect epistemically relevant issues; such a risk was exposed in the comments, presented above, of STEMM professor Brian, whose inadequately supervised doctoral students narrowly missed generating flawed data. In the cases of those who thrive on meeting the challenges associated with pressured professionalism, the findings presented in this chapter expose the risk of fraudulent research practice's reflecting the 'indifference to truth' that Kidd and colleagues refer to, and of provoking 'a desire to interfere with the epistemic agency of others, a sort of epistemic malevolence'. The risk to knowledge production of the practice of strategic co-authoring, or fraudulent authorship claims, is one of potential omission, whereby epistemically worthy knowledge is in danger of being overlooked or eclipsed in the publication-centred dissemination process by knowledge that blinkered, star-struck, journal editors may be persuaded, by virtue of its illustrious authorship, to perceive as more epistemically worthy.

Framing this sketched scenario are more generic epistemically constraining issues, such as that highlighted by van Houtum and van Uden (2022: 200–1):

> [T]he rise of anxious, number-abiding researchers who rather than being stimulated to walk into untraveled terrains are spurred to breed on their secure and fast lane publication and acquisition scores …. What will be researched then is what will be lucratively financeable and/or fairly quickly publishable, which is disturbingly at odds with what the managerial metrical regime was, following its own mission statement, allegedly introduced for, namely to ensure innovative quality.

Concluding Thoughts

Back in 1994 Shirley Fisher warned: '[A]cademics faced with tasks such as lecturing, research, writing research grant applications and organizing administrative tasks, are potentially in overload situations' (Fisher, 1994: 66). In reaching adulthood, the embryonic neoliberal university that she discerned in the early 1990s has, in the twenty-first century, exacerbated the effects of such overload – not least in its demands on professors. Moreover, quite apart from the pressure felt by professors to engage in a wide range of activities – for many of which they may consider themselves unqualified or ill-equipped – this width of focus is having the unfortunate effect of diluting professors' intellectual activity, and impoverishing their (and, by extension, their universities') scholarly output. Added to this troubling image of a university that is failing to get the best out of many of its most senior academics is the issue of holy-grail-pursuit, and its potentially epistemic-worthiness-eroding consequences. Universities may well be labouring under the misapprehension that, apart from the inevitable odd loose stitch and broken thread, they have got performativity all sewn up. Yet Teresa Sullivan's (2014) lamenting the erosion of academe's offering a haven of tranquillity for 'the life of the mind', in which serious scholars sought quiet, calm refuge from the distractions that impeded their creativity may herald a simmering backlash against the frenetic omnifarious activity that defines academic life in today's university. For something must give, and if it turns out to be scholarship, and, by extension, the production of epistemically worthy knowledge, we will have sold academe's soul to the devil.

Are universities aware that he is already pacing up and down restlessly, anticipating the transaction? Or, to experience the transient pleasures of league table successes, have they already entered into a Faustian pact?

Acknowledgements

For clarity and consistency in retaining a singular authorial voice throughout this chapter, I use the singular first-person possessive pronoun – my – in referring to research, and its specific elements, that I conducted with excellent co-investigators, whose invaluable contributions to the *professorial academic leadership study* and the *academic journal editors study* I acknowledge. Dr Justine Mercer (University of Warwick) was the co-investigator of the former project, and Dr Matt Homer (University of Leeds) provided statistical expertise to both projects.

Notes

1 The binary divide in the UK that distinguished universities from polytechnics was abolished in 1992, when the former polytechnics were permitted to become universities. Representing two different mission groups, the 'old', pre-1992,

university sector is traditionally research-focused, whilst the post-1992 sector is traditionally more teaching-focused.
2   Fagan and Teasdale (2021: 775) note that '[t]he majority (78 %) of those who hold the rank of full professor are men', while the Higher Education Statistics Association's figures for the academic year 2019–20 indicate that of 22,810 academics in UK universities who were categorised as professors, 6,345 were women, 16,415 were men and the remaining 50 were identified as 'other' (HESA, 2021).
3   Taking authorial liberties, for simplicity and brevity, here and elsewhere in the chapter I personify the term 'universities' by applying it to denote senior managers and other influential policymakers and administrators who constitute universities' centres of administrative power.
4   The Research Excellence Framework (REF) is the mechanism used in the UK for assessing, approximately every six to seven years, the quality of research carried out by academics in each university that chooses to be entered into the mechanism. Its outcomes determine participating universities' allocations of government funding.
5   The focus of this activity is obscured to protect the interviewee's anonymity.
6   A junior academic grade, equivalent to assistant professor.
7   The subject of the photo referred to has been removed for anonymisation purposes.

References

Angermuller, J. (2017) Academic careers and the valuation of academics. A discursive perspective on status categories and academic salaries in France as compared to the U.S., Germany and Great Britain. *Higher Education*, 73(6): 963–80.

Barnett, R. (1997) A knowledge strategy for universities. In R. Barnett and A. Griffin (eds.) *The end of knowledge in higher education*, pp. 166–86. London: Cassell.

Barnett, R. (2011) Towards an ecological professionalism. In C. Sugrue and T. D. Solbrekke (eds.) *Professional responsibility: New horizons of praxis*, pp. 29–41. Abingdon: Routledge.

Bolden, R. et al. (2012) *Academic leadership: Changing conceptions, identities and experiences in UK higher education*, research and development series, full report to the Leadership Foundation for Higher Education. London: Leadership Foundation for Higher Education.

Castro-Ceacero, D. and Ion, G. (2018) Changes in the university research approach: Challenges for academics' scientific productivity. *Higher Education Policy*, 32(3): 681–99.

Christias, D. (2015) A critical examination of BonJour's, Haack's, and Dancy's theory of empirical justification. *Logos and Episteme*, 6(1): 7–13.

Cropper, W. H. (2004) *Great physicists: The life and times of great physicists from Galileo to Hawking*. New York: Oxford University Press.

Evans, L. (2001) Delving deeper into morale, job satisfaction and motivation among education professionals: Re-examining the leadership dimension. *Educational Management and Administration*, 29(3): 291–306.

Evans, L. (2008) Professionalism, professionality and the development of education professionals. *British Journal of Educational Studies*, 56(1): 20–38.

Evans, L. (2011) The 'shape' of teacher professionalism in England: Professional standards, performance management, professional development, and the changes proposed in the 2010 White Paper. *British Educational Research Journal*, 37(5): 851–70.

Evans, L. (2013) The professional status of educational research: Professionalism and developmentalism in 21st century working life. *British Journal of Educational Studies*, 61(4): 471–90.

Evans, L. (2015) A changing role for university professors? Professorial academic leadership as it is perceived by 'the led'. *British Educational Research Journal*, 41(4): 666–85.

Evans, L. (2017) University professors as academic leaders: Professorial leadership development needs and provision. *Educational Management, Administration & Leadership*, 45(1): 123–40.

Evans, L. (2018) *Professors as academic leaders: Expectations, enacted professionalism and evolving roles*. London: Bloomsbury.

Evans, L. and Cosnefroy, L. (2013) The dawn of a new academic professionalism in the French academy? Academics facing the challenges of imposed reform. *Studies in Higher Education*, 38(8): 1201–21.

Evetts, J. (2013) Professionalism: Value and ideology. *Current Sociology*, 61(5–6): 778–96. https://doi.org/10.1177/0011392113479316.

Fagan, C. and Teasdale, N. (2021) Women professors across STEMM and non-STEMM disciplines: Navigating gendered spaces and playing the academic game. *Work, Employment and Society*, 35(4): 774–92.

Finkenstaedt, T. (2011) Teachers. In W. Rüegg (ed.) *A history of the university in Europe, IV*, pp. 162–203. Cambridge: Cambridge University Press.

Fisher, S. (1994) *Stress in academic life*. Buckingham: Open University Press.

Godin, B. and Gingras, Y. (2000) The place of universities in the system of knowledge production. *Research Policy*, 29(2): 273–8.

Gunn, A. and Mintrom, M. (2022) *Public policy and power: The interplay of knowledge and power*. Cambridge: Cambridge University Press.

Hernes, G. (2021) On the cognitive social contract – will universities survive the 21st century? In S. S. Serger, A. Malmberg and M. Benner (2021) (eds.) *Renewing higher education: Academic leadership in times of transformation*. Sweden-USA Project for Collaboration, Academic Leadership & Innovation in Higher Education (CALIE), pp. 27–49. Lund: Lund University.

Higher Education Statistics Association (HESA) (2021) *Higher Education Staff Statistics: UK, 2019/20: Statistical Bulletin*, https://www.hesa.ac.uk/news/19-01-2021/sb259-higher-education-staff-statistics (accessed 18 November 2021).

Karseth, B. and Nerland, M. (2007) Building professionalism in a knowledge society: Examining discourses of knowledge in four professional associations. *Journal of Education and Work*, 20(4): 335–55.

Kidd, I. J., Chubb, J. and Forstenzer, J. (2021) Epistemic corruption and the research impact agenda. *Theory and Research in Education*, 19(2): 148–67.

Kitcher, P. (2000) Patterns of scientific controversies. In P. Machmaer, M. Pera and A. Baltas (eds.) *Scientific controversies: Philosophical and historical perspectives*, pp. 21–39. Oxford: Oxford University Press.

Kolsaker, A. (2008) Academic professionalism in the managerialist era: A study of English universities. *Studies in Higher Education*, 33(5): 513–25.

Lucas, L. (2006) *The research game in academic life*. Maidenhead: Open University Press & The Society for Research into Higher Education.

Lund, R. and Tienari, J. (2019) Passion, care, and eros in the gendered neoliberal university. *Organization*, 26(1): 98–121.

Marine, S. B. and Martínez-Alemán, A. M. (2018). Women faculty, professional identity and generational disposition. *The Review of Higher Education*, 41(2): 217–52.

Maslow, A. H. (1954) *Motivation and personality*. New York: Harper and Row.

Noordegraaf, M. (2007). From 'pure' to 'hybrid' professionalism: Present-day professionalism in ambiguous public domains. *Administration and Society*, 39(6): 761–85.

Scanlon, L. (2011) 'Becoming' a professional. In L. Scanlon (ed.) *'Becoming' a professional: An interdisciplinary analysis of professional learning*, pp. 13–32. Dordrecht: Springer.

Scott, P. (1997) The crisis of knowledge and the massification of higher education. In R. Barnett and A. Griffin (eds.) *The end of knowledge in higher education*, pp. 14–26. London: Cassell.

Scott, P. (2009). Markets and new modes of knowledge production. In J. Enders and E. de Weert (eds.) *The changing face of academic life: Analytical and comparative perspectives*, pp. 58–77. Basingstoke: Palgrave Macmillan.

Šešelja, J. and Straßer, C. (2014) Epistemic justification in the context of pursuit: A coherentist approach. *Synthese*, 191(13): 3111–41.

Soysal, Y. N. and Baltaru, R.-D. (2021) University as the producer of knowledge, and economic and societal value: The 20th and twenty-first century transformations of the UK higher education system. *European Journal of Higher Education*, 11(3): 312–28.

Stevens, M. L. and Börjesson, M. (2021) Digitization and strategic renewal of higher education. In S. S. Serger, A. Malmberg and M. Benner (eds.) *Renewing higher education: Academic leadership in times of transformation*. Sweden-USA Project for Collaboration, Academic Leadership & Innovation in Higher Education (CALIE), pp. 91–111. Lund: Lund University.

Sullivan, T. A. (2014) Greedy institutions, overwork and work-life balance. *Sociological Inquiry*, 84(1): 1–15.

Švarc, J. (2016) The knowledge worker is dead: What about professions? *Current Sociology*, 64(3): 392–410.

van Houtum, H. and van Uden, A. (2022) The autoimmunity of the modern university: How its managerialism is self-harming what it claims to protect. *Organization*, 29(1): 197–208.

4

Luck and Precarity: Contextualising Fixed-term Academics' Perceptions of Success and Failure

Vik Loveday

Introduction

Mine is a dizzying country in which the Lottery is a major element of reality
(Borges, 1998: 101).

Processes of expansion, marketization and audit have transformed the landscape of the UK's higher education (HE) sector in recent years (Ball, 2012; Brown with Carasso, 2013; Burrows, 2012; Cronin, 2016; Loveday, 2021; McGettigan, 2013; Morrish and Sauntson, 2020; Nash, 2019; Neyland et al, 2019). Existing research on the 'neoliberalizing' sector has shown that academics are experiencing substantial stress, anxiety and pressure to perform (Baron, 2014; Gill, 2014; Kinman, 2014; Loveday, 2018; Morrish, 2019; Sullivan and Simon, 2014), as well as being in increased competition with one another (Knowles and Burrows, 2014).[1] However, while these wider processes undoubtedly impact all employees in the sector, a distinction can be made between what Kimber (2003) terms as a 'tenured core' and a 'tenuous periphery' of academic workers.

In 2019/20, 33 per cent of academic staff working in UK HE institutions were employed on fixed-term contracts (HESA, 2020),[2] and recent research has explored the impact of casualization on teaching and pedagogy (Leathwood and Read, 2020). Yet how do casualized academic employees feel about the temporary nature of their own work? While fixed-term contracts have become increasingly normalized under the guise of flexibility (Barcan, 2013; Bryson, 2004; Sennett, 1998), a number of studies have shown how differential perceptions and experiences of casualized work are likely to be contingent on the intersection of factors such as gender, ethnicity, migratory status and age (Archer, 2008; Bryson, 2004; Ivancheva et al, 2019; Lopes and Dewan, 2014; Reay, 2000; UCU, 2020; Wang, 2020); the variegated nature of the labour market in HE also means that academic discipline may influence career progression, as well as aspirations to remain working within the sector (Vitae, 2013, 2016).

However, while casualization is not experienced in a monolithic way, academic work has become increasingly individualized (Coate et al, 2015; Gill, 2013, 2014; Gill and Pratt, 2008; Leathwood and Read, 2013; Sullivan and Simon, 2014); fixed-term academics experience multiple forms of uncertainty related to their career trajectories, finances, mobility and future plans, but whilst attempting to forge stable academic careers for themselves they are also responsibilized for managing risk (see also Reith, 2004: 397) and coping with uncertainty (Gill and Donaghue, 2016; Loveday, 2018). What, then, might individual academics' perceptions of success and failure tell us about the wider processes at work in the neoliberalizing HE sector and its implications for the future of the academic profession?

Based on eighty-three interviews conducted with forty-four casualized academic employees, the chapter begins by exploring the empirical context of the research before turning to focus on two interrelated facets of the lived experience of employment uncertainty: first, the narrativization of chance and the consolidation of luck as an explanatory factor in making sense of success; and second, the corresponding tendency of the academic participants to individualize failure when expectations have been thwarted. While it is argued that accounts of fixed-term work are suffused with notions of chance and fortune, perceptions of 'luck' remain under-researched within sociology. The chapter thus concludes by considering what 'luck' might offer for a fuller, politicized understanding of processes of subjectification in the academic profession.

Researching 'Casualization' in HE

This chapter emerges from a wider project conducted between 2014 and 2016, which aimed to explore how fixed-term academic staff make sense of their uncertain employment situations, the types of factors that influence their perceptions, and the impact on them of wider processes at work in the UK's rapidly evolving HE sector. Based on a qualitative longitudinal research design, a total of 100 interviews were conducted with forty-four casualized academic staff in three 'waves'; the findings of this chapter are based on the first two waves of interview data comprising forty-four preliminary interviews and follow-up interviews several months later with thirty-nine of the participants.

All participants were employed on fixed-term contracts in UK HE at the beginning of the research and were recruited through personal and professional networks, and the use of snowball sampling. Participants varied in age between their late twenties and mid-fifties; eighteen were male and twenty-six female; twenty-seven were British, but participants from other European countries, Australasia, Asia, the Middle East, North America and the Caribbean were also interviewed. The project aimed to capture and contrast the perceptions of casualized academics working in different types of role (researchers, teaching-only staff, and lecturers) and at different career stages: the most junior participant at the time of interview was only two days into their first appointment post-PhD, while the two most senior participants held professorial positions. Participants were based in different types of university around the UK, and while the majority worked in social science disciplines, academics from the arts, humanities, natural sciences, law and architecture are also represented.

As academics themselves, those interviewed were well-versed in research ethics. The biggest concern was to guarantee the anonymity of those taking part; as Magnus – a post-doctoral social scientist – notes in one of our interviews: 'if there weren't risks to making a big fuss about how shit it is at the beginning of your career, then you wouldn't have to anonymise this'. Due to the participants' considerable anxiety that their interviews might render them identifiable to colleagues and employers, it has not generally been possible to provide precise biographical details in this chapter. Apart from the use of pseudonyms, care has also been taken to work with participants to sufficiently anonymize other details, such as employing institutions. All participants have been provided with copies of their interview transcripts to allay any fears over anonymity, but also to stimulate discussion and reflection during follow-up interviews.

Since the research aimed to explore how the casualized academics make sense of insecure work, interviews were designed to probe participants' subjective understandings of their employment positions (see also Gill and Pratt, 2008; Tweedie, 2013). To capture work histories, the first 'wave' of interviews began by asking participants to describe how they had come to be in their current role, before questions were posed to explore participants' academic identities, future career plans, emotional responses to work, impressions of short-term employment and the effects of work on other areas of life. Follow-up interviews were conducted with as many participants as possible to track changing circumstances and perceptions, but also to allow for the possibility of 'the establishment of a genuine two-way dialogue' (Sinha and Back, 2014: 474).

At the beginning of the project in 2014, I was myself employed on a fixed-term lecturing contract, and the participants were made aware of my contractual situation. Müller and Kenney (2014: 543, following Felt et al) claim that the so-called peer-to-peer interview – based on 'shared membership in the academy' – can facilitate 'trust based on assumed similarity of experiences'. However, Mercer (2007: 6) warns that 'greater familiarity can make insiders more likely to take things for granted, develop myopia, and assume their own perspective is far more widespread than it actually is'. Thus, while I chose to discuss my own position and experiences openly with participants to foster confidence and as a means of establishing a shared stake in the issue of casualization, I was careful in the first wave of interviews not to ask questions that would merely chime with my own impression of fixed-term work in HE as a politicized issue (see UCU, 2016), rather than simply a 'flexible' working arrangement (see Barcan, 2013; Bryson, 2004; Sennett, 1998).

Informed by an abductive approach to data analysis, the research focused on participants' perceptions of academia and their working lives to address the construction of meaning (Tavory and Timmermans, 2014: 21). Interviews were thematically coded and compared across cases, but also diachronically for those interviewed twice. One of the main themes to emerge from the first wave of interview data was the notion of luck; this finding was then explicitly discussed with participants during the second wave of interviews. Interviews are not understood here as having the potential to uncover an objective 'reality', and the participants' opinions are not taken as 'fact'; instead, the interview process is conceptualized as an act of construction between researcher and researched (Hammersley, 2003: 120), and discourse is understood as 'occasioned' (Gill, 2000: 175). Following Strübing (2007: 585), '[d]ata, seen in this way, is not the unhewn material that a researcher starts out with, but rather the *relation* between the field, the research issues, and the researchers established in the course of the analytical process'. In the subsequent section, I explore the connection between perceptions of success, the narrativization of 'luck' in the interviews and the participants' sense of agency.

'Counting my lucky stars': Perceptions of Success

On beginning her first fixed-term humanities lectureship, Alice describes 'counting my lucky stars'. Similarly, when describing getting a job as a teaching fellow in the humanities, Alan notes: 'I was very lucky', and then continues on to describe what he felt was the 'fateful moment' (see also Giddens, 1991) determining his appointment. These types of asides were common during the first wave of interviews conducted: participants tended to construe success in terms of luck – irrespective of variables such as gender, ethnicity or age, or length of contract – so that finding a job or being awarded a grant was often expressed as the result of some fortuitous encounter, series of events or as pure happenstance. Even participants in more senior positions had a tendency to also describe success as a matter of chance, such as Sarah – a social science professor on a fixed-term fractional contract – who describes being head-hunted by a prestigious funder to head up an international project: 'It's sort of like a gift that's fallen out of the sky: I'm just lucky.' In this section, I want to argue that this frequent recourse to notions of luck, chance and happenstance by the participants in this project is indicative of the diminished agency of casualized academic staff in the landscape of UK HE. My interest here is in exploring how academic employees *make sense* of their positions; it is clearly not possible to establish objectively whether the participants have really been 'lucky' and if success has been a matter of pure 'chance'. However, I want to argue that the narrativization of 'luck' is reflective of the tenuous position in which a sizeable proportion of the academic workforce now finds themselves.

There remains a striking lack of sociological literature engaging with notions of luck outside of the sociology of gambling (e.g. Reith, 2002, 2003), which can perhaps be explained by Smith's (1993: 513) contention that 'luck' has remained at the level of a 'residual category' – a 'tacit taboo' (Mattausch, 2003: 506; see also Sauder, 2020). What, then, might be the danger of conceptualizing the concept of 'chance' as being beyond the purview of sociological analysis? Smith (1993: 528) argues:

> [S]ociological models which include chance avoid the assumptions of either total chaos or total regularity. Instead, the three main causal elements of 'agency', 'chance' and 'conditions' are placed within a diachronic relationship where agencies, working within the constraints of logically defined conditions and chance impacts, in turn, modify these circumstances through a combination of intended outcomes and unforeseen chance consequences.

Thus, the acceptance of chance as a sociological concept does not deny the significance of either structure or agency.

My interest here, then, is in using perceptions of luck as a starting point for thinking through the relationship between agency – understood here as an 'individual's capacity for action' (McNay, 2004: 179) – and the wider structural conditions of employment in the HE sector. Reith (2003: para. 2) argues that 'the way we deal with uncertainty is central for understanding how societies operate and organise themselves'. She notes how the application of reason during the Enlightenment sought to eliminate 'irrational' notions such as 'luck', and that the result of such a project was the creation of the new idea of 'risk', or 'the science of uncertainty', as a means of mastering the unknown (Reith, 2003: paras. 13–4; see also Giddens, 1991; Hacking, 1990). Yet Giddens (1991: 130) has argued: 'Notions of fate refuse to disappear altogether, and are found in uneasy combination with an outlook of the secular risk type and with attitudes of fatalism.'

Taking issue with the use of rational choice theory to analyse the relationship between luck and power, Lukes and Haglund (2005: 54) assert:

> 'Luck', according to the dictionary, means either 'chance' or 'fortune, good or ill'. It is hard to see how it can play a useful explanatory role in accounting for differential outcome power (or social inequality) [...] Chance suggests mere accidents and fortune suggests destiny or fate or an act of God. But we are, supposedly, trying to explain [...] the mechanisms that create and sustain inequality in positions or access to resources. Chance, Destiny, Fate and God constitute various different ways of declining to provide such an explanation.

Rachel – a social scientist who had been working as a post-doctoral researcher before being appointed as a lecturer on a permanent contract – also wonders if 'luck' is sometimes used as a convenient way of covering over privilege, as Lukes and Haglund (2005) argue. Yet the narrativization of luck and chance in my research suggests that these concepts were not consciously invoked as a way of denying advantage. Instead, the participants appeared to take recourse to these notions when describing situations over which they felt no control. Byrne (2003: 30) links the narrativization of one's life to 'processes of subject construction'; she argues that an attention to narrative processes is 'likely to offer a key entry point into the "techniques" or "practices" of the self' (Byrne, 2003: 30). In particular, a focus on the context in which stories are produced may provide valuable insight into the production of subjectivities (Byrne, 2003: 32). It was a striking feature of the first 'wave' of interviews conducted that very few of the participants presented voluntaristic accounts of their career trajectories; instead, the vast majority tended to narrate their academic careers as happening *to* them, rather than presenting themselves as agents in control of their working lives.

Daniels (2003: 619) asserts that 'luck implies the existence of agency, good or bad, outside of the control of the human individual', and recourse to the notion of 'luck' when describing fortuitous experiences was one of the unanticipated ways in which participants tended to express a lack of agency. Anne, a social science post-doctoral researcher, comments in our first interview together: 'I guess maybe my interview is quite boring in a way because I was quite lucky to get the job in the first place.' The way in which Anne narrativizes her career trajectory points to a fundamental lack of control: hers is merely a 'boring' story since her appointment is understood as a matter of chance. In a similar manner to Anne, when asked how he had come to be in his current role, Philip – who was also working as a post-doctoral researcher in the social sciences at the time of our first interview together – noted: 'I think I was probably quite lucky in some respects'. He explains: 'I know I should have more faith in my own skills and abilities, but it does feel a lot like luck.'

I want to turn now to the case of David to think through how having 'faith in one's own skills and abilities' might be diminished by the wider conditions in which fixed-term employees find themselves in HE. During our first interview, David had been job-hunting for some time and had applied unsuccessfully for a number of post-doctoral fellowships; his mood was low and he confided that he was questioning his 'commitment' to pursuing a career in academia. However, by the time of our second interview ten months later, David had secured a prestigious post-doctoral position in another EU country where he was shortly due to move.

> David: I keep saying this to people and I believe it when people were congratulating me on getting the [funding] that I do think that it's also a matter of luck in the sense of however you want to define luck: everything [...] that's not within your power to control [...] I just cannot *believe* that my application for the [funding] was light-years ahead than the ones I had done before and that had been rejected.
>
> Author: You said [in the last interview when describing failure], "I tend to personalise it, or individualize it, I tend to bring it down to my own understanding of reality, or my own capabilities and competencies." And I thought that was interesting talking about how when you hadn't had these successes, you individualized that [...] But now you've had a success, you're saying: 'oh, it's luck'.

David: It's definitely luck too. […] me saying it was luck – I'm definitely not saying it was only luck, but me saying that it was also luck, maybe that's actually not necessarily not recognising my efforts or my capabilities, but rather because I had seen before how these efforts, these capabilities had not come to some kind of fruition; I now think that it's not that I got so much better […] Let's say I was good enough. I was good enough. So something else must have happened, been added to the equation.

[…]

But like I said before, attributing chance to one's success maybe has to do with how you develop an understanding of how *hard* things are. Having said that, to be the devil's advocate of what I just said, it's funny because when somebody else has a success […]I don't think 'they were lucky', I think they were fucking good […] The underlying, unspoken message there is that they are so much better than me, to come back to something we were talking about – competition – last time.

While grant applications to research councils in the UK are thought to have grown after the 2014 Research Excellence Framework exercise, success rates have conversely been reported as declining (Matthews, 2015)[3] so that 'once success rates drop below 20 per cent, the process "becomes more of a lottery"' (Martin cited by Matthews, 2015: n.p.). It is hardly surprising, then, that in David's case above, he sees being awarded a grant as a 'matter of luck' due to the wider, competitive landscape of the UK's HE sector. As Knowles and Burrows (2014: 249) warn, 'metricization' runs the risk of 'unleashing new forms of academic competition'. In this competitive environment, David sees the achievement of other academics as being an indication that they are 'fucking good'; yet, he understands his own successful funding application as being merely '*good enough*'. I want to argue, then, that the invocation of 'luck' by David points to a sense of diminished agency for casualized academic employees, but also highlights the lack of entitlement he feels: the suspicion here is that while David has merely been 'lucky', the natural talent of other academics means that they are deserving of their rewards.

While recourse to luck was a common feature of the narrativization of success, participants conversely tended to make sense of their frustrations or failures in individualizing terms, as David notes in our first interview together when he describes trying to come to terms with a fruitless search for jobs and funding: 'I tend to personalize it, or individualize it, I tend to bring it down to […] my own capabilities and competencies.' This seemingly ambivalent position – that is, invoking 'chance' in the case of success, but then taking personal responsibility for failure – is summed up neatly by Imogen, a lecturer in the social sciences, who explains: 'You've also got that small voice in your mind that says: "no, you're a bit shit", or "you're a bit lucky", […] or "you're probably both."' Below I want to consider the individualization of disappointment and thwarted ambition as symptomatic of the wider conditions of the contemporary academy.

'I am my own obstacle': Individualizing Barriers to Success

I have been arguing that for the academic participants in this project, the narrativization of luck is indicative of a feeling of being 'out of control', which is precipitated by the short-term nature of their employment contracts. However, in tandem with the propensity to take recourse to 'chance' in the case of success is the tendency of the participants to individualize failure: while the casualized academics in this research often neglected to take credit for success in the telling of their academic stories (even if they did acknowledge hard work), failure to succeed – for example, in job-hunting, interviews, or publishing – was often attributed to a personal shortcoming, or miscalculation. As Reith (2003: para. 25) notes: 'Ill fortune is no longer seen as a punishment from God, but as a personal failure … attributable to laziness, ignorance or irresponsibility.' In this section, I want to explore the ways in which perceived barriers to success are individualized, so that the most agentic aspect of the participants' narrativization is in the claiming of responsibility for failure or thwarted expectations. This is perhaps most succinctly summed up by Peter – a humanities post-doctoral researcher – who notes in our second interview together: 'I tend to think – does this count as agency? – I tend to think, "I am my own obstacle". So it's not the most empowering version of agency!'

'Imposter syndrome' and feelings of fraudulence are already well documented within research on HE (see for example Barcan, 2013: 191–216; Gill, 2013; Knights and Clarke, 2014; Sullivan and Simon, 2014). Barcan (2013: 192) argues that 'recent decades have produced conditions that have greatly intensified' the phenomenon of feeling like a fraud, and she contends that while 'experienced as a sense of personal inadequacy', fraudulence can be 'linked to the social positioning of the academic and/ or to a critique of institutional organization, pedagogical framework, or disciplinary orthodoxy' (p.195). Karen – who was working on a number of teaching contracts in the humanities during the course of my research – explains:

> I'm losing touch with my own research, I really don't have anything interesting to say, so part of that is the necessity of getting an income – and securing your living position takes you away from your own work – and then you start to feel separate from it and that engenders a feeling of disconnection and fraudulence […] meanwhile you're applying for things and trying to sound smart and not feeling very smart.

Miller and Morgan (1993) examine the production of academic CVs as a kind of 'auto/biographical practice', which must give 'the impression of being a "proper academic" or a "proper scholar"' (p.140); they conclude that 'there is an increasing element of alienation in the production of CVs' (p.142). In their research on female mid-career academics, Coate et al (2015) note the gendering of self-promotion: '[F]eminine "norms" suggest a certain amount of modesty that conflicts with what might be seen as self-promotion' (p.10). However, irrespective of gender, many of the casualized participants in my own research appeared to be uncomfortable with the self-promotional aspect of academia; as Howard – a social sciences researcher – comments: '[M]y goodness, look at all of those self-promotional people still promoting themselves on Christmas Day, and it begins to wear you down.' In their study of business school academics, Knights and Clarke (2014: 340) note, '[W]e were reflexively aware that as academics interviewing other academics, we comprised a specific audience for whom our participants authored particular narratives.' Thus, it was not surprising to me to find a gulf between legitimated forms of public presentation and self-promotion – such as in the CV, the interview, the conference paper or on social media – and how the casualized academics described feeling about their self-presentation during interviews; in this sense, Maclean's (2016) development of Laing's notion of 'double binds' as 'contradictory demands and expectations' is helpful in thinking through such a disjuncture and the way in which particular kinds of discourses are occasioned (see Gill, 2000: 175).

In her research with younger academics, Archer (2008: 282) notes that, 'they were all able to see (at least in part) how their situations were not simply the product of their own responsibilities, successes and failings'. While in my own research the participants were well aware of the wider processes occurring in HE and the implications of these processes for their own careers, there was also a tendency to individualize failure when describing setbacks, and this occurred across the sample irrespective of variables such as gender. This ambivalence can be illustrated by the case of Pedro, a social scientist who was working on a part-time teaching-only contract at the time of our first interview, but was job-hunting when we spoke next nine months later, a process he sums up by noting: '[Y]ou are always a candidate.' He had recently been unsuccessful in an application for a temporary lectureship, an experience which he felt had been lacking in transparency:

> [W]hen you are in a situation like this where you [...] keep getting 'no's, negatives and you keep rearranging your narrative about yourself and putting in question what you are and what you're worth and having to shape it to continuous judgements [...] you obviously want to learn lessons from these failures, so you want to [...] see [...] what was it that I did wrong, what can I improve and therefore it's very easy to fall into that idea that I failed because I didn't do this right, so that's what I have to change. So you get into this cycle of trying to improve yourself as an individual and so trying to find [...] what is wrong in yourself to be improved.

In their critique of technologies of neoliberal governmentality in academia – such as audit – Davies and Bansel (2010: 9) describe how, '[l]ike a well-trained pony, the free individual responds willingly to the smallest signs telling it where it should run and how it should leap'. While the casualized academics in my research are able to be reflexive about the potentially pernicious effects of neoliberal management techniques on both their own lives and the academy, it is nonetheless extremely difficult for the majority of those interviewed to resist such tactics: 'Technologies of audit and surveillance, of self-audit and self-surveillance, are not simply discourses of responsibility and accountability but technologies for the reproduction of responsibilised and accountable subjects' (Davies and Bansel, 2010: 9; see also Leathwood and Read, 2013; Loveday, 2018).

The penalty for resistance is made more acute by the precarious nature of the participants' employment situations, in that failure to comply brings with it the risk of employment contracts not being renewed, appointments not being made, grants not being awarded. I want to argue here that it is hardly surprising, then, that given the wider structural constraints within which academics are currently working, the very little agency the participants do perceive themselves as having relates to the possibility of working *on the self*: of improving perceived deficiencies, of being wily enough to avoid potential mistakes, of playing the long-game even if the future is unthinkable (Gill, 2014; Leathwood and Read, 2020; Ylijoki, 2010). As Katie, a postdoc in non-laboratory-based sciences, explains: 'I treat everything as a potential opportunity where I'm going to screw it up and upset everyone'. She describes having 'agency when it's something that

I'm maybe not doing well enough and I feel like I should be doing [...] better.' Gill (2013: 240) has argued:

> Being hard-working, self-motivating and enterprising subjects is what constitutes academics as so perfectly emblematic of this neoliberal moment, but is also part of a psychic landscape in which *not* being successful (or lucky!) [...] is misrecognised – or to put that more neutrally, made knowable – in terms of individual (moral) failure.

When asked how she had come to be in her present position, Lesley – a research assistant in the humanities – began our first interview by stating: '[W]ell my understanding of my career is that it's all been a bit accidental, I guess.' When I raised this statement with Lesley in our second interview together nine months later, she explained:

> I think a lot of it is maybe an attitude change in that when I was reading [the transcript] I was struck by the same thing, it's like [I] sound like an idiot. [...] I know that's definitely not what you were saying, but saying that everything that's happened is chance [...] it just struck me as stupid. [...] I think it's when faced with these largely inscrutable structures, like universities and hiring systems [...] it all seems quite chance-based, but talking to other people and seeing how they go about things, and realising that actually there's probably been some plan, or I've put myself in a position to be able to react to these good opportunities [...] and trying to be more responsible and mature about how I narrate my life: [...] that would hopefully lead to feeling more empowered about it.

While Lesley gestures towards the 'inscrutable' wider structures in HE, she then goes on to reproach herself for not being 'more responsible and mature about how I narrate my life' – arguably a reaction that epitomizes how the 'regulatory norm of the autonomous, responsible subject' (Rose, 1992: 153) in the neoliberalizing HE sector involves a shift in focus from the conditions that precipitate uncertainty to an incitement to take personal responsibility for setbacks, failure or the anxiety precipitated by such uncertainty (see Loveday, 2018, following Isin, 2004).

I have been arguing that lack of control is keenly felt by the majority of the participants across all career stages, and this is intertwined with the pervasive sense of risk associated with employment insecurity. In order to mitigate this sense of diminished agency, a number of strategies were described by those I interviewed (see also Archer, 2008) in order to impose control on situations in which they felt relatively powerless. For Lesley above, taking individual responsibility is one such route to perceived empowerment. However, the most common way in which the casualized participants – across all disciplines and career stages – attempted to wrest back some modicum of control was through working excessively, and long working hours are also characteristic of the wider sector (Anderson, 2006). For example, Gregory – a researcher in health and social sciences – explains: '[Y]ou feel like you have to do absolutely as much as possible and do absolutely as much as is in your control, which is working as much as you possibly can.'

Yet some of these 'coping mechanisms' have the paradoxical effect of intensifying already disadvantageous situations, such as escalating high stress levels (Kinman, 2014; Loveday, 2018; Morrish, 2019). When I ask Magnus – a post-doctoral researcher – about how much control he feels he has over his working life, he explains:

> [A]ll I can say is that the control that I have [...] is to do the best that I can do [...] and try to do my job as well as I can. But that has limits, and that has effects on the rest of your life [...] But you can also do all that and be the model fucking junior academic [...] and still not get a job [...] the agency I feel like I've got is that I can do that as best as I can [...] even though that can have detrimental effects on other areas of my life, and also just makes me stressed the whole time [...] But then I feel completely agentless in terms of I've got no control over whether a job comes up [...] I feel like I could jump the hurdles perfectly, and do everything exactly as they want, but still there's nothing there.

Adkins (2004: 192) argues: 'One of the most influential ideas in contemporary social theory is that a range of aspects of social life are both characterized by and increasingly require reflexive forms of conduct.' Whilst reflexivity remains a 'contested' concept (Farrugia and Woodman, 2015: 627), Akram and Hogan (2016: 608) define it in terms of how 'agents must engage with their own concerns and negotiate the best course of action for themselves'. They note that reflexivity 'is heightened in periods of breach' (Akram and Hogan, 2016: 608) – and the uncertainty precipitated by employment insecurity can arguably be construed in this manner – yet they caution against equating reflexivity with agency. In their critique of Margaret Archer's work, Farrugia and Woodman (2015: 640) demonstrate that there is reason to be suspicious of 'the valorization of reflexivity within conditions that foreclose the successful establishment of a *modus vivendi*'. Thus, for Magnus above, there is both an awareness of the 'hurdles' that need to be jumped as a 'model' junior academic hoping for a career in academia, yet he perceives himself as having no control over the possibility of securing a permanent job at the end of his current position; while he can attempt to 'negotiate the best course of action' (Akram and Hogan, 2016: 608), the wider conditions in the HE sector under which he is working will determine whether this path is ultimately successful. In this sense,

> Knowledge about risk for these competitive vulnerable subjects is no escape from danger: rather, it is itself dangerous knowledge. It produces an ever-present awareness of the danger of failure to recognise, anticipate, and manage risk. It provides academics with the means for deciding what action to take but also the means by which they might be found to have done something wrong.
>
> (Davies and Bansel, 2010: 15)

The academics in my research are compelled to take individualized choices and risks by virtue of their precarious employment situations; yet, the conditions under which they are labouring radically constrain their outcomes. I want to conclude below by considering the political implications of these working conditions for the academic profession, before proposing that the concept of 'luck' might provide a new locus for resisting the pernicious effects of neoliberalization in the sector.

Conclusion: Puncturing the Neoliberal Logic of Enterprise

I have been arguing in this chapter that my participants' seemingly contradictory responses to success and failure – that is, the invocation of 'luck' in favourable circumstances, but the taking of personal responsibility when things go badly – are indicative of academics' diminished agency, but also of the wider conditions within the changing landscape of UK HE. In this sense, I have aimed to bring together an analysis of chance, agency and structuring conditions (Smith, 1993).

The demands of the neoliberalizing university have created enterprising academic subjects who understand their own professionalism as being increasingly individualized. Academia valorizes the individual successes of 'superstar' academics (Knights and Clarke, 2014: 338) through narrowly prescribed – and often unrealistic – measures of esteem; meanwhile certain forms of labour remain 'hidden' from authorized public performances of capability (Miller and Morgan, 1993: 135), and competent academic selves must relentlessly be promoted for purposes of public engagement, 'impact', student recruitment and career progression. In tandem with the celebration of individualized success comes a creeping responsibilization in the event of failure: suspicions that if only one had worked harder, had the foresight to anticipate and negotiate setbacks, or produced better work, then success might have been possible (see also Sullivan and Simon, 2014). These tendencies are then undoubtedly amplified for those casualized academics who find themselves at the 'sharp-end' of the sector and whose 'capacity for action' (McNay, 2004: 179) has been diminished.

Whilst the HE sector benefits from the intensification of work and the endless striving towards so-called excellence, the individualization of the academic profession has wider political implications beyond its immediate impact on staff. As previously noted, the little agency that the majority of the participants in my project perceive themselves as having relates to work *on the self*; if processes of subjectification in the sector have the effect of focusing the gaze inwards, then the gaze outwards is in danger of becoming blinkered; thus, the real threat of individualization is its capacity to foreclose the solidarity necessary to resist such processes.

However, while Davies and Bansel (2010: 5) caution that 'neoliberal government [...] systematically dismantles the will to critique', there has in fact been a burgeoning of critique aimed at the neoliberalizing university in recent years, and the University and College Union's 'Four Fights' campaign – involving a sustained period of industrial action in 2020 – has sought to highlight the dangers of casualization, even if the dispute currently remains unresolved. Yet, industrial solidarity is not without risk for insecure workers, and some employees will be more constrained in their ability to resist than others; additionally, precarious employees require solidarity not merely from one another, but from those who are positioned in structurally advantageous situations, such as senior managers (see Loveday, 2021). So long as the wider culture of the academic profession upholds the values of 'enterprise' and individual success, then genuine possibilities for professional solidarity will be shut down.

In this chapter, I have been using the invocation of 'luck' in the case of success as a kind of heuristic springboard (see Da Col and Humphreys, 2012: 3) to investigate the production of academic subjectivities in an environment of escalating competition and expectations, and I want to conclude by returning to this concept of 'luck' as a means of puncturing neoliberal discourses of enterprise. While I have argued that perceiving success as a matter of luck points to the gradual erosion of insecure employees' confidence in their own skills and abilities, I believe 'luck' might also have an interesting potential to disrupt those narratives that celebrate the success of the 'superstar' individual, while simultaneously encouraging the taking of responsibility for failure. The notion that successful academic careers are forged through enterprise alone – that is, work on the *self* to develop more ambitious plans, to become more industrious, to manage time better and to take risks in the pursuit of 'excellence' – emphasizes the agency of the individual whilst failing to take into consideration the structural constraints under which academics are labouring, but also the intervening role of chance in mediating success and failure. The open acknowledgement of 'luck' unmoors the neoliberal logic of enterprise: hard work does not always pay off, merit is not evenly rewarded, risk-taking can backfire and the individual academic may have very little control over this. The perception of success as a matter of luck amongst the casualized participants in my project exposes the wider processes at work in the academic profession; acknowledging the role that 'luck' might also play in failure challenges the very logic that underpins contemporary universities.

Acknowledgements

The research was supported by the British Academy [SG142753].

An earlier version of this chapter – 'Luck, chance and happenstance? Perceptions of success and failure amongst fixed-term academic staff in UK higher education' (2017) – was published in *The British Journal of Sociology*, 69(3): 758–75.

Notes

1 I refer to the 'neoliberalizing' sector here to gesture towards neoliberalization in HE as a *process* underscored by competition; competition plays a legitimizing role in the transformation of universities, which are run on market principles but must remain accountable to government (see e.g. Cronin, 2016; Dakka, 2020; Loveday, 2018, 2021; Nash, 2019; Neyland et al, 2019: 76–112).
2 At the time of research, the figure was slightly higher at more than 34 per cent; yet once atypical contracts were taken into consideration, the University and College Union estimated the figure to be closer to 54 per cent (UCU, 2016).
3 In the case of five out of six of research councils (Matthews, 2015).

References

Adkins, L. (2004) Reflexivity: Freedom or habit of gender?. In L. Adkins and B. Skeggs (eds.) *Feminism after bourdieu*, pp. 191–210. Oxford and Malden, MA: Blackwell.

Akram, S. and Hogan, A. (2016) On reflexivity and the conduct of the self in everyday life: Reflections on Bourdieu and Archer. *British Journal of Sociology*, 66(4): 606–25.

Anderson, G. (2006) Carving out time and space in the managerial university. *Journal of Organisational Change Management*, 19(5): 578–92.

Archer, L. (2008) The new neoliberal subjects? Young/er academics' constructions of professional identity. *Journal of Education Policy*, 23(3): 265–85.

Ball, S. (2012) Performativity, commodification, and commitment: An I-Spy guide to the neoliberal university. *British Journal of Educational Studies*, 60(1): 17–28.

Barcan, R. (2013) *Academic life and labour in the new university*. Farnham: Ashgate.

Baron, P. (2014) Working the clock: The academic body on neoliberal time. *Somatechnics*, 4(2): 253–71.

Borges, J. L. (1998) The lottery in Babylon. In *Collected fictions*, pp. 101–6. New York: Penguin.

Brown, R. with Carasso, H. (2013) *Everything for sale? The marketisation of UK higher education*. London: Routledge.

Bryson, C. (2004) The consequences for women in the academic profession of the widespread use of fixed-term contracts. *Gender, Work & Organisation*, 11(2): 187–206.

Burrows, R. (2012) Living with the h-index? Metric assemblages in the contemporary academy. *The Sociological Review*, 60(2): 355–72.

Byrne, B. (2003) Reciting the self: Narrative representations of the self in qualitative interviews. *Feminist Theory*, 4(1): 29–49.

Coate, K., Kandiko Howson, C. B. and de St Croix, T. (2015) *Mid-career academic women: Strategies, choices and motivation*. London, UK: Leadership Foundation for Higher Education.

da Col, G. and Humphreys, C. (2012) Introduction: Subjects of luck – Contingency, morality, and the anticipation of everyday life. *Social Analysis*, 56(2): 1–18.

Cronin, A. (2016) Reputational capital in the 'PR University': Public relations and market rationalities. *Journal of Cultural Economy*, 9(4): 396–409.

Dakka, F. (2020) Competition, innovation and diversity in higher education: Dominant discourses, paradoxes and resistance. *British Journal of Sociology of Education*, 41(1): 80–94.

Daniels, I. M. (2003) Scooping, raking, beckoning luck: Luck, agency and the interdependence of people and things in Japan. *Journal of the Royal Anthropological Institute*, 9: 619–38.

Davies, B. and Bansel, P. (2010) Governmentality and academic work: Shaping the hearts and minds of academic workers. *Journal of Curriculum Theorizing*, 26(3): 5–20.

Farrugia, D. and Woodman, D. (2015) Ultimate concerns in late modernity: Archer, Bourdieu and reflexivity. *The British Journal of Sociology*, 66(4): 626–44.

Giddens, A. (1991) *Modernity and self-identity: Self and society in the late modern age*. Cambridge: Cambridge University Press.

Gill, R. (2000) Discourse analysis. In M. W. Bauer and G. Gaskell (eds.) *Qualitative researching with text, image and sound*, pp. 172–90. London: Sage.

Gill, R. (2013) Breaking the silence: The hidden injuries of the neoliberal university. In R. Ryan-Flood and R. Gill (eds.) *Secrecy and silence in the research process*, pp. 228–44. London: Routledge.

Gill, R. (2014) Academics, cultural workers and critical labour studies. *Journal of Cultural Economy*, 7(1): 12–30.

Gill, R. and Pratt, A. (2008) In the social factory? Immaterial labour, precariousness and cultural work. *Theory, Culture & Society*, 25(7–8): 1–30.

Gill, R. and Donaghue, N. (2016) Resilience, apps and reluctant individualism: Technologies of self in the neoliberal academy. *Women's Studies International*, 55: 91–9.

Hacking, I. (1990) *The taming of chance*. Cambridge: Cambridge University Press.

Hammersley, M. (2003) Recent radical criticism of interview studies: Any implications for the sociology of education? *British Journal of Sociology of Education*, 24(1): 119–26.

HESA [Higher Education Statistics Agency] (2016) Statistical First Release 225 – Staff at HE Providers in the UK. Available online: https://www.hesa.ac.uk/pr/3770-statistical-first-release-225 (accessed 6 September 2021).

HESA [Higher Education Statistics Agency] (2020) What are their employment conditions?. Available online: https://www.hesa.ac.uk/data-and-analysis/staff/employment-conditions (accessed 6 September 2021).

Isin, E. (2004) The neurotic citizen. *Citizenship Studies*, 8(3): 217–35.

Ivancheva, M., Lynch, K. and Keating, K. (2019) Precarity, gender and care in the neoliberal academy. *Gender, Work & Organisation*, 26(4): 448–62.

Kimber, M. (2003) The tenured 'core' and the tenuous 'periphery': The casualization of academic work in Australian universities. *Journal of Higher Education Policy and Management*, 25(1): 41–50.

Kinman, G. (2014) Doing more with less? Work and wellbeing in academics. *Somatechnics*, 4(2): 219–35.

Knights, D. and Clarke, C. A. (2014) It's a bittersweet symphony, this life: Fragile academic selves and insecure identities at work. *Organization Studies*, 35(3): 335–57.

Knowles, C. and Burrows, R. (2014) The impact of impact. *Etnográfica*, 18(2): 237–54.

Leathwood, C. and Read, B. (2013) Research policy and academic performativity: Compliance, contestation and complicity. *Studies in Higher Education*, 38(8): 1162–74.

Leathwood, C. and Read, B. (2022) Short-term, short-changed? A temporal perspective on the implications of academic casualization for teaching in higher education. *Teaching in Higher Education*, 27(6): 756–71.

Lopes, A. and Dewan, I. A. (2014) Precarious pedagogies? The impact of casual and zero hours contracts in higher education. *Journal of Feminist Scholarship*, 7(8): 28–42.

Loveday, V. (2018) The neurotic academic: Casualization and governance in the neoliberalising university. *Journal of Cultural Economy*, 11(2): 154–66.

Loveday, V. (2021) 'Under attack': Responsibility, crisis and survival anxiety amongst manager-academics in UK universities. *The Sociological Review*, 69(5): 903–19.

Lukes, S. and Haglund, L. (2005) Power and luck. *European Journal of Social Theory*, 46(1): 45–66.

Maclean, K. (2016) Sanity, 'madness', and the academy. *The Canadian Geographer*, 60(2): 181–91.

Mattausch, J. (2003) Chance and societal change. *The Sociological Review*, 51(4): 506–27.

Matthews, D. (2015) Success rates: Surge in applications to 'struggling' research councils. *Times Higher Education* 29 October. Available online: https://www.timeshighereducation.com/news/success-rates-surge-applications-struggling-research-councils (accessed 6 September 2021).

McGettigan, A. (2013) *The great university gamble: Money, markets and the future of higher education*. London: Pluto Press.

McNay, L. (2004) Agency and experience: Gender as a lived relation. In L. Adkins and B. Skeggs (eds.) *Feminism after Bourdieu*, pp. 173–90. Oxford and Malden, MA: Blackwell.

Mercer, J. (2007) The challenges of insider research in educational institutions: Wilding a double-edged sword and resolving delicate dilemmas. *Oxford Review of Education*, 33(1): 1–17.

Miller, N. and Morgan, D. (1993) Called to account: The CV as an autobiographical practice. *Sociology*, 27(1): 133–43.

Morrish, L. (2019) Pressure vessels: The epidemic of poor mental health among higher education staff. Higher Education Policy Institute. Available online: https://www.hepi.ac.uk/wp-content/uploads/2019/05/HEPI-Pressure-Vessels-Occasional-Paper-20.pdf (accessed 6 September 2021).

Morrish, L. and Sauntson, H. (2020) *Academic irregularities: Language and neoliberalism in higher education*. New York: Routledge.

Müller, R. and Kenney, M. (2014) Agential conversations: Interviewing postdoctoral life scientists and the politics of mundane research practices. *Science as Culture*, 23(4): 537–59.

Nash, K. (2019) Neo-liberalisation, universities and the value of bureaucracy. *The Sociological Review*, 67(1): 178–93.

Neyland, D., Ehrenstein, V. and Milyaeva, S. (2019) *Can markets solve problems? An empirical enquiry into neoliberalism in action*. London: Goldsmiths Press.

Reay, D. (2000) 'Dim dross': Marginalised women both inside and outside the academy. *Women's Studies International Forum*, 23(1): 13–21.

Reith, G. (2002) *The age of chance: Gambling in western culture*. London: Routledge.

Reith, G. (2003) Living with uncertainty: The construction of 'risk' and the belief in luck. *Organdi*, 6, http://www.organdi.net/article.php3?id_article=69.

Reith, G. (2004) Uncertain times: The notion of 'risk' and the development of modernity. *Time & Society*, 13(2/3): 383–402.
Rose, N. (1992) Governing the enterprising self. In P. Heelas and P. Morris (eds.) *The values of the enterprise culture: The moral debate*, pp. 141–64. London and New York: Routledge.
Sauder, M. (2020) A sociology of luck. *Sociological Theory*, 38(3): 193–216.
Sennett, R. (1998) *The corrosion of character*. New York: W. W. Norton.
Sinha, S. and Back, L. (2014) Making methods sociable: Dialogue, ethics and authorship in qualitative research. *Qualitative Research*, 14(4): 473–87.
Smith, M. (1993) Changing sociological perspectives on chance. *Sociology*, 27(3): 513–31.
Strübing, J. (2007) Research as pragmatic problem-solving: The pragmatist roots of empirically-grounded theorising. In A. Bryant and K. Charmaz (eds.) *The SAGE handbook of grounded theory*, pp. 580–99. Los Angeles and London: Sage.
Sullivan, N. and Simon, J. (2014) Academic work cultures: Somatic crisis in the enterprise university. *Somatechnics*, 4(2): 205–18.
Tavory, I. and Timmermans, S. (2014) *Abductive analysis: Theorizing qualitative research*. London and Chicago: University of Chicago Press.
Tweedie, D. (2013) Making sense of insecurity: A defence of Richard Sennett's sociology of work. *Work, Employment & Society*, 27(1): 94–104.
UCU [Universities and Colleges Union] (2016) Precarious work in higher education: A snapshot of insecure contracts and institutional attitudes. Available online: https://www.ucu.org.uk/media/7995/Precarious-work-in-higher-education-a-snapshot-of-insecure-contracts-and-institutional-attitudes-Apr-16/pdf/ucu_precariouscontract_hereport_apr16.pdf (accessed 6 September 2021).
UCU [Universities and Colleges Union] (2020) Precarious work in higher education: Insecure contracts and how they have changed over time. Available online: https://ucu.org.uk/media/10899/Precarious-work-in-higher-education-May-20/pdf/ucu_he-precarity-report_may20.pdf (accessed 6 September 2021).
Vitae (2013) What do researchers do? Early career progression of doctoral graduates. Available online: https://www.vitae.ac.uk/vitae-publications/reports/what-do-researchers-do-early-career-progression-2013.pdf/view (accessed 6 September 2021).
Vitae (2016) What do research staff do next?. Available online: https://www.vitae.ac.uk/vitae-publications/reports/vitae-what-do-research-staff-do-next-2016.pdf (accessed 6 September 2021).
Wang, B. (2020) Time in migration: Temporary status, precarity and temporal labour amongst Chinese scholars returning from the Global North to South. *Journal of Ethnic and Migration Studies*, 46(11): 2127–44.
Ylijoki, O. E. (2010) Future orientations in episodic labour: Short-term academics as a case in point. *Time & Society*, 19(3): 365–86.

5

Academic Professionalism in the Measured University

Cathal Ó Siochrú, Roland Bloch,
Catherine O'Connell and Jakob Hartl

Introduction

What is it to be professional in a measured environment? What space, if any, is left to be a professional amid the 'metric tide' prevailing on the higher education (HE) sector (Wilsdon, 2015). How these questions are addressed empirically can be a significant factor in highlighting the degree to which spaces for democratic professional accountability can be maintained and developed in contemporary higher education environments.

A research focus on accountability frameworks gives insight into the professional domain and the extent of control and autonomy afforded to professional groups (Wallenberg et al, 2019). As with other professions, academic roles are subject to increasing accountability in form of metrics-based evaluation. This contemporary trend of 'governing by numbers' is associated with both changing modes of state control and a wider social practice (Mau, 2019; Rose, 1991).

The higher education sector in England is widely regarded to be at the extreme end of these developments, and effects of this mode of governance have been studied extensively in this context. The negative effects of this audit culture on academic practice are well documented and a large section of this research literature portrays a dystopian picture of academic professionals as passive actors, disempowered by this mode of scrutiny (Harley, 2002; Oancea, 2008; O'Brien and Guiney, 2019; Smith, 2017; Strathern, 2000) or as self-interested actors exploiting metrics for self-promotional purposes (Blackmore, 2015; Kolsaker, 2008). However, as observed in broader international surveys of the profession (Locke, 2014; Locke and Bennion, 2011; Marini et al, 2019), factors associated with professional dissatisfaction are not uniformly experienced, nor are they directly related to attrition in the profession.

Metrics-based evaluation systems are observed to encourage competitive behaviours between universities yet seem to reproduce existing hierarchies of prestige (Boliver, 2015). Nevertheless, the pressure to perform well in league tables appears to foster risk-averse managerial behaviour which impacts negatively on academic freedom and professional autonomy. However, the broad picture of professional loss, alienation and retreat portrayed in the research literature and wider discourse is challenged by close-up empirical studies which highlight a more nuanced picture of experiences differentiated by age, gender, type of institution and time in profession (Locke and Bennion, 2011; Smith, 2017; Tight, 2014). The measures of teaching and research performance contained within these metrics can reconfigure power relations in unexpected ways that can advantage particular academic disciplines and individuals (Blakemore, 2015; Kolsaker, 2008; Pereira, 2015). There is a contemporary research interest in understanding the elements of these metrics-based evaluation systems which are salient in the re-shaping of academic practices in positive and negative ways (Brew et al, 2018; Locke, 2014), as well as the variety of practices at sectoral, organizational and discipline level which can influence professional practice.

Prevalent critiques of metrics tend to characterize them as a social pathology, intensifying the normative regulation of academic performance and undermining the collegiality of academic practice (Harley, 2002; Oancea, 2008; Smith, 2017; Strathern, 2000). However, such critiques tend to rely on normative assumptions of a prior context historically guided by meritocratic principles. An analytic orientation to the contexts in which metrics are less prevalent can be useful in exploring this assumption. For example, there are other countries where this metricized mode of governance is less developed and there is observed to be a weaker association in HE systems which follow a social-democratic tradition than in anglophone countries (Hazelkorn, 2009).

This Anglo-German study was motivated by an interest to explore the effects of more and less metricized environments on academic practice. Our earlier work explored academic perceptions of fairness of organizational regimes of performance evaluation in highly and moderately metricized environments (Bloch et al, 2021). Underpinned by that work, this chapter examines the perceived impacts of metrics-based evaluation on professional practice.

Comparative Research

This rise of metrics-based evaluation is associated with a trend of devolved state control through mechanisms of output steering (Whitley, 2012). There is a considerable research literature on the effects of metrics-based evaluation in higher education, much of which tends to critique a particular instrument of governance (e.g. research assessment or teaching excellence frameworks). However, this mono-focus on a single system of governance tends to obscure the wider effects and inter-relationships between evaluative frameworks (Gläser, 2010). Universities can be characterized as hybrid organizations (Kleimann, 2019) insofar as there are dual goals of research and teaching and distinct funding streams associated with these activities. The different accountability frameworks associated with these activities can give rise to competing logics (Ibid., 2019) which necessitate institutional work to interpret and reconcile external demands (Wallenberg, 2019). Empirical studies which explore the emergent effects offer a more nuanced view of the varying forms of institutional work associated with responding to metrics that are perceived as being democratic and collegial to varying extents (2019).

Enacting measurement at organizational level may yield ambivalent and partially contradicting effects rather than unfolding as planned (Gunter, 2013). Gläser (2010) advocates a perspective which centers on the actors 'in whose situations and actions governance modes "meet"' (2010: 360). From this perspective, the relative authority and perceived legitimacy of actors are interesting analytically as governance both produces and reconfigures power relations between interdependent actors. This research focus can draw attention to the reconfigured 'authority relations' caused by new modes of governance and the 'degrees of freedom' a governance system may have. Authority relations (Gläser, 2010; Whitley, 2010, 2011) offer a concept that goes beyond formal structures of governance and draws attention to multiple 'authoritative agencies' and how they exercise authority which includes the interpretations and (re)actions of those upon whom authority is directed (e.g. academics, students).

Comparative literature on academic responses to metrics is relatively sparse, however. England and Germany provide interesting comparative contexts as they differ markedly in modes of state regulation, quality and accountability procedures, and in methods of funding allocation. The English 'state chartered' HE system is characterized by higher levels of organizational actorhood due to the extent of devolved control in academic staffing, student recruitment and resource allocation (Whitley, 2012). The Research Excellence Framework (REF), Teaching Excellence Framework (TEF) and the newer Knowledge Exchange Framework (KEF) are technologies that attribute academic performance to the organization, and resource allocation is contingent on these outputs. In this context, performance metrics are constituted at the sectoral level and access to government funding operates at an organizational level, determined according to the outcome of periodic assessment of specified performance metrics. The system of research performance evaluation, initially established in 1983, is administered at subject/discipline level but research monies are allocated at organizational level. The peer-review element of REF has endured throughout the various iterations though with greater prominence now being given to research stakeholders in an impact evaluation component. The system of teaching evaluation has had several iterations since its initial inception in 1996. In the current formulation of the Teaching Excellence Framework (formalized in 2017), student course satisfaction scores and employability outcomes form significant components, reflecting a higher degree of consumer accountability and a reconfiguration of authority relations between students and universities. While the initial policy rationale of linking TEF outcomes to differential fee levels has not fully materialized, TEF metrics are observed to influence enrolment levels due to their reputational value (Gunn, 2018). Relative to other European countries, the national frameworks for teaching and research evaluation create an internally shaped market in which universities have a high degree of strategic control and authority on both staff and student recruitment (Marini et al, 2019). There are currently no limits as to the number of staff or students that can be employed or recruited by a UK university, which creates a market where universities compete to attract as many students as they can.

In contrast, the German 'state contracted' higher education system is characterized by high levels of state control, regulation and input steering (Whitley, 2012). With regard to the allocation of funding in relation to teaching, the staff budget for each university is set down in fixed plans by the state. These fixed budgets determine the number of personnel that can be employed within each university and, owing to fixed staff-student ratios, the number of study-places that can be offered by that university. Only if there are more applicants than study places can access be restricted. There are neither tuition fees nor influential teaching-related rankings of German universities. Under this system, the results from any teaching related performance metrics have no direct relevance to funding and thus may only have implications for the individual level but not the organizational level. In relation to research governance, there has been no direct equivalent to the UK REF. The more targeted 'Excellence Initiative' directs research funds towards a small proportion of universities and does not rely on metrics-based performance evaluation. A key difference between the two academic systems is the 'personal power' (Hüther and Krücken, 2013) and autonomy of the professorial chairs within the German academic system. In Germany, professorial chairholders have complete autonomy within their university with regard to the employment and career progression of academic personnel. They have a high degree of discretion in defining research goals, work contracts, workloads, publishing and so on, within hierarchical master-apprentice relationships. The opinion of the chair is a primary driver regarding the immediate career prospects for academics in their employ. Therefore, career progression within the university is entirely at the discretion of the chair, irrespective of that academic's performance on any metrics. The influence of research performance metrics, in the form of publications and third-party funding, tends to be seen primarily in terms of their reputation in the wider academic community. This can become relevant for the individual academic when applying elsewhere.

Given these divergent contexts it could be expected that metrics would impact on professional practice in more tangible ways in the English context. In Germany, where the use of metrics is decentralized and dispersed, it should not infringe professional autonomy to the same degree and therefore provides a useful comparison of the professional domain.

Methodology

Data was collected through surveys with academics in both England and Germany, who were asked about their attitudes towards the use of metrics to assess performance in both research and teaching. Participants were an opportunity sample, drawn from a wide range of institutions, who were invited by email to participate: 191 respondents in England (109 Education, 82 Economics) and 123 respondents in Germany (61 in Education and 62 in Economics).

Statistical analysis of the survey responses was carried out separately on the English and German samples, in both cases utilizing a cluster analysis to identify any groupings indicated by the responses to the survey (see Bloch et al, 2021 for a detailed account). The responses to the interviews and the survey's open questions were then used to help characterize these groups in both samples.

As a result of this analysis, we identified three groups that were common to both English and German samples and a further two groups that were unique to the German sample. In general, these groups display different attitudes towards the use of metrics in academia. The nature of these groups will be discussed here as well as the factors that might influence which group an academic may become part of. Furthermore, the similarities and differences between the UK and German groups will be discussed in light of what they reveal about the impact that metrics can have on an academic's professional practice.

Similarities

The analysis revealed three groups that were common to both the English and German samples. These groups represented different orientations towards the use of performance metrics in academia: one group who were almost entirely positive about their use, a second who were cautiously positive and a third that were entirely against their use. In addition to the similarities in their overall orientation, the corresponding groups in England and Germany were also similar in terms of the levels of experience and reasons for supporting or opposing the use of performance metrics in academia. While it will be unsurprising to learn that our findings show some academics welcome metrics while others do not, our analysis goes deeper through explorating the role that factors such as experience, authority relations and autonomy might play in shaping these groups and their views on performance metrics.

Young Followers

The first group, who we describe as 'young followers', is composed of early career academics who view performance metrics in an almost entirely positive light. Members of this group included doctoral students, postdoc researchers and those with less than five years of researching or teaching experience in both countries.

The 'young followers' represent those academics who view metrics from a largely uncritical stance. They view the use of performance metrics as a fact-of-life, largely accepted and valued even as a system which can offer structure and guidance, which are valuable commodities at this early point in their career. They see flexibility in metrics both at a personal and departmental level. They also see metrics as providing valuable feedback to the organization, helping to refine practice and avoid complacency or bad habits. They value metrics for their clarity and for promoting discourse at a departmental and institutional level on quality and acknowledge a degree of legitimacy of the role of metrics.

> Identification of some valid concerns raised by students (such as quality, speed of feedback).
>
> (England, Lecturer)

> [performance metrics support] an open dialogue about the quality of teaching, linked to individual opportunities for improving teaching, if necessary with support for optimizing teaching through central positions.
>
> (Germany, research associate, pre-doc)

While the young followers acknowledge that it has been necessary to adjust their practice to meet the requirements of the metrics, they see this as largely compatible with the concept of their own professionalism and as helpful guidance.

> [metrics] provide orientation for academics and potentially help them, especially in the lower ranks, to conceptualize their own academic career, in order to enhance the productivity of research through constructive feedback on self-optimization.
>
> (Germany, research associate, pre-doc)

Overall, 'young followers' view any requirements or adjustments connected to performance metrics from a constructive perspective, bringing about an alignment between the goals of individual academics and the goals of their organization. The results of this process are seen as promoting unity or cohesiveness and the sharing of best practice.

> [TEF] might shift more focus on the quality of teaching, so that everybody is expected to invest in good teaching.
>
> (England, Lecturer)

> It could help to develop some kind of consensus within academic disciplines over the basic principles of ensuring quality in research.
>
> (England, Senior Lecturer)

Autonomous Academics

The second group, who we describe as 'autonomous academics', is composed of more established academics who see performance metrics from a more critical and pragmatic perspective. This is the largest group in terms of both numbers and the range of experience, extending from fixed term postdocs to senior lecturers, with an average experience of between fifteen and twenty years.

These academics believe that performance metrics are facilitating their career advancement; however, they take a far more balanced and critical stance on the merits of the metrics compared to the young followers. Like the young followers, they also perceive flexibility in metrics both at a personal and departmental level yet this flexibility comes at a price in that they feel the need to sacrifice autonomy in some areas in return for having greater control over other areas. Thus, the changes in personal priorities necessitated by metrics are seen as negotiated rather than imposed. As such, they do not see themselves as being locked in authority relations but perceive considerable individual autonomy.

> The indicators are communicated first and foremost to help people to help themselves. It goes beyond this only for explicit problem cases. That is rightly so.
> (Germany, professor)

Autonomous academics also believe that performance metrics help to refine practice and avoid complacency. For example, metrics can force the university to recognize the value of both teaching and research in those cases where either one has been undervalued previously. They also believe that performance metrics can serve as a motivator, pushing them to improve their own performance and stretch themselves. In this way, metrics are compatible with their professional orientation in the sense that they promote high standards.

> The REF has probably enhanced the research culture in many institutions. [...] Allowed me to allocate more time for research.
> (England, Professor)

> That professors who have no competence to teach will not be able to get a call for a professorship.
> (Germany, research associate, pre-doc)

> I am aiming for high quality journals that I might not otherwise have submitted.
> (England, Senior Lecturer)

However, these positive views are combined with concerns over the balancing of priorities and authority within the system of performance metrics. There is some resistance to redefining students as clients owing to the perceived shift in power that this change would represent. There are concerns that the teaching metrics prioritize student satisfaction, thereby devaluing autonomy and professional judgement which are also important parts of their professional identity. However, many of these issues with balancing and autonomy are seen as arising from their institution's implementation of the metrics as much as they are inherent in metrics themselves.

Overall, the adjustments in their practice necessitated by metrics are compatible with their concept of professionalism, but their approval of performance metrics could be said to be transactional. Metrics are seen as acceptable since they facilitate career advancement; they make the 'rules of the game' more transparent. Equipped with this knowledge, autonomous academics think they can play the academic game. In doing so, they evoke a self-concept of empowered individual actorhood which allows them to act self-consciously and strategically with respect to their career (Cannizzo, 2015). However, their willingness to compromise in relation to the requirements arising from the metrics could also be seen as recognition of the fragility of the modern academic profession.

Alienated Academics

The third group, who we describe as 'alienated academics', is composed of experienced academics who reject performance metrics both in principle and in practice. Members of this group are, on average, the most advanced in their career of all three groups, including many senior lecturers and professors who have twenty years or more of research or teaching experience.

These academics are entirely dismissive, even hostile, towards the metrics, seeing them as an unhealthy influence on academic practice and identity. They share a sense of alienation of academia which is pushed by the introduction of new governance mechanisms based on metrics. An important element of their viewpoint is that they see such metrics as reflecting a set of authority relations with little flexibility permitted in relation to metrics requirements either at a personal or departmental level. Rather than representing universalistic academic values, these academics believe that the introduction of performance metrics represents an attempt to impose new values through standardized academic practices. They see the changes to their professional behaviour required by metrics as resulting from coercion, and far from gaining any benefits from these changes, they see them as undermining core principles of the academic professional identity such as autonomy and a search for truth.

> Good research and teaching are central. Everyone should seek to do so first, rather than to indulge in counting, weighing, and measuring.
> (Germany, no status information, Habilitation)

> I focus less on quality and have stopped checking carefully that everything is correct, in order to send papers quickly.
> (England, Associate Professor)

It forces certain people to teach more to allow others to conduct research.
(England, Senior Lecturer)

Discrimination in research time allocation to so-called 'stars'.
(England, Senior Lecturer)

Overall, to these academics, autonomy is an indispensable element of their professionalism and anything which impinges on that freedom is viewed as a threat. As such, it is the restriction of autonomy, which they believe is a result of performance metrics, that is most damning in the eyes of this group.

Every single scientist has to judge his own scientific achievements. [...] Freedom of research and teaching as well as the evaluation of each individual case are the relevant criteria.
(Germany, no status information, Habilitation)

[Concerns regarding the impact of metrics] Forcing the adoption of inappropriate practice and shutting down debate and academic freedom of speech."
(England, Senior Lecturer)

Part of their rejection of metrics is the view that metrics promote an abstracted view of academia which is disconnected from either the principle or reality. From their viewpoint, metrics undermine academic standards of skill and expertise by forcing activities which either contribute little to ensuring these qualities or, worse still, prevent the pursuit of improvement by requiring wasteful performative activities.

The similarities between the English and German responses to performance metrics point to the universalism inherent to academic professionalism. The core activities of the university, research and teaching, may take place locally but have to prove their value globally. Researchers are expected to publish their results, teachers are encouraged to ensure their courses are 'research informed' and universities seek to recruit students internationally. Across the three groups, the responses relate to such ideas of academic professionalism: Young followers perceive performance metrics as helping them to become professional; autonomous academics differentiate effects of performance metrics with regard to academic standards; and alienated academics reject performance metrics on the normative basis of academic values.

One factor may be stage of career, and the share of that career that has taken place within a 'metricized' system and thus the extent to which they are acclimatized to it. Early career academics who have never known any other system may find it easier to accept, since it requires little adjustment, compared to those who have spent the majority of their career outside of such a system. Based on comments from both young followers and alienated academics, a related issue is the extent to which an individual's current practices are compatible with, and thus rewarded by, the system of performance metrics. An individual who can 'play the game' and sees benefits either to themselves or to their institution resulting from their teaching or research via performance metrics is more likely to embrace it or at the very least tolerate it. On the other hand, those who find themselves unable to adapt successfully or whose efforts to adapt appear to provide little reward are likely to become disenchanted and hostile towards the system that undervalues them. This may, in part, explain why those with more positive orientations are early career academics, who have only just begun developing their practices and are doing so in full knowledge of the requirements of performance metrics. By contrast, mid to late career academics may be more likely to be autonomous academics if they are fortunate enough to have practices that are compatible or readily adjustable to those requirements.

However, we cannot overlook the impact that comes from the specific methods of implementing performance metrics which will vary from institution to institution. An implementation which is seen as lacking legitimate authority is likely to influence the view of the academic that experiences it in comparison to another who experiences an implementation which reflects a more flexible and inclusive approach (O'Connell et al, 2021). If performance metrics, as a process, are seen to be imposed by the university without consultation or accommodation, then it's not hard to see why this might produce a negative view of metrics. This may explain one of the key differences between those who are more pragmatic or alienated in their response to performance metrics, where the former retains some sense of autonomy and flexibility in the power relations with the institution that they belong to. Notwithstanding variation at the organizational level, English and German academics are also embedded in different national traditions and organizational structures that shape their views of performance metrics.

Differences

While the three groups previously discussed appeared in the results of the analysis for both countries, it is noteworthy that the analysis of German academics produced a fourth and fifth group that were not found in the English case.

The Subdued Academics

The fourth group, which we describe as 'subdued academics', was composed of mid-career academics on fixed-term positions that include both research and teaching. Although they are similar in their type of employment and career stage to the autonomous academics, their perspective on performance metrics can be characterized as disinterested and disengaged. Unlike the alienated academics, who were unwilling or unable to engage with performance metrics and believe that this disadvantages them, the subdued academics disregard metrics on the belief that they do not apply to them. Faced with a high teaching load they feel that performance metrics are of no consequence. This feeling of being overwhelmed by teaching duties can likewise be experienced by professors. Notwithstanding differences in employment status, academics in this group feel that they are subdued by the sheer quantity of teaching which lets organizational attempts at performance measurement appear futile.

> At our university, only the quantity, i.e. how many students are supervised by whom etc., is measured, and not the quality. There are teaching evaluations but many colleagues do not participate, the results are not made public.
>
> (Germany, professor)

One source of the subdued academics' belief regarding their independence from performance metrics lies in the fact that they report to a professorial chair who sets their priorities and does not evaluate their performance with reference to any performance metrics. They share the latter with professors who feel that their teaching efforts are not appreciated. Rather, their work is fixated on student numbers that must be accommodated with constrained resources. Thus, independence from metrics on these terms does not equate to autonomy, and instead the subdued academics see themselves under the authority of the input-based teaching regime. These authority relations offer no leeway in teaching, neither on the departmental nor on the individual level, and academics feel subdued to them.

> Each chair minds his own business, and at the chair where I work there appears to be little interest in research.
>
> (Germany, research associate, post-doc)

> Teaching performance is second-rate, […], next to publications and third-party funds nothing else counts.
>
> (Germany, professor)

Research performance indicators may play a role transorganizationally, but not within the organization. Here, teaching high numbers of students is the top priority, the university as an organizational actor is considered too weak to change established authority relations. Overall, while the subdued academics may see themselves as independent from performance metrics it is only because they believe they are locked into a twofold set of authority relations – input-based steering of student numbers and unilateral dependence on professorial chairs – that enforce a focus on teaching.

German Mandarins

The fifth group, which we describe as the 'German mandarins', is composed of some of the most experienced academics in the German sample, with the longest teaching experience and the highest shares of professors and permanent employment. Although they have some similarities to the alienated academics in terms of level of experience, they are distinct from this group owing to their tenured positions in comparison to alienated academics who are typically on fixed-term positions. The German chair system is built around them, and they are the main representatives of the academic profession. It is for this reason we are employing the term 'mandarins', based on Fritz Ringer's concept of 'mandarin intellectuals', university professors, who "uphold the standards of qualification for membership in the group, and they act as spokesmen in cultural questions" (Ringer, 1969: 5f). The adoption of the term highlights the dual role of professors as gatekeepers of the German academic career system, in terms of both employment and advancement (Hüther and Krücken, 2013), and as preservers of the Humboldtian idea of the university (Habermas, 1988). From this standpoint, they perceive any organizational attempt at introducing performance metrics as an intrusion into both their recruitment and their academic practice in general.

> I see no advantages [in evaluating research performance].
>
> (Germany, professor)

Given their seniority in the academic hierarchy, academics in this cluster are unlikely to have much interest in performance metrics in terms of their own career progression. Their status allows them to oppose performance metrics fundamentally. Their constitutionally granted autonomy shelters professors from organizational attempts to set strategic goals and implement schemes based on performance-metrics. They are mandarins who 'reign' over their chairs in "solitude and freedom" (transl. Schelsky, 1963), decoupled from formal organization. Therefore, they see no value in the use of performance metrics for themselves or their subordinates, while at the same time any metrics-based targets set by the university have no consequences for the mandarins or the departments they oversee.

The German mandarins further delegitimize performance metrics by criticizing intraorganizational structures.

> No integrated quality assurance – although officially pursued, no incentives to improve teaching quality.
>
> (Germany, professor)
>
> No clear communication, partially unclear decisions resp. unclear basis for decisions (if these are strategic decisions related to research performance).
>
> (Germany, professor)

The organization is criticized for its incapability to introduce, communicate and uphold quality standards. As German universities are still characterized by a strong academic self-governance – with the professors as a group controlling all key positions – achieving consensus is a constant challenge and in many instances is limited to the least common denominator, despite recent attempts at strengthening the leadership in the wake of New Public Management reforms. Under the auspices of collegiality, most university leadership conceive of themselves as belonging to a community of equals, and therefore do not enforce top-down regulation. At the same time, the professorial community lacks group cohesion. Rather, the German university is characterized by its chair system, famously described by Burton Clark (1983: 140) as "small monopolies in thousands of parts" each part with its own interests and veto powers. Under such conditions, it appears to be almost impossible to agree upon standards of performance measurement.[1]

Further reflection as to the nature of these two additional groups led us to conclude that they were complementary. Because of their superior status, the mandarins see performance metrics as an irrelevance, a view that is shared by the subdued academics, yet on the basis of their inferior status. This led us to characterize both of these groups as 'bystanders' in relation to performance metrics in the sense that they do not 'play the game' of metrics and were instead disinterested and impervious to the systems of performance metrics that exist in Germany. Their practice is shaped by structures and demands that are perceived as unrelated to performance metrics, which renders metrics irrelevant to them, albeit for different reasons (professors feel untouched, teachers subdued). Furthermore, the absence of comparable groups in England suggested to us that here structural differences in the academic status system prevent a fully fledged implementation of performance metrics in Germany.

Discussion

In many national contexts research and teaching, as well as other activities, are increasingly being measured along similar standards and indicators. The diffusion of metrics can be seen as part of global organizational expansion (Bromley and Meyer, 2015; Meyer et al, 2006) in which ever-more parts of society are being reshaped along models of rationalized organization. This rationalization de-spiritualizes traditional modes of organization, such as church, guilds or aristocracy, by constructing individuals and rationalized organizations as "the legitimate agent and carrier of authority, responsibility, and capacity to act" (Meyer and Jepperson, 2000: 106). They are transformed into empowered actors who are expected to act for and out of themselves. Organizations implement formal structures that (1) render the organization recognizable as a source of collective action, i.e. as an "integrated goal-oriented project" (Bromley and Meyer, 2015: 139) and (2) make the organization capable of eliciting action.

Metrics represent a rational model of organizing teaching and research and are intended to strengthen the organizational actorhood of universities. Because research and teaching are 'unclear technologies' (Cohen et al, 1972) that cannot be successfully programmed or commanded, universities as organizational actors lack reliable information they could use to shape these activities. Metrics not only promise to deliver this information. They can also be used to render whole universities commensurable along common indicators. Metrics therefore contribute to the transformation of universities into organizational actors, i.e. into "an integrated, goal-oriented entity that is deliberately choosing its own actions and that can thus be held responsible for what it does" (Krücken and Meier, 2006: 241). Metrics allow both intra- and interorganizational competition. They are an essential part of the rationalized university which diffuses globally (Ramirez, 2006). As organizational actors whose actions are based on metrics, universities become ever-more alike across national higher education systems.

Universities, however, already used to be quite similar around the world even before the advent of metrics. For instance, beginning in the nineteenth century, the German model of the research university was adapted in other higher education systems, most notably the United States. This model was based on the freedom and unity of research and teaching but did not conceive of universities as organizational actors. Their main task was to provide the basic infrastructure for research and teaching. Related activities, however, were shaped by the values and standards of academic professionalism, famously described by Robert K. Merton as the norms of universalism, communalism, disinterestedness, and organized scepticism. Merton stressed that these are cultural norms:

> The norms are expressed in the form of prescriptions, proscriptions, preferences, and permissions. They are legitimatized in terms of institutional values. These imperatives, transmitted by precept and example and reenforced by sanctions are in varying degrees internalized by the scientist, thus fashioning his scientific conscience or, if one prefers the latter-day phrase, his superego.
>
> (Merton, 1973: 269)

These norms are not tied to specific organizational structures but are valid across different types of scientific organizations as well as across different national higher education systems. The diffusion of metrics is therefore not directly related to academic professionalism but rather to the strengthening of universities' organizational actorhood. That is, metrics are not intended to shape academic practice but to make the university capable of acting as an organization. Metrics legitimize and enable organizational action. However, our empirical data does not tell a story of peaceful co-existence between metrics and academic practice. Furthermore, the distinction between organizational actorhood and cultural norms of academic professionalism allows us to account for similarities and differences between English and German academics' attitudes towards metrics.

The English higher education system is characterized by higher levels of organizational actorhood. In this context REF and TEF are technologies that attribute academic performance to the organization (and tie it to institutional funding). In contrast, the German higher education system is characterized by high levels of state regulation and input steering. Though the autonomy of universities has been strengthened (Schimank and Lange, 2009), performance measurement is only of secondary importance both intra- and interorganizationally. We would therefore have expected metrics to be more relevant for English than for German academics. The data shows that this is not the case. Though metrics are seen in Germany as less relevant on the organizational level, they seem to flourish in the wider academic community. Like in England, we observe both positive and negative attitudes towards metrics. In both countries, academics appeal to universal academic values to criticize metrics. 'Alienated academics' in England and Germany see academic freedom threatened by performance measurement. For them, the university as an organization should abstain from interfering into academic practice. In contrast, English and German 'young followers' regard metrics as a good way of guiding academic practice. They welcome organizational performance measurement for providing clues to estimate one's own academic performance. Finally, both countries display groups whose attitudes are in-between; English and German 'autonomous academics' attach an emancipatory value to metrics while they are at the same time conscious of the limits of performance measurement vis-à-vis academic professional standards.

Nevertheless, we found two more groups in the German case. In analyzing the authority relations, we have shown that the German system allows for a group that to a large extent can evade metrics – the 'German mandarins'. In fact, they are the most powerful group in German academia because their civil servant status shelters them from organizational influence and they control to a large extent curricula, research agendas and academic careers. The German mandarins regard themselves as the gatekeepers of academic professionalism. Yet it is a professionalism that comes with a strong academic hierarchy. There is a deep divide in German academia between fully fledged professors who enjoy permanent employment and academic freedom and the rest, commonly referred to as academic trainees (*wissenschaftlicher Nachwuchs*) who are still in the qualification process and are therefore only temporarily employed. Only those who have earned a doctoral degree as well as a habilitation, and who have been appointed professor can fully engage in academic professional practice. The subdued academics show that there is a group that has already given up any career ambitions but is still needed to teach vast numbers of students under the conditions of mass higher education. For them, metrics are of no use.

Against this background, metrics can be seen as an opportunity to change authority relations within the scientific community. Instead of leaving assessment to those who rule, metrics render academic performance transparent and commensurable. The organization can use this objective information to frame academic careers. For instance, the newly introduced tenure track in the German academic career system defines clear goals in terms of metrics. If these goals are reached within a predefined time-period, tenure is granted.

Nevertheless, emancipation from traditional modes of academic governance comes with new constraints. Academic performance is limited to that which is measurable. Performance indicators quantify what used to be a matter of quality (Mau, 2020). Especially with regard to the evolution of English measurement systems, it appears questionable whether metrics are able to account for all the nuances involved in professional academic practice. In consequence, academics may limit their practice to that which counts, such as the acquisition of third-party funding or publishing in journals with high impact factors. A new academic habitus may arise that is guided more by valuation than by content (Lenger, 2018).

Conclusions

The pattern of responses in both contexts resonates with earlier studies of changing governance arrangements which observe those who are marginalized, those who make compromises and those who are more aligned to these modes of evaluation (Lock and Bennion, 2011). However, the comparative dimension to this study adds insight into the pervasiveness of metrics even in contexts where metrics are not mandatory at state level. In Germany, where the use of metrics is dispersed and decentralized, many academics experience them as decoupled from organizational practice, serving individual rather than collegial interests and having no practical consequences.

Within the academic community metrics tend to be viewed as a harm to be eradicated. However, our empirical research demonstrates the range of responses and illuminates how deeply we are implicated as organizational and individual actors. Research which avoids privileging 'state actors' and 'purposeful policy' in analyses can reflect the de-centred way in which governance regimes develop at multiple levels (Gunter et al, 2013) and how organizations, subject to the same external regulation, deploy differing responses and, in some cases, 'repair' outside regulation in context-sensitive ways (Wallenburg et al, 2019).

Academic communities in their social organization are characterized by structural inequalities. Hence there can be an emancipatory side of metrics as can be witnessed by the orientations of the 'young followers' and 'autonomous academics' in our study. To varying degrees, these academics welcome the move away from the authority of individual professors as they perceive metrics as more transparent, appropriate and flexible. They trust in a change of authority relations from academic hierarchies to distributed authority at the organizational level. However, the German context also shows that alienated academics may consider metrics as just another regime which impedes academic professionalism and the values associated with it.

Uses of metrics can often be directed towards individual rather than collective interests. The metrics system in England presents a perception of academic benefits at the local level (i.e. my publications and teaching evaluations will benefit me and my institution). An important observation in the English case is that the organization promotes participation and organizational memberhood. If metrics are seen as not being related to organizational positioning but as a practice, this could enable a more participatory approach. For instance, if they were not tied to ranking positions, metrics could be used to initiate an open organization-wide discourse on teaching and research quality that acknowledges both strengths and weaknesses in current academic practice and could be used to legitimize strategies to improve it. Metrics would then not serve external purposes or expectations but relate directly to the core activities of universities, i.e. research and teaching.

In the long run, metrics may alter perceptions of what constitutes good research and good teaching. Due to the higher levels of organizational actorhood in the English context, such a reframing is more likely to be advanced by the organization to a large degree. However, metrics can be seen as an ambivalent technology with various degrees of freedom for organizations and to respond with particular forms of accountability practices which can accommodate or alienate academic professionals to varying degrees. It is however, as the data presented here shows, always a danger of excess; of pushing metrics-based evidencing and positioning into ever-more facets of academic practice and adding an instrumental dimension to what used to be based on the shared values of academic professionalism.

Note

1 Attempts to introduce performance-related payment for professors failed likewise, as faculties decided to distribute performance-related shares evenly between them in order to prevent conflict.

References

Blackmore, P. (2015) *Prestige in academic life: Excellence and exclusion.* London: Routledge.

Bloch, R., Hartl, J., O'Connell, C. and O'Siochru, C. (2021) English and German academics' perspectives on metrics in higher education: Evaluating dimensions of fairness and organisational justice. *Higher Education*, 46(3): 548–62.

Boliver, V. (2015) Are there distinctive clusters of higher and lower status universities in the UK? *Oxford Review of Education*, 41(5): 608–27.

Brew, A., Boud, D., Lucas, D. and Crawford, K. (2018). Academics artisans in the research university. *Higher Education*, 76(1): 115–27.

Bromley, P. and Meyer, J. W. (2015) *Hyper-organization. Global organizational expansion.* Oxford: Oxford University Press.

Cannizzo, F. (2015) Academic subjectivities: Governmentality and self-development in higher education. *Foucault Studies*, 20(20): S. 199–217. DOI: 10.22439/fs.v0i0.4937.

Clark, B. (1983) *The higher education system: Academic organisation in cross-national perspective.* Berkeley: University of California Press.

Cohen, M. D., March, J. G. and Olsen, J. P. (1972) A garbage can model of organizational choice. *Administrative science quarterly*, 17(1): 1–25.

Gläser, J (2010) From governance to authority relations. In R. Whitley, J. Gläser and L. Engwall (Hg.) *Reconfiguring knowledge production. Changing authority relationships in the sciences and their consequences for intellectual innovation*, S. 357–370. Oxford and New York: Oxford University Press.

Grealy, L. and Laurie, T. (2017) Higher degree research by numbers. Beyond the critiques of neo-liberalism. *Higher Education Research & Development*, 36(3): S. 458–71.

Gunn, A. (2018) Metrics and methodologies for measuring teaching quality in higher education: Developing the Teaching Excellence Framework (TEF). *Educational Review*, 70(2): 129–48.

Gunter, H., Hall, D. and Bragg, J. (2013) Distributed leadership: A study in knowledge production. *Educational Management Administration & Leadership*, 41(5): 555–80. https://doi.org/10.1177/1741143213488586.

Habermas, J. (1988) Die Idee der Universität – Lernprozesse. In M. Eigen, H. G. Gadamer, J. Habermas, W. Lepenies, H. Lübbe and K. M. Meyer-Abich (Hg.) *Die Idee der Universität. Versuch einer Standortbestimmung*, pp. 139–73. Berlin: Springer.

Harley, S. (2002) The impact of research selectivity on academic work and identity in UK universities. *Studies in Higher Education*, 27(2): 187–205.

Hazelkorn, E. (2009). Rankings and the battle for world class excellence: Institutional strategies and policy choices. *Higher Education Management and Policy*, 21(1): 55–77.

Hüther, O. and Krücken, G. (2013) Hierarchy and power: A conceptual analysis with particular reference to new public management reforms in German universities. *European Journal of Higher Education*, 3(4): S. 307–23.

Kleimann, B (2019) (German) Universities as multiple hybrid organisations. *Higher Education*, 77(6): 1085–102.

Kolsaker, A. (2008) Academic professionalism in the era of managerialism: A study of English universities. *Studies in Higher Education*, 33(5): 513–25.

Krücken, G. and Meier, F. (2006) Turning the university into an organizational actor. In G. S. Drori, J. W. Meyer and H. Hwang (eds.) *Globalization and organization. World society and organizational change*, pp. 241–57. Oxford and New York: Oxford University Press.

Lamont, M. (2009) *How professors think. Inside the curious world of academic judgment.* 1st pbk. ed. Cambridge, MA and London: Harvard University Press.

Lenger, A. (2018) Socialization in the academic and professional field: Revealing the homo oeconomicus academicus. *Historical Social Research*, 43(3): S. 39–62.

Locke, W. (2014) Shifting academic careers: Implications for enhancing professionalism in teaching and supporting learning. *Higher Education Academy*. https://www.heacademy.ac.uk/system/files/resources/shifting_academic_careers_final.pdf (accessed on 31 October 2021).

Locke, W. and Bennion, A. (2011) The United Kingdom: Academic retreat or professional renewal? In W. Locke, W. Cummings and D. Fisher (eds.) *Changing governance and management in higher education. The changing academy – the changing academic profession in international comparative perspective*, vol 2. Dordrecht: Springer.

Marini, G., Locke, W. and Whitchurch, C. (2019) Centre for global higher education working paper series *The future higher education workforce in locally and globally engaged higher education institutions: A review of literature on the topic of 'the academic workforce'*. Working paper no. 43.

Mau, S. (2019) *The metric society. The quantification of the social world*. Cambridge: Polity

Merton, R. K. (1973) The normative structure of science. In R. K. Merton (ed.) *The sociology of science. Theoretical and empirical investigations*, pp. 267–78. Chicago: University of Chicago Press.

Meyer, J. W., Drori, G. S. and Hwang, H. (2006) World society and the proliferation of formal organization. In G. S. Drori, J. W. Meyer and H. Hwang (eds.) *Globalization and organization. World society and organizational change*, pp. 25–49. Oxford, New York: Oxford University Press.

Meyer, J. W. and Jepperson, R. L. (2000) The 'actors' of mModern society: The cultural construction of social agency. *Sociological Theory*, 18(1): 100–20.

Oancea, A. (2008) Performative accountability and the UK research assessment exercise. *Critical Perspectives on Communication, Cultural and Policy Studies*, 27(1&2): 153–73.

O'Brien, T. and Guiney, D. (2019) *Staff wellbeing in higher education. A research study for the Education Support Partnership*. https://www.educationsupportpartnership.org.uk/resources/research-reports/staff-wellbeing-higher-education [accessed on 31 October 2021].

O'Connell, C., O'Siochru, C. and Rao, N. (2021) Academic perspectives on metrics: Procedural justice as a key factor in evaluations of fairness. *Studies in Higher Education*, 46(3): 548–62.

Pereira M do M. (2015) Higher education cutbacks and the reshaping of epistemic hierarchies: An ethnography of the case of feminist scholarship. *Sociology*, 49(2): 287–304. DOI:10.1177/0038038514541334.

Ramirez, F. O. (2006) The rationalization of universities. In M. L. Djelic and K. Sahlin-Andersson (eds.) *Transnational governance. Institutional dynamics of regulation*, pp. 225–44. Cambridge: Cambridge University Press.

Ringer, F. K. (1969) *The decline of the German Mandarins. The German academic community, 1890–1933*. Cambridge, Mass: Havard University Press.

Rose, N. (1991) Governing by numbers: Figuring out democracy. *Accounting, organizations and society*, 16(7): 673–92.

Schelsky, H. (1963) *Einsamkeit und Freiheit. Idee und Gestalt der deutschen Universität und ihrer Reformen*. Reinbek bei Hamburg: Rowohlt.

van den Brink, M. and Benschop, Y. (2011) Gender practices in the construction of academic excellence. Sheep with five legs. *Organization*, 19(4): S. 507–24.

Schimank, U. and Lange, S. (2009) Germany: A latecomer to new public management. In C. Paradeise, E. Reale, I. Bleiklie and E. Ferlie (eds.) *University governance. Western European comparative perspectives*, pp. 51–75. Dordrecht, London: Springer (Higher education dynamics, 25).

Smith, J. (2017) Target-setting, early-career academic identities and the measurement culture of UK higher education. *Higher Education Research & Development*, 36(3): 597–611.

Strathern, M. (2000) The tyranny of transparency. *British Educational Research Journal*, 26(3): 309–21.

Tight, M. (2014) Collegiality and managerialism: A false dichotomy? Evidence from the higher education literature. *Tertiary Education and Management*, 20(4): 294–306.

Whitley, R. (2010) Reconfiguring the public sciences. The impact of governance changes on authority and innovation in public science systems. In R. Whitley, J. Gläser and L. Engwall (Hg.) *Reconfiguring knowledge production. Changing authority relationships in the sciences and their consequences for intellectual innovation*, S. 3–47. Oxford, New York: Oxford University Press.

Whitley, R. (2011) Changing governance and authority relations in the public sciences. *Minerva*, 49(4): S. 359–85. DOI: 10.1007/s11024-011-9182-2.

Whitley, R. (2012) Transforming universities. National conditions of their varied organisational actorhood. *Minerva*, 50(4): 493–510. DOI: 10.1007/s11024-012-9215-5.

Wilsdon, J., et al. (2015) *The metric tide: Report of the independent review of the role of metrics in research assessment and management.* DOI: 10.13140/RG.2.1.4929.1363.

Wallenburg, I., Quartz, J. and Bal, R. (2019) Making hospitals governable: Performativity and institutional work in ranking practices. *Administration & Society*, 51(4): 637–63.

6

International Student Recruitment: Policy, Paradox and Practice

Sylvie Lomer

Internationalization has taken on plural, contested meanings and its value is often unquestioned, resting on a modernist, globalist sense of symbolic capital, where difference and distance connote value. Thus, recruiting international students from 'across the globe' becomes a worthy endeavour in and of itself: a diverse student cohort is a good one. But it further signifies the capacity of the university and the nation to attract student-consumers from so far away. The picture drawn by policymakers and institutional marketing materials is one of increased campus and classroom diversity, contributing to the financial coffers of universities as well as to the learning experiences of international and home students alike.

However, the uneven distribution of international students across universities, regions and disciplines means that the lived experience of internationalization rarely reflects this idealized depiction. At the extreme peak of international student recruitment, student numbers can fluctuate wildly around predictions, targets and offers, making the planning of academic work and teaching incredibly challenging. Admissions and decision-making around student numbers on particular courses have been centralized, and removed from the academic sphere of influence, separating out questions of curriculum delivery – otherwise known as teaching – from questions of who studies on a course and in what numbers.

Since teaching practices respond to the lived realities, they are shaped by policies and practices of student recruitment. The presence of international students in the classroom has been primarily understood within the framework of internationalizing the curriculum. Internationalizing the curriculum is often taken for granted as an obvious good, evoking narratives of internationalism as a normative value (Byram, 2018). Graduate attributes highlight a nebulous notion of a 'global citizen', aware of their place in the world and capable of working with and learning from the 'Other'. Academics are therefore exhorted to ensure that their curriculum reflects this globalized world, engaging with multiple national contexts. Yet for many international students, the marketing package is sold on exploring a 'British education'. Further, the theoretical literature on curriculum internationalization is often premised on concepts of intercultural learning that assumes all students from the same country know the same things, come from the same culture and share the same attitudes. Intercultural learning is therefore a simple matter of structuring engagement with 'diverse' students. In the contexts described above, these approaches may not be possible. Teachers therefore too often grasp in the dark for practices to respond to the exhortation to 'internationalize' without the resources presumed to be available. Yet deficit narratives dominate the literature, and often, institutional discourses, positioning international students as subaltern petitioners to British higher education, lacking the capacity for critical thought, verbal discussion, independent study and the aptitudes for deeper or active learning (Heng, 2018; Moosavi, 2020; Song, 2016; Wang et al, 2019). These stand in contrast to the claim to value internationalization for its capacity to bring diversity to the classroom.

Instead, contemporary academics may be confronted with one or more of a series of contradictory demands: how to internationalize a locally oriented curriculum with a cohort of mainly home students; how to demonstrate the value of internationalization to home students; how to offer the promised international experience to a cohort of entirely international students; and how to effect intercultural learning between self-segregating or resistant student groups. These endeavours require full epistemic engagement in the intellectual project of globalizing curriculum and teaching, for which many academics lack the vocabulary and time. Further, academics must navigate these paradoxes in the full knowledge that it is the signs, rather than the substance, of internationalization that are valued: consider frequently made marketing claims for how many countries are represented by a diverse student body, for example, or images of international students graduating in their 'traditional national dress'. It is much easier and more cost-effective to achieve a tokenistic representation of internationalization than to break down the intersecting globalized practices of recruitment, admissions and pedagogy, and rebuild them.

The purpose of this chapter is to explore how the contemporary processes of international student recruitment contribute to the ongoing de-professionalization of lecturing and academic staff in highly internationalized contexts. I explore how the inequity of international student recruitment, the specific practices of education agents, the micro-practices around admissions within the university, and the pedagogic practices of HE lecturers teaching international students, intersect to create a highly fractured, tense and problematic environment.

The Inequity of International Student Recruitment

Both marketization and internationalization in the specific form of the recruitment of international students to study physically in a host country have become taken for granted. International higher education is commonly understood as a private good that benefits the individual student, than as a public global good (Marginson, 2016), pursued for the purposes of mutual peace, for example. This rationality legitimates charging tuition fees (Tannock, 2018), which has in turn situated international students as an essential resource for the continued survival of many institutions and indeed sectors in established host or recruiting countries.

The narrative that prioritizes the economic benefits of recruiting international students, who pay far larger tuition fees than do home students in most countries, represents the students as 'cash cows' (Qureshi and Khawaja, 2021). International/home fee differentials privilege the already economically privileged, and marginalized the experiences of less wealthy or struggling international students. These economic benefits are felt predominantly, in Russell Group universities at the higher end of the rankings, and only to a very limited extent in smaller and lesser-known universities. While institutions and countries often contextualize the economic benefits in relation to educational benefits that result from a more diverse classroom, the impact that tuition fees have in shaping this diversity is rarely acknowledged (Warikoo, 2016).

Elite universities are able to charge exorbitant tuition fees to international students, who gain access to limited additional resources and services. Unlike nearly any other marketized commodity, a higher price for an international university experience confers no additional privileges (other than visa support). Even access to in-sessional English support (e.g. the optional academic English classes offered by many institutions) is not dedicated exclusively to international students (nor, from a perspective of equity in widening participation, should it be). International students act as an economic resource for universities but are not themselves offered further resource or support commensurate with their contribution, as far as I am aware. Educational interventions that might help to structure and promote learning through diversity are neither appropriately resourced nor conceptualized. Academic staff feel stretched and exhausted, asked to teach large groups of international students with no additional support or teaching assistants (Lomer et al, 2021). They rely on their best knowledge of inclusive pedagogy, without further training that might help them to organize these principles in relation to an international and globalizing space. However, this knowledge is often premised on a colour-blind frame, that frames race as insignificant and therefore limits the capacity to recognize inequalities (Warikoo, 2016) and engage in transformative change. Instead, universities draw on dominant deficit discourses with reference to international students, constructing them as academically lacking and in need of further support in the form of 'English for Academic Purposes' (EAP) or paid-for pre-sessional or pathway courses. This academic marginalization may help to explain the racialized patterns of student outcomes, which see international students systematically underperforming home and EU-domiciled students. Many universities acknowledge that international students achieve lower grades than home students (Tannock, 2018). Data from HESA (2020) show that over the five years from 2014/15 to 2019/20 international undergraduate students were less likely to achieve a 1st class (20 per cent vs. 26 per cent) or upper second class (43 per cent vs. 47 per cent) degree and more likely to achieve a lower second (27 per cent vs. 18 per cent) or third-class degree (7 per cent vs. 4 per cent) compared to their UK counterparts. While the same analysis cannot be performed on public data or postgraduate taught students, it seems likely that this pattern would also apply. These disparities echo entrenched racial disparities of outcomes for minoritized British students; yet, it is rare for staff to acknowledge that international students are also racialized and minoritized (Madriaga and McCaig, 2019). UK universities therefore rely on international students for their survival; yet, these students pay more to achieve less.

Host countries and recruiting institutions invest in a range of recruitment practices aimed at increasing this income including national branding (Lomer et al, 2016), strategy making (James and Derrick, 2020), target setting and the development of particular products – courses such as pre-sessional programmes which incorporate English language components. The marketization of international higher education has also encouraged the development of a specific profession, the education agent (Feng and Horta, 2021) who mediates between aspiring international students and recruiting providers.

Strategies for Survival

In an ongoing analysis of institutional strategy and internationalization strategy documents from UK universities we identified several dominant discursive patterns (Lomer et al, forthcoming). Reputation dominated as a concern with institutions seeking to position themselves as sector leading or as emerging contenders to overthrow the established hierarchy. Particularly amongst institutions that seem to position themselves either as emerging or as unrecognized or marginalized institutions the predominant emotion was that of fear, typically for institutional survival. In contrast many who position themselves as sector leaders or as emerging contenders had documents which best be described as fuzzy optimism. These contrasted with the more dominant pragmatic narrative with high blown adjectives, few details and proportionately more space given to graphics and images. Documents with a more pragmatic tone whether from sector leaders, emerging contenders or unrecognized institutions tended to have concrete objectives, specific priorities and definite action plans. The recruitment of international students was frequently the first item listed under internationalization strategies whether these were separate documents or embedded within the University's main strategic plan. Despite an ongoing shift away from the language of internationalization and towards the framing of global engagement (Lewis, 2021), numbers of international students on campus or in transnational branch campuses are often taken in these documents to be a primary indicator of their internationalized status. Increasing the number of students recruited was a frequent goal, arguably because it is one of the few quantifiable indicators of internationalization or global engagement. In several documents, this commitment or goal is set in conjunction with an acknowledgement of concerns about the 'quality' of international students.

We see here therefore intersections with national policy discourses. The dominance of the economic narrative that has been the case in the policy context for the last twenty years in the UK is perpetuated in many UK institutions (Lomer, 2014). For many, it is characterized nearly as a matter of institutional survival. For others, particularly established or sector leading HEIs, the financial gains from international students are more taken for granted but are no less 'mission-critical'. The language of marketization and managerialism is fully embedded in these documents, which are overwhelmingly corporate in their presentation, structure and content. Narratives that position international students as a window on the world, educational resources in their own rights, are also present particularly in documents that we characterize as fuzzy optimism. It is however noticeable that few of these documents articulated a coherent vision for how such benefits might be realized through a programme of investment in pedagogy and curriculum (Lewis, 2021). To the extent that it is possible to generalize across a corpus of over a hundred documents, it was far more common to see attention to curriculum related to research rather than internationalization. We also saw little attention given in these documents to investing resources in international students. For example, it was rare to see mention of expanded scholarship programmes, investment in language centres, or simply in hiring more teachers. The lived experience of internationalization therefore rarely reflects the idealized depiction of internationalization in policy.

As the previous discussion of institutional strategies makes clear, internationalization in the UK takes many different forms with different numbers of international students in different institutions in different programs, different levels of engagement in transnational higher education, different levels of institutional commitment to internationalization and global engagement, different understandings of internationalization and so on. When national level policy presents a singular image of internationalization across UK HE, it elides these differences into a fabricated composite.

International student recruitment alone is highly uneven across the higher education sector.[1] On a regional level, nearly 25 per cent of international students in the UK are hosted by London institutions, yet only 1.3 per cent in Northern Ireland. Further variation is evident when sector groups are differentiated: Collectively the Russell Group (which defines itself with reference to its research and research-led teaching) hosts 205,000 international students, and its member institutions average around 8,950 international students. In contrast, the Cathedrals Group (a small group of mostly younger institutions characterized by their religious history), accounts only for 6,155 international students collectively with an average of 410 per institution. While the proportion of international students at Russell Group universities is 31 per cent, at Cathedrals Group universities it is only 5 per cent. The proportion of international students is even higher at specialist institutions, such as the London School of Economics, Royal Veterinary College, and the music and theatre conservatoires, with an average of 39 per cent.

Given that international student fees can be double or even triple home student fees (Oliver, 2020), the economic implications of such different levels of international student recruitment are clear. Institutions able to recruit more international students earn more direct income. They typically rely less on tuition fee income, with a higher proportion of research income (HESA, 2021). The marketization of international student recruitment therefore widens the gap between institutions, with prestigious universities growing larger and richer, and lesser-known universities struggling to recruit students and finance their activities. In the context of ongoing declines in state funding, international student recruitment is, as many of the institutional strategic plans make plain, critical to the survival of many universities.

Practices of Recruitment

It is not therefore surprising that institutions adopt recruitment practices consonant with this fear. In this section, I identify a number of well-known but little analysed practices. Due to the lack of critical scholarship in this area, these are largely based on my own professional experiences. My aim is to highlight how the tensions between policy discourses and the material financial reality of most institutions generate incentives for marketized international admissions practices.

Broadly speaking, with shorter undergraduate and postgraduate degree programmes than the rest of Europe, or than other major destinations such as the United States and Australia, UK HEIs must continuously recruit new students (Ilieva, 2018). There is higher turnover of new international students in the UK than in any other destination; student recruitment and admissions activities are therefore correspondingly more intensive and significant for the sector.

Agents

The removal of admissions work from the academic sphere has been intensified by the increasing activities of education agents, a domain of activity that many academics remain unaware of. Agents or brokers smooth the path of international applications and enable universities to increase their enrolments (Feng and Horta, 2021; Huang et al, 2016; Nikula and Kivistö, 2017; Sidhu, 2002). Agents earn commission from universities, which typically award agents a proportion of the first year or full degree course fees, on average 15 per cent of the tuition fee (Raimo and Huang, 2020). Some agencies, however, charge students as well (West and Addington, 2021). Many agents also provide additional services students may pay for directly such as language classes, visa application support and travel support (Yang et al, 2020). A recent survey suggests 50 per cent of new international students in the UK made use of agents in their application (Edified, 2021), so the size of the sector globally is substantial, but challenging to estimate. Agents are therefore symbiotic with universities, working to expand the international education market.

Universities are willing to share fees with agents because they offer direct access to 'markets' that individual institutions cannot reach effectively, particularly where they have limited international reputations and access to local infrastructure such as in-country offices and market intelligence. Even high-profile institutions engage with this economy of agents, though they may not wish to publicize it (Raimo and Huang, 2020). Agents offer a liaison, a bridging link to help students understand application processes and practices, far beyond what an institutional international office could do on an individual basis. Certain universities establish close partnerships with particular agencies, working closely to organize regular visits to key cities, and even specific local colleges and universities. When the numbers warrant it, they can even offer face-to-face admissions interviews with representatives, for a conditional offer. Indeed, many HEIs reported to a commercial survey that the respondents (primarily international office representatives) wanted agents to do more direct offer-making (Edified, 2021), in other words, to delegate decision-making even beyond the institution. Certain partnerships are so well-established that they offer parallel application systems for students who go through these agencies. These systems are kept solely for communication between agencies and universities. In this extreme example, as Huang et al (2016) conclude, where universities effectively outsource control of decision making to external agencies, they cede power. They also give up the possibility of making strategic decisions about recruitment that might relate coherently to priorities relating to pedagogy and curriculum. In removing decision-making about admissions from not only the academic and the programme level, but even the institutional level, this holistic approach to strategy development becomes impossible.

Agents contribute to accelerating specific patterns of international student recruitment. Where they do not charge fees directly to students, agents can be a way for families to overcome a lack of social capital in terms of awareness of international educational norms and practices. They offer a quasi-insider perspective since many have personal educational experiences of the countries they specialize in, and have access to elaborate specialized databases. Filtering and interpreting information back to potential students and families, with knowledge of cultures, languages and norms of practice, is itself a highly valuable service (Yang et al, 2020).

But it is also a very powerful position for agents to be in, and one in which institutions are effectively blind to the information being disseminated about them and their practices. Stories from alumni, as well as from agents' past experiences, circulate on social media such as Weibo, WeChat and WhatsApp groups, reaching thousands of potential applicants at a time in forums that cannot readily be monitored by monolingual English speakers. Agents can also – sometimes intentionally – block direct communication between the institution and the student. It can be difficult, for example, to gain access to a student's personal contact information before they enrol and agents intentionally filter, parse and interpret the information they receive from universities.

Similarly, the involvement of educational agents in writing personal statements and CVs compromises the role of these documents in the admissions process. They have become carefully crafted documents produced over several years with knowledge of the sector, much like privately educated young people in the UK who can deploy a wider range of social and cultural capital in their statements (Jones, 2013). The centralization of admissions often means that these documents are not interrogated by an academic in any case, but where they are, a formula can often be observed (Hemsley-Brown, 2012). The personal statement is often effectively useless in international admissions, since the intervention of agents makes it impossible to ascertain anything about the student's interests, personality or academic ability, and indeed admissions staff at Russell Group universities claim not to use personal statements at all, finding them 'too engineered' (Houghton, 2019). Likewise, the CV can be a product of intervention, since agents also perform the functions of obtaining relevant internships and work experience opportunities. Sometimes, this can be a useful levelling function, overcoming a student's lack of personal or family connections that often help get access to these opportunities. But in some cases, work experiences are very short, limited practices where students learn little of relevance to their degree courses, and this can be difficult to ascertain from a CV or application form.

In sum the involvement of education agents both facilitates and complicates international admissions. Agents provide a much-needed logistical facilitator, a bridge between different educational systems, but they may complicate universities' ability to assess students' potential and to engage with them directly.

International Admissions Standards

> We conclude that it is simplistic and unsatisfactory for higher education institutions to be seen to rely on the fact that international students continue to apply as evidence that standards are being maintained. It is absurd and disreputable to justify academic standards with a market mechanism.
>
> (House of Commons Innovation, Universities, Science and Skills Committee Students and Universities Eleventh Report of Session, 2008–9)

Admissions standards for international students are best understood as a threshold – much as they are for home students, in fact. In this sense, despite the rhetoric of the policy and strategy documents, no university is recruiting 'the best of the best', because that is not how admissions requirements work (Lomer, 2017). Here is how they do work. The following account is anecdotal, based entirely on my experience at one university, and I cannot claim it to be representative of practices across the sector, since there is limited either grey or published literature on the question.

Academic staff must agree through the quality assurance process what the admissions requirements will be – both academic and English language. The institution typically has a view about minimum requirements, and the admissions team will advise on whether changes are likely to impact recruitment numbers. The admissions team then publishes this on the website, over a year in advance. Students, and agents, review and compare requirements to decide where to apply. Many students, at least those advised by agents, will apply to a shortlist of five to six universities, of which one or two will be a 'reach' (an ambitious goal considering the student's record), one or two reasonable, and one or two 'safe' (see Yang et al, 2022). A top-ranking research university might receive several thousand applications for a single degree course. Where they apply a basic 'standards met', threshold approach, an admissions team will make offers on a rolling basis to *all students who meet the criteria*. There may be an exception, or two depending on the institution: if the English-language standard is not met, a conditional offer will be made such that the student can meet the requirement through independent testing at their own expense. And if the institution has a private pathway provider partnership arrangement (see below), they may make a conditional offer if the academic requirements are not met. While the net effect over years is to increase admissions standards (Ma, 2020), this is not, therefore, a 'competitive' admissions system, despite emphasis in both institutional strategy documents and admissions narratives on wanting 'the brightest students' (Chankseliani, 2018).

At a certain point, for instance when pre-determined recruitment targets are met, offers will cease to be made. There is a complex judgment to be made here, however. Since most applicants will apply to multiple universities, they may hold multiple offers. An institution has no way of knowing how many universities applicants have applied to and what their order of preference would be. These offers may also have different conditions, so an applicant may be in a position of choosing between a safe choice where they already meet the requirements, or a conditional offer involving more fees in the hope of meeting higher requirements. With a conversion rate of somewhere between 20 and 40 per cent, many more offers are made than there are places available. This can result in an unanticipated rise in numbers if not managed very cautiously, with obvious consequences for staff and students. Student numbers can fluctuate by 10–20 per cent in both directions in the two to three weeks around the start of the academic year.

This threshold approach can sometimes mean closing admissions as early as January or February when the requisite number of offers has been made. Applications made via agents tend to be done very early in the academic year to ensure a more positive outcome (see below). This is specifically the case amongst Chinese PGT applicants, who often aim to apply during their fourth year of undergraduate study. Where a course has a particular appeal to this demographic, it can lead to an effectively mono-national cohort of students. As a respondent in Chankseliani (2018) put it, HEIs 'don't want a whole classroom full of Chinese students; [they] need a mix'. But this can only be achieved with a range of indirect strategies such as scholarships, targeted partnership arrangements, and specific marketing, since quota-based admissions are understood to violate British equality legislation.

An alternative approach is to run 'staged admissions', where batches of applications are reviewed and effectively ranked. This comes closer to the 'best of the best' approach as delineated in policy discourse, yet still is held in tension with institutional narratives about financial sustainability. Where international recruitment targets are a factor, the question becomes 'who are the best 50, 100, or 500 of these applicants', where the number is set with reference to the financial needs of the institution – not with reference to the best pedagogic scenario, the best learning experience, or the best chance of all students achieving the desired learning outcomes. Given the scale of applications received, due in part to the work of agents, review can only be cursory and primarily quantitative, contributing to the broader narratives that homogenize international students.

Where this becomes particularly problematic is in the timing and resourcing. Student numbers are often 'unconfirmed' until after registration is complete, which depending on institutional rules can be as late as two to three weeks into teaching. Where institutions withhold resourcing, namely additional teaching and support staff, until these numbers are confirmed, an unanticipated rise in student numbers can lead to a significant shortfall in capacity. Given the lead times on recruiting and appointing staff, this can last for three to four months at least, and often longer. Student-staff ratios on specific programmes or in particular departments can therefore radically exceed those stated on HESA returns or in rankings, since these are institutional aggregate figures. In such a scenario, students' experiences may be completely different from what they might reasonably expect from marketing materials and institutional comparisons.

This scenario is of course not representative of the sector. On the contrary, it is a problem of privilege – the privilege of the internationally renowned university. It is, however, a fairly common experience from staff at Russell Group universities in the UK (Lomer et al, 2021) and one that has immediate and material consequences for professional practice. Unanticipated large numbers change teaching practices, encouraging didactic lecture-based approaches, making small-group interactive teaching impossible without increased resourcing. These dynamics push practice closer to what Hadley (2015) describes as 'sausage factory' institutions. When numbers rise on one programme, they often rise elsewhere in the university simultaneously, creating pressure on physical resourcing such as rooms. Such massification, however, fundamentally changes how teachers can relate to their students, requiring a systemic approach to building community and learning relationships rather than allowing them to emerge organically through unplanned interactions. But such systemic approaches need planning and forethought, not *ad hoc* improvisation, which is what the context of uncertainty around international student recruitment generates.

This scenario is not the product of conspiracy or a lack of care; it is the end-result of intensifying marketization. With international student recruitment seen as a key source of income for universities, there is little to no incentive to limit numbers. Since its primary purpose is to generate income, there is similarly reluctance to resource those areas that do recruit well internationally. Since, as the House of Lords say in the quote at the beginning of this section, the ability to recruit is seen as a sign of success, there is no problem with a course or a department that recruits well but is under-resourced. Reputational damage can take years to filter through, and equally years to undo. With no longitudinal measures of international student success built into metrics or rankings (Hayes, 2019), there is no market-based incentive to financially invest in international students' education. A Russell Group university can coast on its colonial heritage, safe in the knowledge that whatever its pedagogic failings, its historic and contemporary research reputation will secure its competitive advantage in international student recruitment.

In the UK context, efforts to widen access to university amongst minoritized groups with lower rates of participation in higher education have adopted an approach known as contextual admissions (Boliver et al, 2021). This involves using domestic datasets that allow a student's academic achievements to be placed in context with their family, home location and school. A student who gets Bs at a low performing school in a postcode with low rates of university attendance will therefore be rated more favourably in contrast to a student with the same marks from a more advantaged background. This doesn't happen for international students. As Stuart Tannock pithily puts it, concerns about education equity 'stop at the border' (Tannock, 2018). It would of course be an extremely challenging task to obtain such granular data on an international, comparable and reliable scale. But it does mean that international admissions take no account of pre-existing inequalities, such as gender, minority ethnic status, family background, economic status, religion, disability or other factors that the literature amply demonstrates mediates access to and success with education. Any talk of 'raising standards' in reference to international students needs to either confront its elitism or find a way to tackle these intersectional inequalities.

Pre-sessional Courses

As international student recruitment becomes an increasingly important part of financial sustainability and reputation, institutions look for alternative routes to generate recruitment, and pre-sessional courses are an important example.

Most universities in English-language countries offer some form of pre-sessional course (Pearson, 2020), typically a generic English for Academic Purposes curriculum, aimed at students who come close to but miss the English language requirements for admissions. They are intended to offer an intensive course to increase English levels to a minimum appropriate standard for study, by focusing specifically on academic uses of English. Lasting two to fifty weeks, these courses are often part of a conditional offer, including an internal test at the end. Pre-sessional courses are typically staffed by trained and experienced English Language teachers, who are often precariously employed on short-term contracts. Working in pre-sessional delivery requires a high level of temporary domestic and sometimes international mobility from staff, and few will have stable professional relationships with academics in departments. Pearson's meta-analysis suggests a collective pass rate of 96 per cent of those institutions reporting.

The purpose of pre-sessional courses is to fill a gap between the English language level of international students and the admissions requirements of the department and the institution (not necessarily synonymous). Pre-sessional course provision has become a nearly ubiquitous activity for UK HEIs, although this is difficult to evidence. Pre-sessional courses are often made a condition of admission yet cost thousands of pounds. Many offer unconditional progression from the pre-sessional to the target degree course. While the delivery of these courses is intensive and highly professionalized (Pearson, 2020), there is a clear market incentive from institutions to ensure that students progress appropriately. Indeed, it may not be possible for academic departments to review results or reject pre-sessional students. However, Pearson also found that students who do pre-sessional courses do not perform as well on their degree programme as students who are made an offer through direct entry. In other words, pre-sessional courses do not fully remediate the gap between those who meet admissions standards at the outset and those who fall short.

The incentives to offer large pre-sessional courses are clear: it opens up a large additional potential group of students who would otherwise not meet admissions criteria. Unfortunately, this means there is also a powerful incentive to pass students.

From the perspective of a subject academic, these pre-sessional courses generate an additional level of uncertainty. Students will likely be juggling multiple offers from different universities with a range of different conditions. An imaginary case might look like Table 6.1.

One of the earliest indicators of numbers on a course is therefore how many students (or rather what proportion) take up the longest pre-sessional course on offer at that institution but increasing conditional offers may result in a fall in student numbers if they obtain unconditional offers at a competitive institution.

In addition to pre-sessional courses, some universities now offer 'pathway courses'.

Table 6.1 Hypothetical example of a student's offers. Author's compilation

Offer type	University type	Location	Additional cost
Unconditional	Non-Russell Group safety choice	Campus-based safe but unknown location	
Conditional	Russell Group	Tourist city outside London (i.e. lower cost of living, perceived as safer)	Five-week pre-sessional required charging an additional £2,300
Conditional	Russell Group	London (high cost of living, not as safe but more cultural attractions and work opportunities)	Twelve-week pre-sessional charging £7,000

Private Pathway Providers

Often delivered through private providers such as INTO, Kaplan, Navitas and Study Group, these foundation or pre-masters programmes offer alternative routes of access to students who do not meet academic and/or English language entry requirements (Lawton, cited in Bell, 2021). Typically, their curriculum covers both Academic English and subject specific content (the latter is often generic, at the 'science and mathematics' or 'business and social science' collective discipline level). It is currently challenging to get a sense of the scale and scope of these activities, since there is no obvious mandatory reporting requirement to HESA and it is not clear whether the courses and students would be considered under the host institution or the private provider. Likewise, there is very limited academic literature exploring or problematizing their practices.

Students who do not meet the direct entry requirements for an institution with such an arrangement would then typically receive a conditional offer specifying their requirements to study on the pathway course. Students often perceive these as part of the university itself, but partnership arrangements are often quite distant, with curricula developed by the private provider and only quality assured by the institution, for instance. Teaching staff are employed entirely separately and not on academic contracts, often having little to no engagement with the relevant academic departments the pathway students would go on to study in.

For large providers, this arrangement is highly lucrative, since fees would be split in a profit-sharing arrangement between the private provider and the host institution, and full-cost fees are charged. Not only does this add up to a year of fees to every student who successfully matriculates from the pathway college, it also opens up an entirely new market of otherwise ineligible students. As with pre-sessional courses, the financial incentives are clear. However, the absence of statutory reporting requirements resulting in public data means that the size, scale and profitability of this part of the sector cannot be made transparent, and there have been criticisms of this area of the sector. For example:

> Admissions criteria and the quality of courses being offered are severely compromised. Staff are under huge teaching workloads, unable to engage with vital development work and research.
> (University and College Union, 2010)

Such courses may be a substantial benefit to students, of course. Particularly for PGT students on intensive twelve-month courses, the time available to acclimatize to local academic norms and practices is potentially invaluable, and the teaching is often very demanding, with curricular and pedagogic practices sometimes ahead of HE sector norms (Wildavsky, 2012).

The existence of private pathway providers, like agents and pre-sessional courses, is material evidence of the intensification of market-based practices in international student recruitment (Hadley, 2015). Hadley refers to these as Student Processing Units, divested of professional criticality and scholarship, McDonaldized (Ritzer, 2013) approaches to uniform instruction and curriculum, with mechanistic managerialist approaches to language learning. Agents, pre-sessional courses and private pathway providers all represent a distancing of academics and applicants in the admissions process. By first centralizing, and then outsourcing, much of the international admissions process now happens completely outside the control of academics, and without the additional support of algorithms that might support contextual admissions for the purposes of equity as in the domestic context. When they get into the classroom, academics must then respond to a huge range of unknowns, with limited resourcing. The following section details how academics respond to this challenge in context in their teaching practices.

Pedagogies

During a nation-wide interview-based study with UK academics (Lomer et al, 2021), we explored their perceptions and experiences of teaching with international students, and the results illustrate tensions between pedagogic practice and recruitment practices. In an ideal scenario, as depicted in much of the internationalization of the curriculum literature, an international classroom is taken to mean a group of students from multiple different countries, accessing a curriculum that draws on literature and cases from multiple global contexts, and drawing on each other's varied sets of cultural knowledge to augment this curriculum. Formal learning opportunities therefore consist of facilitating this exchange and putting it into dialogue with the curriculum content, ideally within smaller group interactions guided by a subject expert lecturer. This isn't what participants told us was happening in their classrooms.

Internationalization and the presence of international students were consistently reflected by our participants as a positive and well-established characteristic of teaching in UK higher education. This was often discussed from the perspective of career fulfilment, that teaching international students added greater joy and variation to a career in HE. Teaching international students was also framed as an opportunity to reflect on teaching practices and challenge assumptions they had made about areas of their expertise. It was viewed, as one participant noted, 'a real privilege' (Participant 41), 'that invigorates us' (P24), 'like a breath of fresh air' (P25).

But many participants alluded to how the wider higher education landscape structures and limits pedagogic possibilities. This was often made in reference to issues of neoliberalism and austerity, reflecting on practical implications of national policies towards higher education: 'Actually, to be honest, it is, I think, the current UK higher education position, with years of conservative austerity, is that we're exhausted and there's no resources' (P38).

Other concerns from participants centred on entry requirements outside the control of teaching staff (and, frequently, their departments), pressures to increase student numbers, financial restrictions on investment in teaching and staff, limited engagement from senior leadership in the 'chalkface' issues of internationalization and increasing workload. Thus, there was a palpable and often explicit sense of fatigue from staff, not wholly attributable to COVID-19 (but often exacerbated by it): 'I feel like my job is unethical. And it shouldn't be' (P10).

For many, the will to invest in pedagogic innovation and continuing professional development was stymied by a lack of institutional investment and time, as well as a lack of support for experimentation and failure. Emphasis on metrics, such as the National Student Survey (NSS), and teaching evaluation questionnaires left particularly early career staff feeling vulnerable to negative reviews and unwilling to take risks in teaching. Constraints imposed by timetables, room styles, student numbers and lack of additional staff made options limited for many. Yet the determination to create positive and enriching learning experiences for their students remained and pedagogic innovation was, in many ways, required. Although participants expressed views similar to those of policy discourse, in terms of an unproblematized commitment to a diverse classroom leading to an 'international education', this did not come about easily, due to a range of obstacles.

Several participants positioned their own positive attitudes towards international students in contrast to a more problematic culture in the institution or department. One described it as 'the old mindset' (P1) of an 'unkind' deficit approach, while another described a faculty committee meeting where staff suggested they only work with international students 'because we have to' (P22). Another explicitly linked this to admissions requirements: 'There's definitely a vocal minority that is upset, and honestly, with decent reasons, because, like, at my university, we have very low entrance requirements' (P33). Participants saw themselves as pushing against the tide and often isolated as 'the international' or 'the pedagogy' person. Where international students are seen as a burden to bear, they are unlikely to be taught well.

While many academics acknowledged the complexity of the international students' transition experiences, some situated their practices as 'nationality-blind', stating that it was a point of principle not to 'change' their teaching approaches for international students. Despite a frequent recognition that international students might need transitional support, embedded skills development and supplementary language input, few participants felt they had been part of a systematic departmental level conversation about teaching with international students: 'There's never been such a discussion ... or a change of approaches' (P37). The absence of such a discussion raises concerns about how international students might equitably access the curriculum, whether they might not be fundamentally disadvantaged, as persistent outcomes gaps referred to in the introduction might suggest.

Despite the superficial positivity towards international students, we saw a recurrence of the deficit model, depicting them as 'unadapted' to British-style pedagogies, which are still taken to be a one-size-fits-all best approach. Participants particularly focused on interactive teaching in seminar style discussions to be where international students struggled. Some participants attributed this to 'cultural differences', though many almost immediately re-framed this as 'different learning experiences'. The trope of the 'silent Asian student' was still apparent in our interviews, which was seen as a source of challenge for lecturers: 'The challenge will be just to keep up the engagement. Just hopefully, somebody will say something' (P3). One lecturer highlighted the change over the course of their career, that as student numbers increased, they had to implement greater structure into their seminar discussions, moving away from traditional 'You know, you've been given a question and a reading list, come and tell me what you think' models (P29). Many participants suggested that the presence of international students in the classroom made more obvious the weaknesses and shortcomings of this traditional approach, namely: uneven engagement; reliance on vocalized participation; absence of structure connecting the discussions to the learning outcomes of the unit/module; reliance on implicit norms of discussions; failure to acknowledge the intersectional class, race and gender dynamics of turn-taking and discussion, which can further marginalize non-traditional student groups: 'I do think that sometimes this kind of communicative Eurocentric Western approach likes the performative element of a discussion' (P22). This suggests that innovation is needed to understand what appropriate interactive teaching looks like in an internationalized classroom, that is not always a model of diversity.

But universities do not make it easy to develop more interactive teaching approaches. Timetables were seen as constraints when they categorized a session as a lecture and a follow-up session as a seminar, which structured students' expectations (P31). Pre-agreed timetable structures limited possibilities such as blocking extended periods for activity-led teaching. Similarly, classroom structures such as the availability of whiteboards, being timetabled in a tiered lecture theatre (P3), or with fixed seating, limited options for moving students around or organizing group work, whereas flat spaces facilitated this. Student numbers also constituted a barrier (P16) for several we interviewed at higher-ranking institutions, who described attempting to deliver seminars to groups of sixty to eighty students. Where institutions do not invest in resources such as staff time and additional classroom space, small-group teaching cannot follow, and it is in small groups facilitated by subject experts that the dialogic model of intercultural exchange takes place.

In this way, there was a recognition that internationalization itself was not problematic, but that it, combined with the massification of student numbers, made more apparent existing challenges to teaching norms and assumptions.

Conclusions

This chapter has attempted to summarize a scenario that will be familiar to many academics teaching in UK universities today. We have given up control of our admissions processes to central bodies. We are held hostage to targets set at institutional levels. International admissions take no account of contextual information and do not seek to widen participation or aspire to equity. The uncertainty surrounding international admissions means it is almost impossible to plan for the academic year since we can never know how many students we will have, what their needs might be, and even if we were it would be unlikely that the resources would follow at such short notice. We recruit international students at extortionate fees and are not able to provide them with commensurate support. We know they are unlikely to achieve equal outcomes under these circumstances, and we do not have the time or willpower to critically interrogate the assessment and evaluation practices that make this so. We have a shared vision of what good international education looks like and how it should be delivered, but despite the billions of pounds international students bring to the sector, we rarely have enough rooms, training or teachers to deliver it. The reputation that attracts students is built almost exclusively on research, and hardly at all on the actual teaching practices experienced by international students. The divorce between international student recruitment and admissions practices, and academics and teaching practices, generates this ethical dilemma.

International higher education is marketized in both its practices and its discourses. This is unlikely to change soon. What reflexive professionals in this context can achieve is a considered critical awareness of the forces that structure international student recruitment, to reflect on the ethical tensions that emerge in our daily practice. Such a practice requires overcoming the artificial barrier established between academics and professional support staff and particularly in this case admissions. It requires offering both teachers and professional support staff access to training and professional development opportunities premised on an understanding of critical internationalization. These trainings need to address the inequalities that structure the field, from both the student and institutional perspective. They also need to make transparent the professional practices of both teachers and admissions staff. Workload models need to account for the time needed to incorporate professional reflexivity that attention to these critical issues fosters. Management structures need to adapt to the innovations and adaptations that such reflexivity will generate. And institutional strategies need to be guided by the expertise of professionals who can determine what is possible and what is necessary. Contemporary working environments seem intentionally designed to stymie such reflexivity and professionalism, through chronic overwork, devaluing the work of professional support teams, inflating low-value administrative tasks, centralizing services, and fostering a divide between academic and professional support staff. Internationalization generates further pressure on an already-stretched system, and solutions that ignore the humanity, creativity and resilience of its staff and students are doomed to fail.

Note

1 This analysis is based on a synthesis of publicly available datasets: HESA, THE rankings and sector group memberships as part of a British Academy/Leverhulme funded project. This report is forthcoming.

References

Bell, D. E. (2021) Accounting for the troubled status of English language teachers in higher education. *Teaching in higher education*, 1–16.

Boliver, V., Gorard, S. and Siddiqui, N. (2021) Using contextual data to widen access to higher education. *Perspectives: Policy and Practice in Higher Education*, 25(1): 7–13.

Byram, M. (2018) Internationalisation in higher education – an internationalist perspective. *On the Horizon*, 26(2): 148–56. https://doi.org/10.1108/OTH-11-2017-0090.

Chankseliani, M. (2018) Four rationales of HE internationalization: Perspectives of U.K. universities on attracting students from former soviet countries. *Journal of Studies in International Education*, 22(1): 53–70.

Edified. (2021) *A partnership for quality: A route to a UK quality framework with education agents.* British universities International Liaison Association and the UK Council for International Student Affairs. https://www.buila.ac.uk/news/2021/ukcisa-and-buila-launch-sector-wide-agent-quality-framework.

Feng, S. and Horta, H. (2021) Brokers of international student mobility: The roles and processes of education agents in China. *European Journal of Education*, 56(2): 248–64.

Hadley, G. (2015) *English for academic purposes in neoliberal universities: A critical grounded theory.* Cham: Springer.

Hayes, A. (2019) *Inclusion, epistemic democracy and international students: The teaching excellence framework and education policy.* Basingstoke: Palgrave MacMillan.

Hemsley-Brown, J. (2012) 'The best education in the world': Reality, repetition or cliché? International students' reasons for choosing an english university. *Studies in Higher Education*, 37(8): 1005–22.

Heng, T. T. (2018) Different is not deficient: Contradicting stereotypes of Chinese international students in US higher education. *Studies in Higher Education*, 43(1): 22–36. https://doi.org/10.1080/03075079.2016.1152466.

Higher Education Statistics Agency. (2021) *Higher education student enrolments and qualifications obtained at higher education providers in the United Kingdom 2019/20 | HESA*. Statistical First Release. https://www.hesa.ac.uk/.

Houghton, E. (2019) Impersonal statements: Aspiration and cruel optimism in the English higher education application process. *International Studies in Sociology of Education*, 28(3–4): 279–98.

Huang, I. Y., Raimo, V. and Humfrey, C. (2016) Power and control: Managing agents for international student recruitment in higher education. *Studies in Higher Education*. https://doi.org/10.1080/03075079.2014.968543.

Ilieva, J. B. (2018) *Five little-known facts about international student mobility to the UK. Analytical summary for UUKI*. https://core.ac.uk/download/pdf/199233467.pdf.

James, M. A. and Derrick, G. E. (2020) When 'culture trumps strategy': Higher education institutional strategic plans and their influence on international student recruitment practice. *Higher Education*, 79(4): 569–88.

Jones, S. (2013) 'Ensure that you stand out from the crowd': A corpus-based analysis of personal statements according to applicants' school type. *Comparative Education Review*. https://www.journals.uchicago.edu/doi/abs/10.1086/670666?casa_token=Xv eraDbpWAkAAAAA:RxxlI1xMGltOOpfS1mVgYIkyiFmFszvlFJwq3TSyY4v0qwvEb J47oq0-os2ubajangtIMH2CcZ8.

Lewis, V. (2021) *UK universities' global engagement strategies: Time for a rethink?* Vicky Lewis Consulting. vickylewisconsulting.co.uk/global-strategies-report.php.

Lomer, S. (2014) Economic objects: How policy discourse in the United Kingdom represents international students. *Policy Futures in Education*, 12(2): 273–85.

Lomer, S. (2017) *Recruiting international students in higher education: Representations and rationales in British policy*. https://link.springer.com/content/pdf/10.1007/978-3-319-51073-6.pdf.

Lomer, S., Mittelmeier, J. and Carmichael-Murphy, P. (2021) *Cash cows or pedagogic partners? Mapping pedagogic practices for and with international students* (Issue October). Society for Research in Higher Education. https://srhe.ac.uk/research/completed-award-reports/.

Lomer, S., Papatsiba, V. and Naidoo, R. (2016) Constructing a national higher education brand for the UK: Positional competition and promised capitals. *Studies in Higher Education*, 43(1): 134–53.

Ma, Y. (2020) *How Chinese college students succeed and struggle in American higher education*. New York City: Columbia University Press.

Madriaga, M. and McCaig, C. (2019) How international students of colour become black: A story of whiteness in English higher education. *Teaching in Higher Education*, 1–15. https://doi.org/10.1080/13562517.2019.1696300.

Marginson, S. (2016) *Public/private in higher education: A synthesis of economic and political approaches*, pp. 1–26. University College London: Centre for Global and Higher Education.

Moosavi, L. (2020) 'Can East Asian students think?': Orientalism, critical thinking, and the decolonial project. *Education Sciences*, 10(10): 286–306. https://doi.org/10.3390/EDUCSCI10100286.

Nikula, P. T. and Kivistö, J. (2017) Hiring education agents for international student recruitment: Perspectives from agency theory. *Higher Education Policy*. https://doi.org/10.1057/s41307-017-0070-8.

Oliver, C. (30 March 2020) *Reddin survey of university tuition fees*. Complete University Guide. https://www.thecompleteuniversityguide.co.uk/sector/insights/reddin-survey-of-university-tuition-fees.

Pearson, W. S. (2020) The effectiveness of pre-sessional EAP programmes in UK higher education: A review of the evidence. *Review of Educational Research*, 8(2): 420–47.

Qureshi, F. H. and Khawaja, S. (2021) Is COVID-19 transitioning cash cows international students into cats?. *European Journal of Education Studies*, 8(7). https://doi.org/10.46827/ejes.v8i7.3816.

Raimo, V. and Huang, I. Y. (17 November 2020) *Why do many UK universities keep their work with international student recruitment agents secret?* https://www.hepi.ac.uk/2020/11/17/why-do-many-uk-universities-keep-their-work-with-international-student-recruitment-agents-secret/.

Ritzer, G. (2013) *The McDonaldization of society: 20th anniversary edition*. Sage. https://play.google.com/store/books/details?id=GWmuSztNeCsC.

Sidhu, R. (2002) Educational brokers in global education markets. *Journal of Studies in International Education*, 6(1): 16–43.

Song, X. (2016) 'Critical thinking' and pedagogical implications for higher education. *East Asia*, 33(1): 25–40. https://doi.org/10.1007/s12140-015-9250-6.

Tannock, S. (2018) *Educational equality and international students: Justice across borders?*, pp. 1–234. Palgrave Macmillan and Basingstoke: Springer International Publishing.

University and College Union. (2010) *Kaplan: A UCU briefing*. https://www.ucu.org.uk/media/4601/Kaplan-A-UCU-briefing-Jul-10/pdf/ucu-cme-Kaplan-briefing_jul10.pdf.

Wang, S. and Moskal, M. (2019) What is wrong with silence in intercultural classrooms? An insight into international students' integration at a UK university. *Journal of Comparative & International Higher Education*, 11: 52–8. https://papers.ssrn.com/sol3/papers.cfm?abstract_id=3747308.

Warikoo, N. (2016) *The diversity bargain*. Chicago, IL: University of Chicago Press.

West, E. and Addington, L. (2021) *International student recruitment agencies: A guide for schools, colleges and universities*. Arlington, VA: National Association for College and Admission Counseling.

Wildavsky, B. (2012) *The great brain race*. Princeton, NJ: Princeton University Press.

Yang, Y., Mittelmeier, J., Lim, M. A. and Lomer, S. (22 June 2020) *Chinese international student recruitment during the COVID-19 crisis: education agents' practices and reflections*. https://www.research.manchester.ac.uk/portal/files/173092496/Ying_et_al._2020_final.pdf.

7

University Management as Court Society: A Processual Analysis of the Rise of University Management

Eric Lybeck

Vive l'Université!

In 1789, the king of France, Louis XVI, had a financial crisis on his hands. To resolve this via new taxation, he convened the Estates-General for the first time in 175 years, a decision that quickly devolved out his hands and into those of the people of France. After the Estates' first meeting, a question of representation emerged regarding whether votes should be tallied according to head or order, with the former proposal suggesting one house consisting of the first (clergy), second (nobility) and third (middle and popular classes) estates, and the latter proposal recommending an upper chamber for the first and second and a lower for the third. Decamping to a nearby tennis court, the third estate declared an oath that they would remain assembled until a constitution was established. Soon thereafter, the representatives declared themselves a National Assembly. In the following month, the king sacked his finance minister, Jacques Necker, for publishing documents revealing the fully debased state of the kingdom's financial health, which the population perceived as an act directed against the National Assembly. Riots ensued, culminating in the storming of the Bastille prison, a potent symbol of royal power. The French Revolution had begun. It was not long before all special privileges of the first and second estates were abolished, and the equal rights of Man were declared.

Without the same level of international political significance, a more recent event can be recounted here for comparison. In 2018, the University and College Union (UCU), representing over 100,000 university staff in the UK, balloted to begin strike action to prevent changes to their Universities Superannuation

Scheme (USS) pension after negotiations with university 'employers' represented by Universities UK (UUK) stalled. This led to the largest and longest industrial action in British university history, with more than a million students affected by the withdrawal of over 575,000 teaching hours during the month of sustained strike action. While changes to pensions were the proximate cause, the strikes soon took on a broader, critical dimension against sector-wide trends within UK universities towards more marketization, performance management and unaccountable decision-making.[1]

In the run up to strikes, reports emerged of a disproportionate influence played by constituent colleges at the universities of Cambridge and Oxford. Focused attention was accordingly directed at Oxford ahead of a 6 March meeting of congregation – the 'supreme governing body' of the university, consisting of all academic staff – which sought a vote on changing the university's position vis-à-vis the pension dispute. Hitherto, the university's vice chancellor, Louise Richardson, towed the USS line, and, though she was abroad at the time of congregation, her office arranged for suspension of debate using a legislative technicality. This resulted in outraged members of the governing body staging an *ad hoc* meeting outside, where a vote was taken of 442–2 against senior management. Two days later, the vice chancellor adjusted the universities' formal position in light of the 'depth of feeling'. Thus, just as the tennis court oath taken by members of the third estate asserted their representation of the people vis-à-vis the monarchy in the French Revolution, at least for this moment – and within a much more limited institutional sphere of university, rather than national governance – academics at Oxford performatively re-asserted their control of the university vis-à-vis university management.

Since their foundation in the Middle Ages, universities have been autonomous, self-governing institutions of higher learning. How was it the case that, in 2018, the gulf between management/employers and academics/employees had grown so wide as to necessitate such a dramatic and contentious event? In this chapter, we can learn even more about the dynamics driving present higher education policy and practice, if we retain parallel analysis of the French Revolution. Drawing particularly on the social theory of Norbert Elias, but extending this within a broader processual sociology of higher education, we can see that changes within the governance and management of universities have structural homologies with the court society that developed in the decades prior to the storming of the Bastille in 1789.

Processual Sociology of Higher Education

The following analysis of university management as court society applies theoretical concepts and frameworks developed in my recent book, *Norbert Elias and the Sociology of Education* (Lybeck, 2019). Despite being a well-known, if initially neglected, sociologist of the twentieth century, Elias' social theory is not widely applied within education studies. This is due to his own neglect of the topic area within his otherwise comprehensive analyses of modern society, certainly compared to more familiar social theorists, Pierre Bourdieu and Michel Foucault. The book introduces readers to Eliasian – or figurational – sociology, as it is called, including several concepts and analyses introduced in less detail here, namely 'court society', 'game models' and figurations/processes, in general. Indeed, the most important contribution Elias adds to our understanding of social phenomena is recognition that these are all processes. In other words, historical interpretations are essential to capture the unplanned, temporal dimensions of social configurations, structures and identities, particularly those that occur over long timescales.

The period under consideration – the decades prior to 2018 – certainly involves tremendous changes to the linkages between and across universities, the government, professions and markets, which have had internal and external effects within the ways universities operate and are governed. The dramatic growth of functions, including new demands to accommodate expanding numbers of students enrolled in higher education (Marginson, 2016), to produce economic growth through technology transfer and professional skills development (Block and Keller, 2009), as a leading cultural institution projecting soft power overseas (Lomer, 2017), as a presumed contributor to the ecological transformation of a warming planet (McCowan, 2019) and more, means higher education institutions have become more and more complex. Smelser noted the way in which universities develop via a form of 'structural accretion' in which new functions are added without functions being removed, becoming bulging, unwieldy structures with dramatically increased complexity (Smelser, 2013).

Drawing on Elias, this can all be interpreted using his theory of 'game models'. As explained in greater detail in both Lybeck (2019) and Elias' original essay itself (Elias, 1978: 71–103). The model begins using a simple example of a 'primal contest' in which two groups are competing over food, one (A) being stronger than B. Though A can dominate in certain regards, B does have room to manoeuvre, thus highlighting that no power imbalance is absolute and the figuration consists of the relations between the groups as much as the qualities of any group independently. Elias adds more and more complex examples to highlight ways in which multiple groups can become involved in coalitions for and against a more dominant actor, who may lose control of both their own room for manoeuvre and their control of the overall rules of the game. Thus, paradoxically, as the distance between power actors diminishes, more chaos and uncertainty can emerge. This might necessitate articulation of a second-tier – something like a parliamentary government – which establishes representatives of the population and groups competing on the first level, but now engaged in competition, coalitions and power struggles on the second-tier. In oligopolistic configurations, the second tier might distance itself entirely from the people, as in aristocracies or out-of-touch political establishments whose genuinely relation to the people becomes increasingly nominal. This can result in a power contest across the tiers, resulting in a revolution or democratic reform. The tennis court oath, for example, amounted to a reclamation of the rights of the 'people' to be represented fairly relative to the out-of-touch, unelected and privileged estates in the French clergy, aristocracy and monarchy.

The monarchy in France, prior to the revolution, had played aristocracy and bourgeois classes against one another via what Elias called the 'royal mechanism'.

> When the situation of the bulk of the various functional classes, or at least their active leading groups, is not yet so bad that they are willing to put their social existence at risk, and yet when they feel themselves so threatened by each other, and power is so evenly distributed between them, that each fears the slightest advantage of the other side, they tie each other's hands: this gives the central authority better chances than any other constellation within society.
>
> (Elias, 2000: 320)

With dominated groups competing amongst themselves, rather than directing their power collectively against the king, the central authority has greater control over the rules of the game. From this vantage, they can better observe the overall field of power and make strategic moves and interventions more predictably and effectively. During the long-term 'civilizing process' across the early modern era Elias (2000) described, monarchs managed to secure the monopoly of violence through the elimination of territorial rivals, generally by fielding large standing armies. To pay for these armies, the monarch introduced currency into the economy, thereby contributing to the ascent of the bourgeois classes of merchants and financiers in towns and cities. However, as military and naval campaigns became more extensive and unpredictable, this led to fiscal crises and arbitrary taxation patterns that proved unacceptable to the bourgeoisie. In many ways, their demand for greater rights in parliament on behalf of the 'people' meant control over public finance: in other words, seizure of the monopoly of taxation from the unaccountable monarchy.

Meanwhile, during the civilizing process, the monarchs not only had to eliminate foreign rivals through territorial expansion, they needed to remove the existing military power of local aristocracies, who historically emerged from warrior classes. Securing the monopoly of violence meant defanging the existing aristocracies so these could not function as viable counterpowers. In *The Civilizing Process*, Elias traced the long-term change in manners and ideas of 'civility' that occurred as the upper classes learned new standards of acceptable behaviour, reflecting the sublimation of their more violent instincts in the form of etiquette. Drawing on his earlier study of court society under Louis XIV, Elias demonstrated the way in which the sun king managed to remove aristocrats from their territorial homes by making them participate in increasingly elaborate rituals of etiquette and style within the court of Versailles (Elias, 1983).

Elias captured the fundamental lack of freedom – that is, constraint – within this particular figuration.

> Etiquette and ceremony increasingly became ... a ghostly *perpetuum mobile* that continued to operate regardless of any direct use-value, being impelled, as by an inexhaustible motor, by the competition for status and power of the people enmeshed in it – a competition both between themselves and with the mass of those excluded – and by their need for a clearly graded scale of prestige ... No single person within the figuration was able to initiate a reform of the tradition. Every slightest attempt to reform, to change the precarious structure of tensions, inevitably entailed an upheaval, a reduction or even abolition of the rights of certain individuals and families. To jeopardise such privileges was, to the ruling class of this society a kind of taboo. The attempt would be opposed by broad sections of the privileged who feared, perhaps not without justification, that the whole system of rule that gave them privilege would be threatened or would collapse if the slightest detail of the traditional order were altered. So everything remained as it was.
>
> (Elias, 1983: 93)

Thus, we can see the manner in which social constraint became embodied as self-constraint. Even if a particular individual wanted to change their manners and habits, they would risk so much – effectively, excommunication from the central court society – so, they did not even consider this as an option. Further, to reject these patterns of behaviour would be to, in effect, criticize the very status one held; in a sense, this would amount to rejecting one's self and one's identity. The result was an ultimately highly conservative structure that was nonetheless constantly changing in terms of new participants, new events, even new manners – as the textbooks of manners reveal changes occurring over the long term.

The aristocracy bought into and assimilated into this system through a range of incentives including retention of historic rights to be exempt from taxation. However, the high expense of retaining position in court, including extensive gambling, socializing, formal dancing and currying favour with the monarch and his inner circle, often debased the wealth of aristocracies. All the while, the disgruntled bourgeois classes demanded representation and positioned themselves and their values (of utility, prudence, industry) against those of what the decadent aristocracy had become.

In terms of game models, we can see the initial (all unplanned and long-term) moves made by the monarch to gain control over a complex field of territorial power by spatially constructing and concentrating rivals within court – effectively a second tier made manifest within the royal palace. From there, he could view the entire field of power ostensibly represented by the territorial rulers competing for his favour. Enlisting a burgeoning class of advisors, often from educated members of the clergy, bourgeois and aristocratic classes, he and his cabinet could gain an overview of the second-tier. One could interpret this as a limited third-tier observing the second – but, one ultimately dependent on the reduction of complexity provided by the physical space of court, the willing participation of members of court society in rituals of deference, and the wider relations that linked those representatives to the growing nation's far-flung territories. Once these relations and conditions had broken down, the opportunity for revolution emerged, resulting in a new configuration of games, tiers and processual openings, including, I argue elsewhere, the rise of the modern higher education system (Lybeck, 2020).

Combining the various theoretical insights introduced here before turning to the recent rise of university management, we can see the value of adopting a processual perspective in order to see the unplanned and initially partly disconnected developments that produce a particular configuration. The figurational game models demonstrate the way in which changing power relations can produce multiple tiers, which provide different power actors with better or worse knowledge of the overall game, which may be leveraged into greater power chances. In the early modern era, this resulted in the consolidation of absolutist courts as monarchs managed to pacify the aristocracy through separation of this class from its territorial constituents on the first tier, as well as the ascending bourgeois classes, by encouraging their competition over style and favour on an increasingly detached second-tier. This established new patterns of behaviour, selection mechanisms and socialization, which influenced not only the courtiers, but their enemies who defined themselves in opposition. This highlights the relational character of such power figurations. Finally, we have seen the way complexity itself begins to increase due to functional differentiation – and, indeed, through power equalization and fragmentation itself – which may compel articulation of further tiers in order to get a (potentially illusory) reflexive grasp on the situation on a lower tier. All of these insights will inform our analysis of the recent consolidation of university management as a kind of court society.

The Rise of Management as a Third Tier

Drawing on the game model theory provided by Elias, we can arrange our study in order to observe and interpret certain aspects of recent history. Within the topic area of university management we are interested in the ways in which management begins to distance itself across a differentiated tier – on the one hand, claiming to represent the masses of academic staff upon whose authority they govern; on the other hand, becoming involved in their own patterns of behaviour just as Louis XIV organized in his absolutist court. Methodologically, our challenge is how to capture this history and the manner in which these unplanned processes developed over time. My aim in this initial scoping study was not to 'prove' the theory, but rather to demonstrate proof of concept: to demonstrate the potential adopting an Eliasian perspective can facilitate our looking for new materials in a way that helps explain the outcome of interest, that is: the USS strike of 2018. Accordingly, the methods here are rather tentative and historical. Still, in this initial study, I opted to study documents in sequence, akin to Elias' study of books on manners (Elias, 2000). These included Senate and Council documents in the archives, and policy and regulation documents available online. I compared these to similar documents at other universities to gain a sense of broader trends. However, this comparison was not systemic and, as noted in conclusion, a more robust comparative historical study can be envisaged to further refine and confirm the findings tentatively presented here.

The following narrative provides an account of a pseudonymized university's history based on a number of qualitative sources – largely interviews and archival material – as well as experiences gained through personal efforts at university reform within and beyond particular institutions. It would be difficult to provide reference to much of this material without revealing the identity of the institution and actors therein. Effort has also been made to integrate similar events, policies and experiences from other institutions to further disguise the case, which should be understood as an ideal type in any event. The narrative should accordingly be understood as a story, rather than as a specific historical instance, although the story is rooted in real historical events and should illuminate more generalizable processes. By narrating a story of one institution, we can better see the many contingent and unplanned ways in which the process developed locally and in relation to broader contexts.

As Elias noted, no social process ever really has a beginning, since one could always point to the significance of prehistory. However, for present purposes, we can begin in the mid- to late-1970s at a time just after the broad expansion of higher education in Britain following the Robbin's Report (1963), the establishment of new plate glass universities, and the coming-of-age of student radicals from the late 1960s and early 1970s. Our university, called here the University of Wessex, was founded as a plate-glass university in order to provide higher education within an underserved region. Initially drawing on Oxbridge and University of London professors and graduates as its first generation of lecturers, the original dons wore robes and segregated themselves by gender in a club-like atmosphere. In this condition, self-governance was presupposed and relatively smooth due to the similarities of social backgrounds, values and assumptions of the professoriate. Organized and chartered as a Council and academic Senate, which managed the curriculum and research, the faculty also elected department chairs, deans and the vice chancellor, who was drawn from their ranks and managed a small executive committee accountable to the governing board (Council).

The first signs of strain emerged internally as a younger generation of lecturers from different social and institutional backgrounds, often more politically leftwing, having come of age within the era of student activism, rejected the culture and governance arrangements wherein the professoriate dominated decision-making, often at the expense of more junior lecturers and students. Indeed, demands for devolution of more representation below the professorial level were concurrent with student demands to establish a robust students' union and to obtain representation on university committees, including council. By the end of the 1970s these efforts to formally and culturally democratize the university were successful, and for a decade or so, the same activists who led initial reforms encouraged wide participation in governance, including a larger academic Senate akin to Oxford's congregation mentioned above. By the 1980s, however, participation rates began to wane, not least due to the continued expansion of academic staff numbers, resulting in unwieldy staff meetings dominated by unrepresentative, oppositional academics and lingering, conservative dons, who retained interest in Senate proceedings.

Concurrent to this internal decline, the broader political context of Thatcherism put pressure on the governing Council as well and public pressure on the academic profession, demanding both wider student participation and more economic utility to be delivered with fewer resources, new accountability exercises including the Research Assessment Exercise and diminishing long-term security. This began to tie university vice-chancellors together across the sector, in order to consider means of defending themselves, collectively, in a context of increasing uncertainty. The significance of Universities UK as the committee of university vice-chancellors grew, eventually culminating in the Jarratt Report published in 1985 as an attempt to thwart further Thatcherite interference in the sector, by voluntarily submitting to self-organized accountability mechanisms and moves towards what would later be called 'neoliberal' university management organized around targets and performance management (Deem, 2004; Parry, 1999). Consolidation of the position of the older universities, including ancient, redbrick and plate glass institutions, was deepened with the formation of the Russell Group in 1994 after a large number of former polytechnic institutes were granted university status in 1992.

Increasingly, university senior managers saw themselves as a distinct tier representing their institutions in policy and business sectors. At Wessex, this was evident in the distinctions between roles – with the vice-chancellor's (VC) workload involving 'external' partnerships, with a Provost managing internal institutional issues. As Jarratt articulated, academics were to be thought of less as self-governing members of autonomous corporations pursuing higher learning, but as shop-floor producers delivering educational and research services to customers, be they students or external partners. Throughout the period, resistance could be observed here and there, but as the scale of activities increased, it became more difficult for academics to gain an upper hand on management within their institutions or on a national bargaining platform beyond trade union issues of pay as the newly formed UCU obtained in 2006.

Locally, at the University of Wessex, we see a gradual and largely unplanned chipping away at the authority and rights of Senates and academics, often under the guise of plausible practicalities, such as the unwieldy size of a Senate consisting of the entire faculty. Instead, departments were allowed to elect representatives to Senate, where ex officio members of the executive group, including deans, who were also elected, joined them. As further rapid changes developed externally, council and executives became wary of the delays inherent in waiting for approval and deliberation amongst Senates that might meet only three or four times a year. Increasingly, committees began to proliferate to progress certain agendas, for example, research, education, engagement, finance and so on. Each of these committees was linked to members of the executive team, each of which might involve a new role – Director or Deputy Vice Chancellor of Research, etc. These members too would be represented as ex officio members of Senate and often Council.

Following a poor performance in the Research Assessment Exercise (RAE), resulting in a dramatic withdrawal of government direct grant funding, concurrent with a scandal that saw the elected VC involved in minor, but embarrassing corruption surrounding use of staff and resources, the governing board opted to invest in obtaining a visionary leader for the executive. The new Chief Executive Officer, as he would come to be called, modelled himself on an idea of business leaders dominating the corporate economy, despite having no non-academic, business experience himself. The VC/CEO's first priority was to 'see' the institution and hired the most innovative technicians in data analytics who developed statistical models enabling forecasting. Together with the Chair of Council, a former executive at one of the leading logistics companies, he created a set of twenty key performance indicators (KPIs) by which he would be judged year by year, including global ranking position, number of students, staff satisfaction, grant income and so forth.

Of course, such indicators largely measured the performance of others – academic and non-academic staff – and so to increase performance meant 'change' amongst departments, finance offices, human resources and so on. Few activities that did not contribute to the 'bottom line' were cut, including departments, local history associations, staff meeting rooms. Meanwhile, growth areas were identified by deploying a 'SWOT' analysis to identify strengths, weaknesses, opportunities and threats. These included mergers with nearby institutions, including art schools, polytechnics and teachers' colleges, to incorporate their successful programmes, while eliminating deadweight and obtaining new estate. At the same time, ambitious plans to develop new buildings, many show-stopping student-facing venues to attract new applicants, resulted in complex financial arrangements involving large loans obtained by international investment banks at not particularly attractive interest rates.

Still, the university was growing. The executive team hit their KPIs, and initial resistance by academic staff had diminished as the appearance of financial security and success as more and more students enrolled. Still, not every policy travelled smoothly through Senate, and department heads continued to irritate the executive committees with parochial demands that failed to see the bigger picture revealed by the data. In 2009, the university council and executive group conducted a wholesale revision of the governance of the statutes, ordinances and charters. They re-applied to the Privy Council to move many provisions from statutes to ordinances, where changes could be made without further re-chartering – that is, internally, amongst council, senate and executive committees.

While nominally retaining departments, these were merged in more-or-less arbitrary configurations to fudge KPIs and to diminish the authority of department heads. The departments were reorganized into five different schools consisting of anywhere from two to eight departments. The deans of these schools were renamed pro-vice-chancellors (PVCs). Each PVC was provided with an executive committee that mirrored the top. A few years later, without notice, ordinances were changed so PVCs were no longer elected, but hired via executive search. Another ordinance change dramatically reduced the number of academic senators in Senate, allowing for only four per school for a total of twenty. Meanwhile, ex officio positions had grown to such an extent that academic senators amounted to less than half of the voting members, most of whom were directly accountable to the CEO/VC.

Concurrently, since the VC had been in office for so long, the appointment of external governors had been conducted to ensure that, although governors were ostensibly responsible for holding the executive to account, none would dramatically challenge the strategy, reports or activities of the senior management. By this stage, little visible resistance to the chief executive remained – all reports demonstrated progress, especially after the metric measuring staff satisfaction (hovering between 20 and 30 per cent) was removed as a KPI. Everyone surrounding the VC agreed with the direction of travel. The restructuring of governance via committees and a defanged Senate meant decisions and policies could be prefigured entirely by deputy VCs; Senate meetings took the form of information delivery, wherein powerpoints explained what was going to happen, without asking questions about 'what should happen?'

At every level, all involved used metrics they knew were incredibly flawed, including surveys with completion rates in the single digits. But, none would dare draw attention. As in the absolutist court of Louis XIV, organized around etiquette, in this instance, measurement became the ritual around which internal compliance was ensured. If one challenged these, they exposed themselves as an individual at odds with the entire configuration. Many preferred the option of resigning and returning to academic work rather than push against the machine that ran according to its own logic. The roles demanded that the actor submit to the emergent hierarchy in order to survive within it – if one stepped out of line, s/he was selected out and replaced by a firm believer in both the validity of the metrics and the suzerainty of the VC/CEO as the captain of the great ship Wessex.

Breaking the Social Contract

The crisis that enveloped the universities in the wake of the 2018 USS strike should be understood within the context described above – which, although based largely on one institutional history, was common across the sector. Homology was partly due to institutional isomorphism (DiMaggio and Powell, 1983), in which universities copied one another's 'best practices' in order to deal with common challenges on the market and with respect to increasing governmental regulation. As complexity increased, many relied on consultants, including lawyers, accountants, human resource gurus and so on, to provide advice about how to, for example, remove statutes and reposition these in ordinances; how to establish 'interdisciplinary institutes' in order to avoid the insularity of 'academic tribes'. As these consultancies linked themselves together within the burgeoning networks created within Times Higher Education summits, HE expos; as the consultants themselves developed collective consciousness amongst themselves as 'wonks' as defined within the blog WonkHE established in 2012; a new layer of technicians and 'professional service' administrators were introduced into universities' operations. On the frontlines, these workers might identify with, interact with and sympathize with academics, but many would enter the senior management courts, promising to deliver 'change' regardless of whether such change was good or bad for the institution or sector.

Through UUK, university executives coordinated their actions vis-à-vis the government and international markets, although many would remain competitive as each institution struggled for advantage in rankings and governmental metrics. Thus, just as the court society established in Versailles was emulated across European courts, down to the level of minor princes in German or Slavic speaking states, so have university courts become a national – indeed, international – society operating on its own tier.

However, this tier was becoming more and more detached from everyday experiences of the academic staff and stakeholders who the VCs ostensibly represented. It became ever-more difficult, even for professional associations and government ministers to determine whether VCs spoke for their own interests or for their institutions. The most evident public expression emerged during the 2017 scandals over VC pay, leading to the resignation of Dame Glynis Breakwell as leader of the University of Bath. It appeared not even the titles and honours VCs helped confer upon one another could protect an individual 'bad apple' who made their cohort look bad. Meanwhile, nearly all had participated in the scandalous activity in question: namely, sitting on the pay committees that determined their own extravagant pay – all of which consisted of members of court.

Operating on an increasingly autonomous tier meant university leaders had become less aware of conditions on the ground – particularly amongst academic staff, who had been disenfranchised and were losing control of their conditions of professional work. Academics had been, by and large, unaware of these changes themselves, and experienced only a general dissatisfaction with the direction of travel and local frustrations. Finding no suitable outlets for expression of grievances, the profession knew that something was wrong, but felt powerless to do anything. The cut in pension benefits was the final straw that broke the camel's back.

Obliviously, the chief executives of universities and UUK thought the matter would be quickly resolved; none expected the scale of industrial action taken. Once academics came out on the picket lines, they established themselves as truly interdisciplinary cohorts; they established collective consciousness and shared local grievances, which became recognizable as general patterns. All became increasingly aware that the pensions crisis was merely a symptom of the deeper problem: namely, that the social contract that linked the tiers together had been broken. The VCs claimed to speak on behalf of universities, but as the dramatic vote at Oxford demonstrated, the universities themselves begged to differ.

Still, this was only possible at Oxford insofar as the governance structures had not changed as radically as those at the University of Wessex, in part due to their antiquity, in part due to tradition, and in part due to the sustained defence of academic decision-making Oxford academics made during the entire period in question, even when they faced similar problems of participation and large congregations. Now, in the wake of the 2018 strikes, with the pension dispute still unresolved, when academics have returned to their offices, back to similar conditions of work as before, the question remains whether we can point to any similarities between the revolutions of 1789 and the present. More than likely, beyond some minor reforms – and some greater attention paid by courts to their nominal constituencies – the court society structure that had developed before remains in place today.

Academics on the lower tier – historically tasked with the self-governance of our institutions – need to determine a path forward. Do we continue to demonstrate deference to our university courts and their monarchs? Do we look to establish alliances or clashes with the growing body of professional service administrators and consultants coming between us and the management tiers? Do we revitalize and reform the remaining institutions for academic decision-making and resistance that have been defanged? Senates. Departments. Unions. These are choices yet to be made. But, only by first understanding and, indeed, observing that, due to a range of unplanned processes such a structure now exists can we hope to regain some agency in the ways our universities and our work are run.

Note

1 The USS pension crisis was complicated due to the lack of transparency surrounding the way the USS firm prepared its valuation, projecting a contested deficit of £17.5 billion. This led employers (UUK) to replace the defined benefits scheme with a defined contribution scheme. During the course of the strike, members of UCU calculated alternative valuations which not only projected no deficit, but even interpreted the scheme as being in surplus. The eventual resolution to the industrial action involved creation of a Joint Expert Panel to assess these contradictory valuations.

References

Block, F. and Keller, M. R. (2009) Where do innovations come from? Transformations in the US economy, 1970–2006. *Socioeconomic Review*, 7: 459–83.

Deem, R. (2004) The knowledge worker, the manager-academic and the contemporary UK university: New and old forms of public management? *Financial Accountability & Management*, 20: 107–28.

DiMaggio, P. J. and Powell, W. W. (1983) The iron cage revisited: Institutional isomorphism and collective rationality in organizational fields. *American Sociological Review*, 48: 147.

Elias, N. (1978) *What is sociology?* New York, NY: Columbia University Press.
Elias, N. (1983) *The court society*. New York: Pantheon Books.
Elias, N. (2000) *The civilizing process: Sociogenetic and psychogenetic investigations*. Malden, MA: Blackwell Publishers, Oxford.
Lomer, S. (2017) Soft power as a policy rationale for international education in the UK: A critical analysis. Higher education. *The International Journal of Higher Education Research*, 74: 581–98.
Lybeck, E. (2020) *The university revolution: The academization process and the emergence of modern higher education since 1800*. London: Routledge.
Lybeck, E. (2019) *Nobert Elias and the sociology of education*. London: Bloomsbury Academic.
Marginson, S. (2016) The worldwide trend to high participation higher education: Dynamics of social stratification in inclusive systems. *Higher Education*, 72: 413–34.
McCowan, T. (2019) *Higher education for and beyond the sustainable development goals*. New York, NY: Springer International Publishing.
Parry, G. (1999) Education research and policy making in higher education: The case of Dearing. *Journal of Education Policy*, 14(3): 225–41.
Smelser, N. J. (2013) *Dynamics of the contemporary university: Growth, accretion, and conflict*. Berkeley, CA: University of California Press.

Re-imagining the Place of Professional Education in the University

Vivienne Baumfield

Historical study shows professional education to have occupied an important position central to the activity of a university since the earliest medieval European institutions:

> The universities' primary goal, the reason for their creation, was ... to prepare professionals to maintain and lead the established social order, secular as well as religious.
>
> (Axtell, 2016: 18)

Commitment to professional education informs the original purpose of elite American universities, such as Princeton, to promote social mobility by transforming the sons of farmers into prospective members of professions such as law, medicine and also teaching, albeit as tutors of the children of wealthy families. In due course, under the influence of German universities, the importance of teaching in universities based on the lecturer's original investigations gained prominence and being an academic itself became a profession (Turner, 1972). In more recent times, the general trend internationally is for this close coupling of teaching and research in the core activity of universities to be displaced by the emphasis on being 'research intensive' as a marker of status to the detriment of a focus on professional education. At this point it is appropriate to consider the objections raised by Thorstein Veblen in the early 1900s to the provision of vocational education within a university. He is often cited as being vehemently opposed to the inclusion of 'practical' learning in the university but a closer reading of publications such as 'The Higher Learning in America: a memorandum on the conduct of universities by business men' reveals a more nuanced perspective. Veblen opposes the use of education for personal gain by an individual and this is what he takes 'practical' to mean. What was important was that higher education should be for the good of society and this requires the fostering of inquiry and a 'scientific spirit' rather than the ' ... clamorous conformity to current prepossessions of respectability or an edifying and incisive rehersal [sic] of commonplaces' Veblen associated with provision for vocational education (Veblen, 1918: 177). As we will see, this is a view shared by those engaged in professional *education* in universities today and is the basis of their objection to its reduction to a narrow form of training.

Being a graduate continues to be a marker of status linking the professions with higher education but the nature of this association does not remain static and interests can become more or less closely aligned. As the purpose of universities and what it means to be a professional are both subject to change over time, taking a 'long view' can provide perspective on the dynamics of the relationship. The focus of this chapter is the provision for teacher education within the university and the wider implications of the location of professional education for the relationship between practice and research, academics and the public and ultimately for democracy. The argument draws upon insights from the study of professions using an ecological model of professionalization as complex and contingent with actors competing in particular contexts over claims to specific tasks rather than a linear process and in which, as conflict involves knowledge claims, universities are bound to play a role (Abbott, 1988, 2005). Taking a long view also means taking account of the interaction of different time scales and durations of natural time, social time and individual time affecting particular events (Elias, 1983). In short, a historically informed awareness of past, present and future is necessary to provision of the best means of orientation to 'sort things out' (Lybeck, 2020). Teacher Education is an interesting case for our purposes, as an international study of provision has shown:

> Teacher education and training has become contested territory with complex pedagogic and ideologic forces interacting with historical structures and ideas. Teacher education is a relative newcomer to the work of universities. It does not have the historical lineage of medicine or law, and teacher preparation is a large-scale, mass, not elite, endeavour.
>
> (Moon, 2016: 1)

The resulting 'quest for legitimacy' throws into sharp contrast the elements of what counts in terms of becoming established within academia and how this has changed over time. Consideration of academics engaged in professional education can be illuminating given that they occupy a liminal position and so can inform our understanding of where boundaries might lie and what may be necessary to respond to contemporary challenges to both the universities and the professions.

Professional Entanglement

It is beyond the scope of this chapter, and the competence of its author, to engage fully with Abbott's concept of linked ecologies; complex and contingent social processes composed of simultaneous, numerous adjacent events. However, the heuristic idea of *hinges*, strategies that work as well in one ecology as in another whilst yielding different rewards, and *avatars*, whereby a profession reproduces a version of itself within an adjacent ecology rather than seeking an alliance, could offer the means of navigating the accounts of developments in professionalism impacting on the modern university (Abbott, 2005). Such heuristics are helpful when faced with an entanglement of professional education in universities and the 'new professionalism' of administrators in the New Public Management university. The strategies for achieving status and recognition through professionalization reveal similar features but different outcomes for academics engaged in professional education and for administrators. However, jockeying for position within universities when the institutions themselves are in a competition determined by the metrics of international league tables is likely to favour the infiltration characteristic of an avatar rather than collaboration in the formation of academic professional identities.

Professionalism

The expansion in the number of occupations laying claim to being a profession was commented on by Wilensky in the 1960s when he asked if what we were experiencing was the 'professionalization of everyone?' (Wilensky, 1964). He predicted that the development of knowledge societies would lead to even greater demand for professionals whilst at the same time creating barriers for the achievement of strong forms of professionalism. Features of the neoliberal climate associated with knowledge societies (flexible specialization, emphasis on consumers, cost control, performance management) make the autonomy of professions hard to maintain although the element of evidence-based practice has been used in the professionalization of 'semi-professional' occupations (Noordegraaf, 2007). The example of nursing is cited and similar developments can be seen in teaching, but in this case, moves to be an evidence-based profession have not necessarily strengthened the role of the university in teacher education. The tendency to interpret evidence as meaning performance data rather than the product of inquiry, antipathy of policymakers in some national contexts to the involvement of educational researchers in school education, referred to by one Secretary of State for Education in England as 'the blob', and competition from non-HEI 'itinerant experts' (Barley and Kunda, 2004) combined can impact negatively on the case for university-based teacher education. We can concur with the analysis of professionalization as a matter of contradictory and controversial attempts to get a grip on occupational control and that 'we do not really know how to make sense of professional control in anti-professional knowledge societies with changing public sectors' (Noordegraaf, 2007: 764). As Evetts has argued, the meaning of professionalism is not fixed and how the concept is being used is dependent on the context in which occupational change is taking place (Evetts, 2003). Noordegraaf draws upon the work of Schon to develop the idea of 'hybridized professionalism' as the form relevant to the contemporary context in which professionals are 'reflective practitioners' for whom their links with outside worlds are integral to maintaining a sense of a collective identity based on an epistemology of practice (Noordegraaf, 2007). The 'reflective practitioner' is a concept frequently employed in the characterization of teaching as a profession, some might argue overused and underdefined. Establishing the importance of linking professional education with universities for the blending of scientific and intuitive, experiential learning the development of an epistemology of practice requires remains an attractive if elusive endeavour.

University Challenge

According to some commentators the social contract with the public and policymakers establishing the purpose of universities is broken and those of us working in higher education are living in the 'in-between times'. Grant presents such times as moments of change in which the future can be either one of destructive negativity or take a more humanitarian, sustainable turn (Grant, 2021). In his advocacy for the latter course of action, Grant suggests that we should embrace the concept of 'new power' (Heimans and Timms, 2018). New Power enables the university to:

> ... resolve the very real tensions in the trade-offs that shape its purposes, including social versus economic goods, universalism versus elitism, collectivism versus competition, autonomy versus system dependence.
>
> (Grant, 2021: xvi)

It is able to do so because it opposes the formal structures, centralization and managerialism of 'Old Power' institutions with networks of governance characterized by participation and radical transparency. According to this analysis, professionalism as expertise and specialization is associated with 'old power' and inconsistent with the 'do-it-ourselves' ethic and maker culture of 'new power'. Grant identifies a new cohort of 'third space professionals' breaking down unproductive academic versus professional staff dualism as one of the main drivers of the staffing model central to the development of the university of the future. The concept of a 'third space professional' is based on the identification by Whitchurch in her study of changes in the higher education workforce of an expanding 'third space' between the usual activity of professional staff and that of academic staff (Whitchurch, 2008). Institutional projects such as Student Transitions, Partnership and Professional Development were creating a demand for 'blended professionals' with mixed backgrounds and a portfolio comprising elements of both professional and academic activities. The trend is for the demand for such professionals to increase and for their roles to be embedded in the staffing structures of universities. Grant predicts that expansion of the 'third space' will result in professionals working across traditional academic/professional boundaries becoming the dominant cohort in the 'New Power' University. This vision of the university of the future essentializes the identities of current staff, polarizing their roles and positing a new form of professionalism. In doing so, it risks failing to take sufficient account of the expertise and experience already present in the work of academics not easily characterized by such binaries, and which challenge such dichotomies from within existing university structures.

Creating a new cohort of staff threatens the position of academics engaged in professional education and may not be beneficial for anyone taking up the new positions; a recent study found that people in such roles felt isolated and like 'ghosts in the machine' (Watermeyer and Rowe, 2021). Whilst Grant's vision of the 'New Power' University may be problematic, universities are certainly under pressure to find their place in an increasingly global knowledge economy where knowledge transfer is high on national policy and research council agendas and feel the need to 'reformulate' their societal rationale (Wiewel and Broski, 1997). Gibbons charts a course of action based on becoming part of a larger and denser network of knowledge institutions that extend into industry, government and the media (Gibbons, 2000). One approach to extending the scope of the university is to take advantage of the opportunities available through the natural connection between schools and universities. In 2014 Research Councils UK and the National Co-ordinating Centre for Public Engagement commissioned the School-University Partnership Initiative (SUPI) Learning Project with the aim of learning from existing work on school-university partnerships and exploring the potential for a programme of work to enhance quality and impact (Greany et al, 2014). They concur with the findings from a review of literature on partnerships intended to achieve the renewal of teacher education that although high hopes have been held for school-university partnerships, their complexity means those hopes have remained unfulfilled (Smedley, 2001). School-university partnerships are social enterprises (Day et al, 2021) and so require participation in a hermeneutic dialogue (Beyer, 1988) to build knowledge through relationships. Successful management of the process, therefore, entails a commitment to being open to learning and space for uncertainty. Whilst such relational knowing can be transformative in building the capacity of individuals and teams for deeper organizational change, it is hard to achieve. Despite the difficulties encountered, it is the potential to re-imagine the intellectual and relational dynamics of institutional cultures that co-producing knowledge in partnerships create (Lieberman and Grolnick, 1996) that continues to captivate (see McLaughlin et al, 2015 for further discussion of the opportunities and challenges of school-university partnerships). However, even when the focus is on the potential of promoting closer school-university partnerships, the location of the professional education of teachers in the university is not necessarily central or secure. The RCUK initiative did not highlight the role of university-based teacher educators when funding projects linking academics with schools and the literature review and interviews conducted for the initial Learning Project identify a gap whilst seeming to be unaware of the existence already within universities of a group of academics who could fill it:

> The role of brokers, match-makers and translators – professionals who catalyse partnerships and who empower others to engage in dialogue – has been highlighted throughout the project. Is there a case for greater investment in this intermediary level, for example through a national network, professional training or award scheme?
>
> (Greany et al, 2014: 14)

Not all of the SUPI-funded projects linked academics directly with schools without considering the involvement of university-based teacher educators for whom mediating between the university and schools was their daily work. The 'Empowering Partnerships: Enabling Engagement' (EPEE) project adopted a distributed leadership model with groups of triads composed of an educational expert, subject expert and teacher expert. The education experts were academics that had been teachers and were currently teacher educators going into schools on a regular basis to work with teachers. The four-year project achieved a number of successes and produced guidelines and tools for others to use when setting up a partnership. EPEE demonstrated that involving teacher educators was a positive feature of school-university partnerships and can enable existing structures to be a starting point for the development of extended knowledge exchange networks.

Jurisdictions: The Case of University-based Teacher Education in the UK

Jurisdiction is a concept that informs the argument in this chapter in two ways: the case presented for consideration is an account of how situating the education of school teachers in the university to improve the status of teaching as a profession involves university-based teacher educators in a struggle for legitimacy with other academics; secondly, the case is set in the context of provision for teacher education in the UK, and how the interplay of the four devolved nations as policy jurisdictions produces different configurations of the relations between teachers, teacher educators and universities.

Finding a Place in Academia

The incorporation of teacher education into universities in the UK resulted in friction between teacher educators, previously based in Colleges of Education, and educational researchers already located within departments or institutes of education in universities (Furlong, 2013). The 'logic of mergers' (Dickson, 2015) was as likely to be resisted initially by the teacher educators concerned about threats to their autonomy as by the educational researchers who sought affinity with academics from other disciplines by distancing themselves from the practice of teaching. What counts as success in the university is represented in the criteria for career progression and these mainly reward publications and research income rather than contributions to professional practice. In America, a report on Schools of Education (Holmes Group, 1995) concluded that staff newly incorporated into universities became isolated from the world of schools as they sought recognition from the academic community by engaging in research that was not focused on the professional work of teachers. The result was a pivot towards a sociology of education more concerned with critique of macro-social forces than the enactment in pedagogy as the dominant form of research amongst teacher educators. Recent international analysis of the policy and practice of teacher education considers this to have resulted in major fault lines in the present structure exacerbating attempts to achieve alignment of theory and practice (Moon, 2016). Such is the clash of values between the university and the professional formation of teachers that university-based teacher education has been described as a 'field of tensions' (Elstad, 2010). Tension is not in itself necessarily a bad thing; raising awareness of points of difference can lead to new insights, but it does require commitment to seeking resolution without closing down debate prematurely. One source of tension resides in the debate about the relationship between theory and practice in professional learning. Different conceptualizations of what being a teacher requires influence perspectives on the question of the legitimacy of the location of professional education in the university. Is it a craft primarily concerned with the development of skilful practice or is it an intellectual pursuit requiring the development of a distinct and robust body of knowledge? Whilst it is possible to find opinions expressing such starkly opposed positions on whether teacher education has a place in academia, it is more productive to consider the relationship between the amount and quality of practical experience required and how it is, and could be, integrated into initial and continuing professional education. Current debate presents ideological concerns in a rhetoric about quality and relevance when what is needed is the re-imagining of teacher education processes and structures to disrupt established and outsider relations in the academy. Moon's exploration of competing narratives around teacher education identifies one narrative line drawing upon the idealism of bringing the education of teachers into the university fusing political and professional development so that '[e]ducation was about creating a better and more equitable society and teachers needed the professional skills to help in the process' (Moon, 2016: 252). The impetus for this change was largely driven from the university by educationalists such as Dewey in America and Montessori and others in Europe. Changing social and political conditions associated with the rise of neoliberalism led to the supplanting of this narrative by one more attuned to the ethos of education as a commodity acquired by individuals to improve their prosperity and promote economic success. According to this view, the role of teachers was to enable individuals to advance, and if they failed to do so, the fault lay in the quality of teaching. The remedy was to make teacher education more practically focused on the classroom and outcomes measured according to metrics of student performance determined by governments.

Regulation of the professional accreditation of teachers is another area on which changes to quality assurance and accountability processes have consequences for the extent to which universities are perceived to have, or would want to have, a role in teacher education. The dual accreditation of teachers in the UK who are awarded a university qualification, Post Graduate Certificate of Education (PGCE) or Diploma (PGDE) in Scotland, and accreditation as a Qualified Teacher (QTS) by the professional body or in England the Department for Education (DfE) represents an alliance of interests in what constitutes professional education but is open to challenge as recent developments in England have shown, the use of Initial Teacher Training (ITT) as opposed to Initial Teacher Education (ITE) should also be noted:

> Building on the development of school-led ITT, DfE should work in collaboration with those involved in ITT to consider the way in which teachers qualify, with a view to strengthening what has become a complex and sometimes confusing system. We would like applicants to understand that QTS is the essential component of ITT and that a PGCE is an optional academic qualification.
>
> (DfE, 2015: 13–14)

The 're-imagining' of the role of teacher educators (Dickson, 2015) necessary for the full potential of the university's contribution to the formation of teachers to be realized is jeopardized by the impact of narrowly conceived accountability structures and competition for scarce resources. For some the challenges arising from the nature of the university as the context within which the contestations to assert agendas take place are such that 'tough decisions have to be made as to whether one should try to reform institutions, or imagine others that are more fit for purpose' (Sultana, 2016: 102). Before abandoning commitment to the location of teacher education in the university, we need first to attempt a challenge of the theory versus practice dichotomy in which preferences for school-based or university-based professional education reside. In 2013, the Higher Education Academy (HEA, now known as Advance HE) convened a summit of experts on 'Learning to Teach', which concluded that the university can play an important role in supporting the development of new practice in response to the changing world in which we live (Florian and Pantić, 2013, p. Part 2.4). Rather than a simple theory versus practice binary, the issue is the extent of the commitment to the 'contestability of knowledge', and instead of requiring an either school or university-based approach to teacher education we need to think about how boundaries between schools, colleges, industry and universities can be less sharply drawn (Furlong, 2013: 8). The relationship between educational research and practice in the professional development of teachers has been disputed in England for some time, less so elsewhere in the UK as we shall see, and was given added impetus by the controversial lecture by a university Professor of Education sponsored by the Teacher Training Agency (TTA, a government quango responsible for the recruitment and training of teachers) berating spending on educational research as having little impact on practice and promoting the self-improvement of schools (Hargreaves, 1996). It is a debate based on premises that continue to generate more heat than light and one that has been instrumental in undermining the position of university-based teacher educators in England. The negative view of the contribution of universities to the improvement of schools is all the more remarkable in the face of conclusions from research into school-university research partnerships, also funded by the TTA in the 1990s. The School-Based Research Consortia initiative showed the value of educational research for schools when they are able to engage in critical inquiry into the meaning and purpose of education in a collegial community composed of teachers, teacher educators and researchers (Baumfield and Butterworth, 2007). The stress on the opportunity to question and challenge ideas is an indicator of where the tension may actually lie.

Analysis of national contexts with the highest level of satisfaction with teacher education shared by policymakers, teachers and parents and the lowest level of satisfaction confirms that the issue is not the privileging of practice over theory as measured by the proportion of school-based versus university-based provision. If we compare Finland, the country with the highest level of satisfaction, with England where it is very low shows that *less* time is given to school-based practice in teacher education courses in Finland. The issue is not the quantity but the quality of the practical experience or, as Dewey would argue, the extent to which the experience is 'educative'. Focusing on improving the practice of teaching need not diminish the role of the university but has implications for the integration of theory and practice in courses and the role of educational research in informing the initial and continuing education of teachers. In answering the question 'Do Universities have a role in the education and training of teachers?' Moon argues that for there *not* to be a role for the university would be to the detriment not only of teachers but also of academics. If the meaning and purpose of education are to remain open to inquiry, teacher education has a place in the university, which has the important task of building strong professional communities and frameworks:

> Where this has not happened, other stakeholders (governments, business) are stepping in, sometimes 'shoving out' the university. I think this is unfortunate. Teaching is an intellectual and professional task, and deep connection with the university ought to be at its core.
>
> (Moon, 2016: 261)

Members of the UK's Universities' Council for the Education of Teachers (UCET) recently initiated a study to develop a better understanding of the contribution made by teacher educators in Faculties of Education to the strategic aims of their institutions (https://www.ucet.ac.uk/). The intention of the study is to direct attention towards the position of university-based teacher educators as members of academic staff and their expertise in core institutional activities including: supporting professional and practitioner learning; reflective practice; developing conducive learning environments and cultures; pedagogy, curriculum development and assessment. The capacity of teacher educators to use their knowledge and skills to support community engagement, partnerships, widening participation, access and employability is also highlighted. But concerns are raised in the preliminary report that the positioning of Faculties of Education within university structures, due in part to the history of the incorporation of Colleges of Education and to the persistence of strong disciplinary identities, may be masking knowledge, skills and expertise that could be valuably deployed within the sector. The pro-active approach taken in the UCET initiative to making the case for the importance of teacher education for the mission of the contemporary university is encouraging. It will be important as the study develops to widen the perspective further to consider professional education as a provocation and disrupter of assumptions regarding the relationship between the university and the professions. Forging alliances with academic colleagues also engaged in professional education, in Law, Health and Engineering for example, will extend and strengthen the case; it will also be necessary to engage with the changing role of administrators and the implications of the emergence of 'hybrid professionalism' to find scope for collaboration. Shifting perspective to look within the university to establish a common ground for the different professional interests builds on previous research on the role of teacher educators in bridging and brokering relationships between universities and schools (Baumfield and McLaughlin, 2006) by extending understanding of the relationship as one of mutuality:

> To get Education right in higher education, indeed, in order to get teaching as a profession right, we need to do something about the work of HEI-based teacher educators.
>
> (Ellis and McNicholl, 2015: 149)

Faculties of Education must contest their position on two fronts: their relationship with other faculties within the university and their relationship with schools. In the current political climate, it appears to be those education systems with the confidence and independence of spirit to conceive a broad vision of teaching that offer most support for the involvement of universities in the formation of teachers in which teacher educators continue to play a vital role. Variations emerging across the four jurisdictions of the UK provide a glimpse of the alternative possibilities that different values and policy contexts can yield.

Teacher Education in the Devolved Nations of the UK

The devolved nations of the increasingly (dis)United Kingdom provide a 'laboratory' for the observation of the interaction of global trends, national contexts and local circumstances in 'Home/International' studies (Raffe et al, 1999). Hulme and Menter in their report of a Teaching and Learning Research Programme (TLRP)-funded scoping study comparing provision for ITE and Early Professional Development (EPD) in post-devolution UK explored the extent to which learning to teach can be characterized as a technical or an ethical process. Analysis of policy documents was followed up in regional seminars where the similarities and differences across the four nations were discussed and refined. They conclude that whilst there are powerful transnational forces leading to convergence, there are also differences resulting from the different political values and 'shaping myths' that inform policymaking post-devolution (Hulme and Menter, 2008). The distinction between 'travelling' and 'embedded' policy (Ozga and Jones, 2006) is employed to identify these similarities and differences. The 'travelling' policies influencing the conceptualizing of teacher professionalism include the development of integrated frameworks for qualification, aspirations for all teachers to be qualified at masters' level and a drive to 'modernize' the profession. However, generic travelling policy is embedded in particular national contexts, in which 'history, political culture and the professional voice of the mediating community' (Hulme and Menter, 2008: 50) support a degree of divergence.

Examples of 'embedded' policy divergence across the four nations identified by the project that are relevant to this chapter include: the extent to which the profession itself has been able to shape professional standards, the level of educational literacy expected of teachers, the degree to which the expression of the standards includes an emphasis on critical reflection and the extent to which the teacher's role includes interaction with the wider community beyond the school. In the period under review they found that England afforded the least 'scope for agency' as sustained emphasis on a reductive view of practice and the promotion of multiple routes into teaching, which marginalized universities and risked the 'pedagogical deskilling' of the profession (Robertson, 1996). In Wales teachers were more engaged in determining the future development of standards, and the decision not to link continuing professional development directly with pay was an indication that teacher learning was intrinsic. The restructuring of the ages and stages of schooling in Wales and the development of the Welsh Baccalaureate also signalled a commitment to pursuing a distinctive Welsh approach to teaching and learning. However, the need to ensure that Welsh qualifications are recognized across the border in England was a constraint. In Northern Ireland, the review of teacher competencies conducted by the General Teaching Council Northern Ireland (GTCNI) in 2005 provided the opportunity to directly involve the profession in defining the attributes of a teacher for the first time. The GTCNI also led the way in establishing an integrated model of professional development. In Scotland, where a degree of autonomy in educational matters had been in place since the signing of the Act of Union in 1707 and the General Teaching Council Scotland was established in 1965, there is model of educational policymaking that seeks to promote consultation and collaboration. Certainly, the development of the Standard for Initial Teacher Education would appear to support this view: a benchmarking group composed of representatives from HEIs, schools and local authorities drafted the standard, which was then moderated through discussion at a national seminar.

How has the divergence across the four nations of the UK developed since this scoping study? Four years later, in 2012, following the coming to power in England of a coalition government, the Minister of State for Education, Michael Gove, stated his views of teaching as a 'craft' best learned in a classroom through an apprenticeship model and this diminishing of any intellectual elements of pedagogical processes was reflected in the implementation of new *Teachers' Standards*. The first thing to notice is that any aspiration for greater integration of teacher professional learning across a career had been reduced to a set of standards that will apply to the 'vast majority of teachers regardless of their career stage'. The standards define the minimum level of practice expected, and while professional judgement is not entirely removed the context is one of evaluation to ensure conformity with the scope for action construed in terms of conforming to the ethos of the school and upholding 'British' values. Subsequent developments in England leading up to the most recent 'market review' of ITE (DfE, 2021) are a continuation of this approach with university-based provision marginalized by policymakers.

In Wales commitment to a model of teaching and learning that is not subject to the influence of the English system but is 'Made in Wales' has strengthened. Teaching is recognized as a profession in which the sharing and testing of beliefs and understandings with colleagues in professional learning communities are central and the knowledge required of teachers includes an awareness of the United Nations Convention on the Rights of the Child, not simply subject knowledge. The scope for action for the teacher is also broadly conceived and includes contributing to the community as a whole. The GTCNI continues the work of re-establishing teachers as 'lead intellectuals' in their local communities begun in the review of the standards. The conception of the teacher as a public intellectual goes beyond setting an example, as in the English configuration of 'upholding public trust', to embrace the commitment to the radicalism that construing teaching as a reflective profession entails and incorporate activism for positive social change. The policy context in Northern Ireland is, however, threatened by the current economic situation post Brexit and the concomitant political tensions. In Scotland, the Donaldson Review (Donaldson, 2011) of teacher education recognized teaching as a complex and challenging profession in which both excellence and equity are important factors and the tradition of the 'democratic intellect' upheld (Benn, 2012). The centrality of research-informed practice in teaching and teacher learning is sustained by the key role played by universities; in fact, closer links are formed by extending engagement beyond Education Faculties to encompass the wider university. The drive is for greater partnership between schools, and universities with no appetite for multiple routes into teaching or wholly school-based provision.

The British Educational Research Association (BERA) in partnership with the Royal Society for the encouragement of Arts, Manufacture and Commerce

(RSA) commissioned an inquiry on the role of research in teacher education and school improvement. The inquiry concluded:

> While the idea of teaching as a research-based-profession is increasingly evident in Scotland, Northern Ireland and Wales, it seems that England, at least in respect of the political rhetoric, recent reforms and explicit definitions, is fixed on a contrastingly divergent trajectory towards the idea of teaching as a craft-based occupation, with a concomitant emphasis on a (re)turn to the practical.
> (Beauchamp et al, 2015: 154)

Teacher education in UK higher education exists in a contested and ambiguous space. England has experienced the strongest pull away from university-based ITE, and pre-service education has been largely school-based with an evolving inspection framework which prioritizes statistical data over other indicators of quality since 1992 (Ellis, 2010). Universities themselves have come under significant scrutiny in terms of neoliberal accountability measures, formalized in the 2016 White Paper, Higher Education: Success as a Knowledge Economy. Recent policy changes in England (DfE, 2021) leave ITE provision in universities under sustained threat while continued attempts to commercialize ITE in other parts of the UK reflect challenges to the combined university and school-based model more generally.

Why Professional Education Is Important for the Contemporary University

How the question of whether teacher education should continue to have a place within the university is addressed is an indication of the position taken on the nature of teaching as a profession. Pivotal to an evaluation of what would be a satisfactory answer is the extent to which teachers are to be trained as providers of a technical service or educated to become agents of educational and social reform (Sultana, 2016). However, the location of teacher education has radical potential not just for teacher professionalism; provision for their learning also has implications for how the purpose of the university is understood and how its relation to the professions is shaped. The status of a profession is dependent on establishing claims to specialist knowledge acquired through higher education, experience sustained through life-long learning and a commitment to a code of ethics. Integral to a professional's daily work is the requirement to draw upon evidence to exercise judgement in determining the best course of action in complex, problematic situations; it is on this basis that they establish their authority and earn trust. Positioned at the intersection of research, policy and practice professionals can mediate between experts and the public. The ideal type of the professional can be represented as a 'public intellectual' (Giroux, 2010) equipped to be an advocate for democracy in their service to the community. The reality, of course, may fall short of fulfilling this potential but does not diminish the pivotal role of professionals in the axis of global trends, national contexts and local circumstances.

Recognition of multiple narratives in contemporary society may erode the idea of a single 'public' but has increased the need for education that can promote critical engagement. The description of public intellectuals as needing to operate within multiple tensions, including those between theory and practice, between elitism and mass appeal and between academic specialization and generalist inclusiveness (Schweizer, 2008), will resonate with academics involved in professional education as well as the members of the professions they teach. The close association of critical pedagogy with the function of the public intellectual can be found in the writings of Dewey and Freire and in reflections on the obligations of academics and professionals (Hill, 2012; Parsons, 2013). The importance of the university-based teacher educator is crucial in resisting restricted notions of teaching as a technical service driven by market forces, and their liminality accords with the view that public intellectuals work best as outsiders whose lives unsettle others (Said, 1996). Whilst focusing on the case of the teacher educator does not offer full illumination of the issues affecting the contemporary university, it can highlight how a 'space within' existing structures challenges binaries to create sufficient tension to offer new possibilities. The situation of teacher education in higher education serves as a reminder that for Bhabha the most potent binary is that of inclusion/exclusion (Bhabha, 1994). The debate has a wider resonance not simply with other forms of professional education but also for the contribution of the university in contemporary society.

References

Abbott, A. (1988) *The system of professions*. Chicago: University of Chicago Press.
Abbott, A. (2005) Linked ecologies: States and universities as environments for professions. *Sociological Theory*, 23(3): 245–74.
Axtell, J. (2016) *Wisdom's workshop: The rise of the modern university*. Princeton: Princeton University Press.

Barley, S. R. and Kunda, G. (2004) *Gurus, hired guns and warm bodies: Itinerant experts in a knowledge economy*. Princeton: Princeton University Press.

Baumfield, V. and McLaughlin, C. (2006) Bridging and bonding: Perspectives on the role of the university in SUPER. In C. McLaughlin (ed.) *Researching schools: Using school-university partnerships in educational research*. London: Routledge.

Baumfield, V. and Butterworth, M. (2007) Creating and translating knowledge about teaching and learning in collaborative school–university research partnerships: An analysis of what is exchanged across the partnerships, by whom and how. *Teachers and Teaching: Theory and Practice*, 13(4): 411–27.

Beauchamp, G., Clarke, L., Hulme, M. and Murray, J. (2015) Teacher education in the United Kingdom post devolution: Convergences and divergences. *Oxford Review of Education*, 41(2): 154–70.

Benn, M. (2012, Monday 27th August) Why Scotland's approach to publicly funded education works. *Guardian*. Retrieved from https://www.theguardian.com/education/2012/aug/27/scotland-supports-publicy-funded-education (accessed on 1 August 2022).

Beyer, L. (1988) *Knowing and acting inquiry, ideology and educational studies*. Lewes: The Palmer Press.

Bhabha, H. K. (1994) *The location of culture*. London: Routledge.

Day, C., Gu, Q., Townsend, A., & Holdich, C. (2021). *School-university partnerships in action: The promise of change*. London: Routledge.

DfE. (2015) *Carter review of initial teacher training*. London: HMSO.

DfE. (2021) *Initial teacher training (ITT) market review report*. London: HMSO.

Dickson, B. (2015) Scotland: Radical alternatives in teacher education. In C. Brock (ed.) *Education in the United Kingdom*. London: Bloomsbury.

Donaldson, G. (2011) *Teaching Scotland's future: Report of a review of teacher education in Scotland*. Edinburgh: Scottish Government (Scotland).

Elias, N. (1983) *The court society*. Oxford: Basil Blackwell.

Ellis, V. (2010) Impoverishing experience: The problem of teacher education in England. *Journal of Education for Teaching*, 36(1): 105–20.

Ellis, V. and McNicholl, J. (2015) *Transforming teacher education: Reconfiguring the academic work*. London: Bloomsbury Publishing.

Elstad, E. (2010) University-based teacher education in the field of tension between the academic world and practical experience in school: A Norwegian case. *European Journal of Teacher Education*, 33(4): 361–74.

Evetts, J. (2003) The sociological analysis of professionalism: Occupational change in the modern world. *International Sociology*, 18(2): 395–415.

Florian, L. and Pantić, N. (2013) *Learning to teach. Part 2: Exploring the distinctive contribution of higher education to teacher education*. York: Higher education academy.

Furlong, J. (2013) *Education – An anatomy of the discipline: Rescuing the university project?* London: Routledge.

Gibbons, M. (2000) Mode 2 society and the emergence of context-sensitive science. *Science and Public Policy*, 27(3): 159–63. DOI:10.3152/147154300781782011.

Giroux, Henry A. (2010) Bare pedagogy and the scourge of neoliberalism: Rethinking higher education as a democratic public sphere. *The Educational Forum*, 74(3): 184–96. DOI: 10.1080/00131725.2010.483897.

Grant, J. (2021) *The new power university*. London: Pearson.

Greany, T., Gu, Q., Handscomb, G., Varley, M., Manners, P. and Duncan, S. (2014) School-university partnerships: Fulfilling the potential. Summary Report: October 2014.

Holmes Group. (1995) *Tomorrow's schools of education*. East Lansing, MI: Holmes Group.

Hargreaves, D. H. (1996) *The teacher training agency annual lecture in: teacher training agency*. London: Teacher Training Agency.

Heimans, J. and Timms, H. (2018) *New power: How it's changing the 21st century – and why you need to know*. Australia: Macmillan.

Hill, M. L. (2012) Beyond 'talking out of school': Educational researchers as public intellectuals. *International Journal of Research & Method in Education*, 35(2): 153–69.

Hulme, M. and Menter, I. (2008) Learning to teach in post-devolution UK: A technical or an ethical process? *Southern African Review of Education with Education with Production*, 14(1–2): 43–64.

Lieberman, A. and Grolnick, M. (1996) Networks and reform in American education. *Teachers College Record*, 98(1): 7–46.

Lybeck, E. (2020) *Norbert Elias and the sociology of education*. London: Bloomsbury.

McLaughlin, C., Cordingley, P., McLellan, R. and Baumfield, V. (2015) *Making a difference*. Cambridge: Cambridge University Press.

Moon, B. (2016) *Do universities have a role in the education and training of teachers? An international analysis of policy and practice*. Cambridge: Cambridge University Press.

Noordegraaf, M. (2007) From 'pure' to 'hybrid' professionalism: Present-day professionalism in ambiguous public domains. *Administration and Society*, 39(6): 761–85.

Ozga, J. and Jones, R. (2006) Travelling and embedded policy: The case of knowledge transfer. *Journal of Education Policy*, 21(1): 1–17.

Parsons, J. (2013) The ethical academic: Academics as public intellectuals. Retrieved from https://eric.ed.gov/?id=ED539258.

Raffe, D., Brannen, K., Croxford, L. and Martin, C. (1999) Comparing England, Scotland, Wales and Northern Ireland: The case for 'home internationals' in comparative research. *Comparative Education*, 35(1): 9–25.

Robertson, S. (1996) Teachers' work, restructuring and postfordism: Constructing the new 'professionalism'. *Teachers' Professional Lives*, 2: 28–55.

Said, E. (1996) *Representations of the Intellectual: The Reith Lectures (1993)*. New York: Vintage Books.

Schweizer, B. (2008) Introduction: Twentieth-century writers as public intellectuals. *Studies in the Humanities*, 35(2): 121–37.

Smedley, L. (2001) Impediments to partnership: A literature review of school-university links. *Teachers and Teaching*, 7(2): 189–209.

Sultana, R. (2016) Universities and the preparation of teachers in the Mediterranean: Cautionary tales from the Global South. In B. Moon (ed.) *Do universities have a role in the education and training of teachers?* pp. 85–106. Cambridge: Cambridge University Press.

Turner, R. S. (1972) *The Prussian University and the research imperative: 1806–1848* (PhD). Princeton: Princeton University.

Veblen, T. (1918) *The higher learning in America: A memorandum of the conduct of universities by business men*. New York: B. W. Huebson.

Watermeyer, R. P. and Rowe, G. (2021) Public engagement professionals in a prestige economy: Ghosts in the machine. *Studies in Higher Education*. DOI: 10.1080/03075079.2021.1888078.

Whitchurch, C. (2008) Shifting identities and blurring boundaries: The emergence of third space professionals in UK higher education. *Higher Education Quarterly*, 62(4): 377–96.

Wiewel, W. and Broski, D. C. (1997) *University involvement in the community: Developing a partnership model*. Chicago: Great Cities Institute, College of Urban Planning and Public Affairs, University of Illinois at Chicago.

Wilensky, H. L. (1964) The professionalization of everyone? *American Journal of Sociology*, 70(2): 137–58.

9

The Power and Beauty of the Disciplinary Infrastructure of Our Culture

Julian Williams

Introduction

I start and will conclude this chapter with an answer to the question 'What should our universities be for?': I will claim they should be for the power and beauty of the disciplines in maintaining and developing our cultural infrastructure, i.e. for their 'use value' in the 'public good' or public interest. This is, I argue for the 'cultural use value' of our disciplines, for example, in the problem solving required for the survival of human cultures in the pandemics and other global eco-challenges upon us and yet more to come.

The thinking behind this chapter began with Collini (2012) who seriously asked, 'What are universities for?' Then I developed his approach for a conference on Higher Education at Hope University in 2019, and came to this point of development during the pandemic of 2020 and 2021. Collini has fun with the then current fatuous policy documents on higher education (HE) in the UK, and the 'excellence' frameworks for the assessment of and metrics for researching and teaching (known here as REF and TEF). He takes this from the Browne report (cited in Collini as from page 182), selling us their marketization of HE with this vacuous tautology:

> Students are best placed to make a judgment about what they want to get from participating in Higher Education.

In response, Collini hopes that a university-educated person in possession of critical faculties would ask 'and why should society resource such students' participation in HE?' But for Browne this is not up for discussion, as the student market (even though funded by government) is supposed to drive university provision, even while the employment market is supposed to drive the student market, motivating the student to consume education for their enhancement of the value of their labour power later (i.e. for capital).

What Universities Should Be for: The Public Good?

Rather, Collini seriously posits instead the intrinsic 'public good' of the arts, humanities and universities' disciplines as a whole. He works particularly on the public good of the arts and humanities that have been devalued in policy and even fee structures; he argues that each generation must revisit the great questions posed by art down the centuries, how can we live together, what do we value in life and so on. And, indeed who can say that he was wrong, now that we see human cultures under the pressure of a pandemic? And, if we can imagine the pandemic is just the first ripple of the coming eco-cide as oceans rise, continents turn to desert, the reefs die and wars over water break out, it's hard to imagine a future when all goes back to 'business as usual' in the economy, in politics, in the university or in the arts and humanities.

But Collini's argument needs to be extended to the whole of the university's disciplinary offerings. The crisis is not only in arts and humanities. Big science, technology and medicine are also in serious trouble as the commercial imperatives and markets bite deep into their activity at the same time as they engage in destroying the environment. I will argue that the commonality in the decay of the disciplines – most visible ironically in their failure to work interdisciplinarily – arises due to their alienation from labour, from work outside academe, and so alienation from their use value to society and to our cultures. Collini rightly calls this out as alienation from the 'public good', but my argument will take a disciplinary and interdisciplinary problem-solving approach. I want to formulate the public good or interest in the cultural use value of our work, and counterpose it to cultural capital.

Here from my conference powerpoint is the list of some 'public goods' in the Hope University seminar, 2019:

> The public good?
>> to get vaccinated,
>> to make sure everyone has good health care,
>> to prevent the carrying of weapons to school,
>> to maintain a clean environment, or …
>> to ensure the survival of the planet?

Since then I have reflected on the 'survival of the planet': I know the planet will survive, I think the human genome will likely survive, but I am not sure that our 'humanity' – or better our humanities – will survive (I use cultures and humanities in recognition that these are many and varied, even if they might share in some common enemies). I have also come to the conclusion that technology alone won't be adequate, we humans first and foremost have to change ourselves and our relationship with each other as well as with the planet itself, as a whole: education (writ large) has become the central political, social, cultural project for those of us committed to making a sustainable environment for future generations.

Clearly, humanities, the arts and education will have a central role, I argue. But this is, or must become, entangled with science (especially social science), technology and medicine in tackling humanities' problems in the emerging global crises.

As I make this argument, I am conscious of how much the experience of the last two years has sharpened and radicalized my thinking: I will be referring to this context to strengthen my argument. All is political now.

The Functions of the University: What Universities Are Really for

Perhaps before one goes to 'should be for' in more detail, one should consider 'what are the universities for?' in fact, currently, other than corporate interests.

Looking at the objective social functions of schools and universities, one can see mass institutions for the orderly babysitting of unemployed youth, and then also cultural centres and dating agencies for the reproduction of the next generation.

Preparing graduates for the labour market is clearly there too, producing a stratified and largely compliant workforce that industry can somewhat cheaply train in their particular ways to make labour add surplus value to their production and capital.

Additionally, universities argue they provide for publicly funded employment in town and city centres, and bring communities and cities cultural capital.

Finally, universities are subsidized to conduct research that offers Capital cheap (in a sense free) knowledge that reduces costs of production (think of the public money that went into virus and vaccine science that private industry is now exploiting).

This is a short and surely incomplete list of separate functions, and they are not obviously connected in a coherent way, except perhaps through their functional support for Capital. Additionally, now that universities are run as corporations by managements that prioritize the bottom line, each of these functions brings money to the corporate university coffers. Indeed, this corporate control of universities exerts a contradictory effect, because it means universities actually lose control over what they do. Every programme has to turn 'a profit' (if not economically, in some wider sense of accumulation of cultural Capital), and every academic appointment has a 'business case', even if that means employing and exploiting academics on precarious contracts, to the point where they find themselves earning less than the minimum wage to 'prove themselves' fit for the increasingly proletarianized academic labour market.

Reflecting on Bourdieu's analysis of the cultural fields, however, including education, one can make a convincing case that these functions all provide for the 'reproduction' of the social conditions of production in society: reproduction of oppression, ideology, with the labour force stratified and primed for Capital, compliance and so on. Bourdieu offers us some tools to understand this capital as cultural capital, and his analyses of educational (and many other) fields show how this is managed. My colleagues and I have developed this idea of capital for education in particular into a cultural commodity model: each student's learning and knowledge becomes a cultural commodity, through a 'credit system' that the university and students use to measure the 'value added' to labour power for employers to 'use'. (This partially explains the emphasis in educational institutions on the rigour of examinations and assessment at the expense of doing any useful work.)

But then I always ask: where is the 'use value' in the cultural commodity, and don't we want to consider 'use' in the universities' activities, functions and knowledge production? A simple answer would be to claim that the 'use' of all this education is in the value of the students' labour power to Capital, exploited in their subsequent careers (see some details in Williams, 2011).

While this is valid, the long list of objective social functions above suggests that this economic analysis is rather too simple, and in fact abstract. The uses of cultural commodities and cultural capital are not captured in their inscription as exchange values, but in fact develop in a dialectical contradiction of use with exchange value (Black et al, 2021).

In a critique of some limitations in Bourdieu's work (and in Bourdieu and Passeron in particular), Williams and Choudry (2016: 16) put it thus:

> Thus, when Bourdieu emphasises the arbitrary nature of cultural capital, he prefaces his theory of class reproduction with the qualification 'insofar as' pedagogy/capital is arbitrary. 'All pedagogic action is, objectively, symbolic violence insofar as it is the imposition of a cultural arbitrary by an arbitrary power' (Bourdieu and Passeron, 1977/1990, p. 5). But if one allows pedagogy,

knowledge, and competence – even schooled knowledge – to have some functional use value in practice one might refer to that aspect of knowledge as having a 'cultural use value' as well as 'exchange value' (i.e. Bourdieu's capital), and one that is potentially consumable in non-exploitative and non-dominating work. Thus we propose ... to add to Bourdieu: 'Insofar as pedagogic action invites learning of useful mathematical competences and the power to use these critically in practice, it objectively undermines the imposition of the cultural arbitrary by any arbitrary power'.

The notion that knowing (and identity) is commodified in the cultural fields leads us to consider the dialectic of knowledge, identity and competence as commodity, or knowing, identifying and practising as processes invoking commodity relations (see Black et al, 2021 for more details).

The value of 'disciplinary' knowledge and identities will need to be considered in this light. Advanced warning for the reader here, I will argue that it becomes essential to repair the alienation of disciplines from labour (and from each other) and that this involves turning disciplinary work to solving humanities' problems. Some of this will seem obvious to interdisciplinary research teams, but I will argue this is universal, and applies as much to teaching-learning as it does to such current research.

A New Disciplinary and Interdisciplinary Problem-solving Conceptualization of What Universities Can and Should Do

Barring the babysitting and partying/match-making functions alluded to above, which actually Bourdieu in his argumentation in 'Distinction' would give great credit to as functional for reproducing class privileges, all these functions might be brought under the mantle of disciplinary infrastructure. Thus, as I argued in the Hope conference:

> Universities and educational institutions have largely taken on, and should take on, the role of maintenance and development of the intellectual (and disciplinary) infrastructure of a cultured society.

However, one immediately needs to caution that the disciplines themselves have largely become alienated from the social practices where they can be most socially useful. In particular, the alienation of learning (or 'research', too) from teaching has increasingly become dangerous, allowing students to leave universities with little experience of significance about how their discipline can be of wider use, solve problems or engage with other disciplines. Similarly, it leads professors to compartmentalize their research at a distance from teaching. Additionally, in order to solve many social or technical problems it becomes essential to develop interdisciplinary teams, something universities are not always very good at doing, so compounding the fact that students may get little experience with it.

The nature of 'discipline' as a concept in practice does need some examination. Historically, according to Williams and Roth (2019) the concept of discipline has roots in the armed forces of antiquity, through the medieval religious orders and guilds to 'modern' notions of the education of professions, and nowadays to science. Adopting a discipline was meant to enhance one's power by devoting oneself to a set of practices, norms or orders that gives agency to the disciplinary authorities one serves. I am conscious while writing these very words that each sentence gives to Caesar that which is Caesar's – it adopts an academic voice while it is (and to some extent because it is) obedient to the disciplinary norms of academe, which by the same token cut these words off from audiences I might wish to communicate with.

I am therefore an agent for my 'discipline' as much as an agent for 'my' discipline, i.e. I am a voice for 'other authorities' as much as for an other voice in 'myself' – and this then raises the question of contradictions in my self and my identity/ies. [I am both the product and the perpetrator of the discipline: for more on Bakhtinian multivoicedness, see Holland et al, 1998.]

This reminds me of the question of the 'academic' (and so academically disciplined) and 'everyday' conceptions which so engages Vygotskyans, of which more soon. But there is a similar question involving interdisciplinary communication in collective problem solving, since the alienation of a discipline from its social use in solving problems and meeting needs goes hand in hand with the alienation of one discipline from another. This then requires a massive effort to stitch labour back together again through interdisciplinary working. In everyday practices this is often a given and not much of a problem, but in the academy which has developed disciplinarity as its main rationale (the 'teaching' of one's discipline) it becomes a massive, almost insurmountable problem.

Considering interdisciplinarity in problem solving, Williams and Roth (2019) suggested a spectrum from less to more complexity in the conception thus:

Mono-disciplinarity →
    multi-disciplinarity →
        inter-disciplinarity →
            trans-disciplinarity →
                → meta-disciplinarity?

It would be wrong to suggest that monodisciplinary problem solving is of no or even less use due to this lesser 'complexity'; however, on the contrary, much good practical problem solving does not require interdisciplinarity, and in fact it is usually a sufficient knowledge and understanding of the problem context (rather than lack of interdisciplinarity) that limits the mono-disciplined problem solver (see Williams and Goos, 2013).

Arguably, unnecessary interdisciplinary complexity can be bad for problem solving: better to keep things simple if the occasion warrants. The bane of the monodisciplinary or multidisciplinary academic practice lies rather in this: the failure to engage the discipline with the everyday context in which the interesting problems arise. (Whose 'interest'? More on this later.)

But then the need for more than one discipline is increasingly part of real-world problem solving: the 'multi-disciplinary team' that focuses on a particular problem (e.g. the wellbeing of a child/adult in the school/health clinic) is now ubiquitous. And this is of course not new, in that the division of labour in production is older than human civilization.

The specific 'inter-'quality carries the more complex connotation that the disciplines involved can interpenetrate, so mathematical biology is both mathematical and biological, but its mathematics is of a certain kind, and the biology is similarly an arena where mathematical models become prominent. Then 'trans' in this context implies the relative disappearance of the boundaries between disciplines in the service of the problem being worked on. In school projects like 'cleaning up the creek', the children may not even consciously identify the science, language or mathematics curricula being brought into their collective activity, at least until this is deliberately brought to their attention by the scholars or teachers. These terms might be unfamiliar to readers, more can be found in Doig et al (2019).

However, it is the 'meta' which is most important here. At all levels, a vital product of the joint activity of learning-teaching is the growth of metacognitive knowledge and associated self-regulation. Following Vygotsky, as I read his work now, this is only achieved when there is problem solving involved, generally arising from outside the disciplinary fields and outside academe, where interests and success criteria might be negotiable between all those engaged in the activity.

Vygotsky saw this as being a point of contact or dialectic, and what we might today call an entanglement, of the practices of the 'academic' with the 'everyday'; at this point the teachers/instructors may offer a wider experience of the discipline than the novice, but all students as well as instructors may have their own interest and partial expertise of the 'everyday' issues at the roots of the

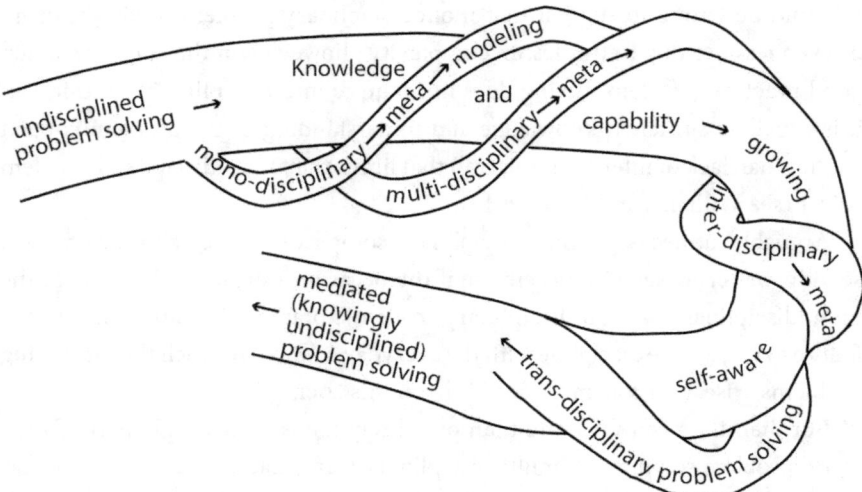

Figure 9.1 How metacognitive reflection has a role in each of the levels (from Williams and Roth, 2019: 31).

problem. Both students and professors then may learn and teach each other as part of the process of joint problem solving. Vygotsky used the word 'obuchenie' for the single, joint, activity of learning and teaching: I will refer to it as teaching-learning. It involves a communication in which the learner also teaches the teacher (about their 'everyday' practices and interests), and the teacher thereby also learns from the students. This is what is required to overcome the alienation of the academic discipline from the students' everyday practices and know how through teaching-learning.

This is also how teaching, learning and indeed 'research' all come together: for the researcher is a learner too: being 'taught' by engaging in the problems and objects of their research about how to practise and extend their discipline. A good example is offered by an environmental scientist of the ecology of the forest – she says that it is the forest that taught her almost everything, though the indigenous peoples' practices were also significant, as Simard (2014) says in *Finding the mother tree*.

Gone is the alienated activity of the classroom where the teacher delivered 'their' discipline to the learners, whose role was to absorb and regurgitate it in ways that earn them capital. Instead, there is joint activity, joint communication about problems of interest and the role of the disciplines in helping to solve them. Here, I emphasize again, the professor has as much to learn as the student, especially when the problems are non-trivial, i.e. requiring research and inquiry.

Recently, the market has brought hundreds of students from China to my classroom where I talk about educational theory: but what do I know about their everyday experiences of education that theory can engage with? Not much, and I'd better find out, not just for the sake of my students' satisfaction ratings, not just for the students' deepening understanding and formation of 'true concepts', but for the sake of my own research and my own formation of true concepts.

This is not to say of course that joint activity does not involve a division of labour, and that the experienced problem solver or disciplined practitioner has nothing special to offer. But it does suggest that in such cases the resources at the collective's disposal should not be restricted to the teachers' expertise and interests, and the experience and even research of the students can be seen as a strength of the collective enterprise, especially in their diverse richness of social and cultural experience.

During such collective problem solving the boundaries of the discipline(s) may become apparent; it is in their use in important problem solutions that their cultural use value may become apparent. This meta-knowledge is essential to development of the intellectual infrastructure, and it is a shame that so little of it goes on in academe (we give them exams instead). An effective problem solver needs not only to have some disciplinary skills and knowledge, they need to know when these might be useful to deploy, and where to go if they need to learn more. They also need to know when NOT to do so, to be 'knowingly undisciplined' (Williams, 2016).

I try to forget the authors' names but I once read about how to use maths to calculate how many partners (did they actually say 'girl friends' back then?) I should have before marrying one – I'd say this is one use of the discipline I would personally rule out as an option. But certainly, there are many others, perhaps a growing number now (e.g. how to deep-mine coal, drill for oil, optimize logging in the forests or steal an election).

All this meta-knowledge is relevant to the spectrum of complexity of inter-disciplinary problem solving in different ways. Even in a monodisciplinary context, knowing when to consider a discipline relevant or irrelevant has its place (i.e. in 'modelling' of a problem context for a disciplined approach). One has all this new data since the pandemic on all these questions, now. In evidence to the House of Commons, we hear that the government did not understand what mathematicians call 'modelling', in that they did not think it necessary to check the models their advisors were graphing for them (of cases, hospitalizations and death rates) against the actual emerging data. Either the advisors also did not understand, did not know what data was available, or they failed to do an effective job of teaching the politicians – perhaps a combination of all three. The scientists' committee is known as 'SAGE' in the UK: a name that one suspects might come back to haunt them.

But in multidisciplinary contexts, especially when there is a division of labour within the collective, a different kind of awareness comes to the fore, one that Wenger refers to as 'knowledgeability', and others call 'relational' awareness in multidisciplinary teams (e.g. the consultant, the anaesthetist, the nurse, the social worker, the cleaner, in surgery). This involves an awareness of the practices and knowledge of 'others' in the division of labour, and how their disciplines and work interpenetrate with one's own role or discipline. More, it involves a certain suppression of one's disciplinary identity in favour of the joint activity's achievement of a collective outcome. In short, one has to grow up a bit to perform effectively in an interdisciplinary or interprofessional team.

The reader may feel that all the above language of 'problem solving' and disciplines is redolent of the sciences and technology, but I see it as equally valid in the professions (medicine, nursing, education, engineering, etc.) and the arts and humanities. As suggested above echoing Collini, the arts and humanities require each generation to rethink the old questions and problems: 'How shall we live with each other?' 'What is freedom, today?' and perhaps also, 'How can we change our ways of living and being to produce a sustainable relationship with our environments?'

The Case of Mathematics: Power and Beauty Come Together?

The case of pure mathematics is particularly interesting: the pure mathematician Hardy famously waxed lyrical on the theme of elegance and beauty as the sole criterion and motivation for his work, and this seems particularly alienating to many who understand mathematics as useful. And yet pure mathematics has repeatedly proved its value as useful, often decades after its invention (e.g. Boolean logic, non-Euclidean geometries, number theory, symmetry or fractals). It turns out that the driving force of mathematical 'elegance', intuition and proof is a key feature that makes it powerful in practice.

Pure mathematics is also driven by problems, and increasingly these are engaging teams who come from different specialties within pure mathematics: everything said about interdisciplinary work is here reproduced as inter-speciality working within the discipline. Only a few work in research across these boundaries, but wicked problems demand an assembly of a team. Fields medallist Terence Tao has written about this, cited in Williams and Roth (2019).

Collini was right to criticize the facile developments of the UK government's assessment and accountability processes, the 'employability' narratives and accountability policies, and their discourses. But he poses 'intrinsic values' of the disciplines as the victims, while I posit their beauty and power, which I argue make them useful in the public good, to our cultures and our interests. I admit that in pure mathematics the discourse of 'intrinsic value' is seductive, and 'use value' in contrast feels, well, rather utilitarian and indeed commodified. But even pure mathematics research in practice is commodified, someone is paid for the labour required to do it. As the Indian, more or less unschooled mathematician Ramanujan said in his letter to Hardy in Cambridge, he needed the 'leisure' to do his mathematics.

Furthermore, I'd like to suggest that what Collini calls 'intrinsic' can be read in a discourse of 'power and beauty'. We ask each generation of students to re-think Shakespeare and the value of his work for the coming experiences of humanity, and we share our understandings of previous generations and of our research/scholarship for the present. But if the students don't see the beauty and enjoy the theatre, there is little hope of superseding the alienation that the universities' deployment of its metrics and examinations deliver.

In the last years of Vygotsky's life, he was much exercised with the dialectic of emotion-cognition. Emotions and cognitions were in traditional 'bourgeois' psychology and medicine (and everyday common sense as inscribed in our language) dichotomized and even alienated. This alienation is still visible today in the trivialization of mental health (second only perhaps to the neglect of the aged). But for Vygotsky every thought, every action and every word entangles emotional and cognitive parts (Hegel calls them moments in a dialectic, and Vygotskyans insist they are such, and not merely mechanically interacting 'elements'). I cannot say the word 'mother' – though I know some would have it down as a simple biological or social relation – without its emotional entanglements with my life experience of my relationship with my mother, or that of my daughters with their mother and my grandchildren. And for Vygotsky, these moments are essential to processes of development of the person (and I'd argue the development of the collective 'character' of the discipline, too).

In 'the problem of the environment', Vygotsky began to develop a unified concept for this entanglement and how it might be used to understand development, and many scholars have worked on this since. On the basis of this work, I venture to suggest that the dominant 'we' in education take emotional engagement for granted, and focus on cognitive outcomes at great cost. The astonishment of the mathematician (professional or child) who becomes aware of a beautiful pattern may only be a moment, but it may be transformative for their future engagement and so development. (Astonishment is a much undervalued emotion – one that is unique in being sometimes positively delightful and sometimes negatively horrific.)

Contrast this with today's dominant curriculum, that sometimes seems to have been written by or for Gradgrind[1] – as alive today as when Dickens imagined his discourse on 'facts' some time ago (following a science stream at school, I didn't get Dickens until adulthood – shame!). A critical reader can argue that we now in many places have a wider range of cognitive curricular outcomes – we can add procedures, concepts and heuristic processes. But without a pedagogy that engages emotionally with the individual's and collective's interest in some project, the difference is not so great.

Why is this so? It is in the essence of alienation of our individual and collective labour from our needs. It is our emotions that connect our needs to our actions. If there were only cognition, I could watch my body starve to my death with pure intellectual curiosity. It is the pain of hunger that drives me to eat. A similar lack of emotion in the classroom allows students to disengage with equanimity.

In fact, of course there always IS emotion in the mathematics classroom, but rather too often not of the kind we would wish an emotional curriculum to prescribe. I speak of fear, anxiety and loss of esteem, rather than joy, beauty and astonishment.

Thus, the cultural use values of disciplinary power (the enhancement of our capacities to understand and work, whether paid or unpaid) and emotions due to its beauty and hence the joy of learning through work, leisure and understanding are what we 'professionals' are, or should be, about in education and the university. Let us think what a transformation it could be if this were made central to our curriculum and pedagogy.

The Source of the Professional Workers' Struggle with Capital

I argue then that in all that we education-workers do, in research, learning and teaching – altogether let's agree to call it 'scholarship', we are a professional working class potentially working for the public good and in the public interest, and as professionals, we should work with the communities and other institutions and with students and researchers to this end. This feels particularly urgent now as we deal with local crises and global challenges that threaten our cultures and humanities.

However, we also have to address these crises and challenges in the immediate conditions where activity and labour have to be paid for. In terms of monetization, we argue that our labour in the public interest provides the reason why our profession and institutions should be funded, and this should cut across the notion of a student market in HE provision, our production of industrial patents, etc. The public interest demands funding our collective scholarship, which in turn demands student engagement, whether this is marketized or not. This reverses the current ideology implying that universities need to market themselves to the student-customer base to fund its 'essential' work, i.e. that of a rarefied, alienated activity, or research which is presumed to serve the 'economy', i.e. capital.

This means de-prioritizing some activities, perhaps defunding, like decolonizing some of our curriculum. The current dominance of indices of student 'satisfaction', chasing funding through industrial or narrowly functional competitions for funding, would then need to be proven in the interest of the public and our survival. Revisiting the notion of the cultural arbitrary, cultural use values could be monetized, thus producing cultural commodities of use rather than cultural Capital for the sake of Capital.

The engagement of scientists in the discovery and production of new vaccines shows what can be done, and how capital and patent can ruin all this good public work, ensuring that cheap or free vaccines don't reach the poor, so that the pandemic continues to swirl round the world unnecessarily and to potentially deadly effect.

Capital and their puppets won't like this message but the profession must ask itself, i.e. the professional workers must ask themselves, individually and collectively, what and who our activity and labour is for, and we need urgently to do so now in the new context of ecological breakdown that threatens survival of our cultures – maybe even the species – in the coming generation.

The Sharpening of Academic Workers' Struggle with Capital in the Coming Era

Every day the struggle between labour and capital is sharpening, and this is cultural labour and cultural capital as much as it is economic: everything starts to appear more clearly in this pandemic, as it will increasingly do as we confront the climate and other global eco-crises.

We witness locally: (i) the failure of government to connect with epidemiological expertise, even in terms of its own previous research; (ii) the bailing out of business so they don't go bankrupt in the pandemic (rhetorically 'saving jobs' in the furlough schemes) and (iii) the failure to support local public health organizations in favour of national big business (failing Personal Protective Equipment, and funding Track and Trace big businesses, sometimes corruptly associated with government commissions).

But what is not even visible is the intentional privatization and associated hollowing out or destruction of every 'public good' and institution, in health, education, environment, the arms trade, policing, etc. In one week as I write this there are UK government bills to finally privatize/Americanize the National Health Service, to make legal the currently illegal dumping of sewage in our rivers, and to similarly protect our police/military from prosecution for war crimes.

Simultaneously the academy and academic freedom are under assault: the right to critique is not just discouraged (through want of government and business funding and grants) but the very act of speaking out is under threat. This is most clearly notable in the case of Palestine, but it perhaps only takes one example like this to 'encourage the others', and there are similar difficulties emerging across the cultural spectrum: in schools it is suggested that it is improper to discuss certain ecological concerns, and in many contexts there seem to be threats to discourse on gender, LGBTQ+ identities, racism and imperialism.

However, it might also be recognized that the universities' undermining of the traditional assertion of academic freedom, when coupled with the proletarianization of the academic worker (including the huge expansion in precarious contracts, and erosion of academics pay and pensions), might lead to a degree of radicalization. In the UK, the Universities and Colleges Union (UCU) has led more strikes than almost all other trades unions (as of 2021). This seems to have been fed by the universities' corporate governance and politics: the universities are now some of the biggest businesses, with some of the highest top salaries in UK cities.

It is worth examining the university corporate management's behaviour during the last year or so to see the result. As soon as it was legally possible to get students – maybe they are thought of as customers – back to campus the student residences were flooded with visitors from all over the country and internationally. This coincidentally met the needs of many students whose social lives had been stilted for some time (COVID parties were said to be common in some places) but also the economics that demanded the students commit to fees as soon as possible. Where was the care for the communities which subsequently experienced upticks in infections, the vulnerable workers exposed to dangerous infections, or in fact the mental health of students who were later, quite predictably, trapped in new lock downs in crowded housing and residences with minimal support? The accusations await future inquiries, by which time the current incumbents will have moved on, even if some relatives of the dead might think the deaths the universities have been responsible for demand justice.

We now have to look to the network of contradictions between government, university governance, academics, students and their families and communities, and the wider public, perhaps the working classes and oppressed allies thereof. It is too late for many COVID victims, but perhaps not for those likely to perish in the coming storms (see Malm, 2018, 2021).

Conclusion

I have built on Collini's critique of the current mind-numbing drift in the universities' and their political masters' perceptions of the proper functions of higher education, and directed the argument for the 'public good' through the maintenance and development of the disciplines and their (largely interdisciplinary) functions in cultural use. This places emphasis on the 'intrinsic' value of the study of the arts and humanities, but also on the power and beauty of all the disciplines in a healthy, outward facing university. I argued that the alienation of the disciplines in academe is an alienation from production/labour and from its use value to society, and this should lead the disciplines to interdisciplinary problem solving and understandings in increasingly complex ways, but also to a metacognitive 'freeing' from the disciplines, which I call knowingly undisciplined work with the disciplines.

Can universities achieve this programme? There are massive contradictions in the use/exchange dialectic that one can see as the ultimate source of the universities' demise if they don't. What is involved is effectively a re-emergence of their use value for the public good, in the public interest. This requires a programme of reform, a dismantling of the quasi-markets imposed through pseudo-measures of exchange value, and that means effectively a governmental re-nationalization of the universities.

Is this even thinkable? The pandemic has made many things thinkable again: a conservative government that discovers the magic money tree (OK, mostly for their chums), re-nationalization of the railways, and yet billions spent on private consultancy firms and furlough to keep business in business, awaiting the return to normal capitalism.

But it is also not unthinkable that this century will see the end of the universities as leading contributors to such developments, if they are allowed to continue down the dead-headed, dreary, bean-counting path that the governments and their yes-men (yes, mostly men) in university leadership teams seem determined to follow.

Therefore, I conclude it is surely now thinkable that universities might be re-ordered to prioritize learning and research (e.g. vaccines but also the sociology of public health, i.e. epidemiology), or educate the population about their significance to our survival. Let's start from this seed, and then contemplate the role of universities, e.g. in new technologies replacing fossil fuel and carbon-based building material, in the cultural use value of the arts and social science, and education. Thence to consider developing new patterns of living, eating, travel, holidays, exercise, communications, entertainment, fashion and arts that prioritize health, joy and the good life.

Note

1 Thomas Gradgrind was the notorious school board Superintendent in Dickens's 1854 novel *Hard Times* who was dedicated to the pursuit of profitable enterprise.

References

Black, L., Choudry, S., Howker, E., Phillips, R., Swanson, D. and Williams, J. (2021) Realigning funds of identity with struggle against capital: The contradictory unity of use and exchange value in cultural fields. *Mind, Culture, and Activity*, 1(14). https://doi.org/10.1080/10749039.2021.1908364.

Bourdieu, P. (1984/2010) *Distinction*. Abingdon, UK: Routledge.

Bourdieu, P. and Passeron, J.-C. (1970) *Reproduction in education, society and culture*. London: B&P, Sage.

Brown et al. (2010) *Securing a sustainable future of higher education*. Switzerland: IdME, Springer www.independent.gov.uk/brown-report.

Collini, S. (2012) *What are universities for?* London: Colln, Penguin.

Hardy, G. H. (1940) *A mathematicians apology*. Downloadable (October 2021) from https://www.math.ualberta.ca/mss/misc/A%20Mathematician's%20Apology.pdf.

Holland, D., Lachicotte, W., Skinner, D. and Cain, C. (1998) *Identity and agency in cultural worlds*. Cambridge, MA: Harvard University Press.

Malm, A. (2018) *The progress of this storm*. London: Malm Verso.
Malm, A. (2021) *How to blow up a pipeline*. London: Malm Verso.
Simard, S. (2021) *Finding the mother tree*. London: Penguin, Random House.
Williams, J. (2011) Toward a political economic theory of education: Use and exchange values of enhanced labor power. *Mind, Culture, and Activity*, 18 (3): 276–92. DOI: 10.1080/10749031003605854.
Williams, J. (2016) *Becoming undisciplined with science and mathematics*. Deakin University conference paper. http://stemedcon.deakin.edu.au/wp-content/uploads/sites/25/2017/05/Proceedings-Julian-Williams.pdf (uploaded 2/8/2022).
Williams, J. and Goos, M. (2012) Modelling with mathematics and technology. *International Handbook of Mathematics Education*. DOI: 10.1007/978-1-4614-4684-2.
Williams, J., and Goos, M., (2013) Modelling with mathematics and technologies. In M.A. Clements, A.J. Bishop, C. Keitel, C. J. Kilpatrick, and F. K. S. Leung, (eds.) Jul 2013, *Third International Handbook of Mathematics Education*, pp. 549–69. New York: Springer Nature. DOI: 10.1007/978-1-4614-4684-2.
Williams, J. and Choudry, S. (2016) Mathematics capital in the educational field: Bourdieu and beyond. *Research in Mathematics Education*, 18(1): 3–21.
Williams, J. S. and Roth, W.-M. (2019) Theoretical perspectives in interdisciplinary mathematics education. In B. A. Doig, J. S. Williams, et al (eds.) "*Interdisciplinary mathematics education*, pp. 13–34. (open access https://link.springer.com/book/10.1007%2F978-3-030-11066-6).

10

Epilogue: The New Class (Room) Struggle in the Neoliberal University

John Holmwood

The different chapters in this volume have all addressed the current status and role of the academic profession and future prospects. In this epilogue, I want to place the discussion into the institutional context of changes to the university and how that is determining new relationships between academics and students and academics and senior managers. I will suggest that the academic role is becoming 'de-professionalized', but that is not a simple matter of it becoming 'deskilled' and subject to worsening conditions. The integration of the academic role into general employment processes has been longstanding and the issue is at least in part the changing nature of those general processes.

Max Weber (1948 [1918]), for example, wrote in the early twentieth century about how the academic role was shifting from being a vocation to being a form of employment within a university that was itself increasingly like a capitalist corporation. Later sociologists represented this development somewhat differently and rather more positively. According to Parsons, for example, the academic vocation had become collective, represented by the professional association and its ethics (Parsons, 1971; Parsons and Platt, 1973). Even the convergence between the university and other large-scale corporations could be presented in a positive light once it was recognized that the separation of ownership from control had opened a space for the corporation to represent interests other than profit-maximization. This, for Parsons, allowed bureaucratic organization to be moderated by collegial relations. On this understanding, then, the corporation was becoming like the university as much as the university becoming like the corporation. Finally, professional ethics were also increasingly 'socialized' as the political and industrial revolutions of modernity were joined by an educational revolution incorporating social rights of citizenship (for a full discussion, see Holmwood, 2017).

The current crisis confronting the academic profession in a number of countries is primarily a consequence of dramatic changes of finance and function in higher education. These have significantly disrupted the narrative just presented. 'Shareholder value' now dominates the modern corporation, and any convergence between the university and large scale corporations is at odds with collegiality. These changes are profound within Anglophone higher education, especially in the UK, Australia and the United States. From the point of view of teaching, the changes are associated with a decline in direct public-funding of undergraduate degree programmes and its replacement by a fee-based system supported by student loans. From the point of view of research, the shift has been towards its management to secure government objectives, primarily for its commercialization or its service to approved beneficiaries. As a short hand, I will characterize these developments as involving the construction of a neoliberal knowledge regime.

This is frequently understood in terms of the 'marketization' of higher education, but we should also understand that this involves the absence of the profit motive, for which is substituted 'revenue maximization'. In this short piece, I want to consider the neoliberal knowledge regime in terms of the relations between students, staff, senior management and government, and how the functions of the university are shaped by these relations. I will do so through the lens of a rather old and now forgotten text by C. B. Macpherson, namely his Massey Lectures for the Canadian Broadcasting Corporation in 1965, published as *The Real World of Democracy* (1966).

One part of Macpherson's argument was to consider the potential contradiction between liberal democracy and the market principle of the 'myth of maximization'. Liberalism, for him, was primarily a system of power based on property rights and this was in tension with the principle of equality integral to democracy. 'Maximization' gave rise to inequalities that would conflict with democracy unless checked. It is this tension, I shall suggest, which is currently playing out within higher education in Anglophone countries. Macpherson was conscious of the rise of the public sector, within which he located the growth of higher education. He has interesting comments to make about the nature of the class relation intrinsic to any public sector activity. Class relations involve a transfer from workers to property owners, but he asks 'to whom, then, is the transfer made in the case of those working in the non-profit sector?' (1966: 49). Notice, he is assuming that labour markets will generally operate to regularize payments across workers of similar levels of skill and qualification whether employed in the private or public sector. But, 'teachers and social workers, librarians and civil servants, are not obviously having part of their powers transferred to others who are owners of their means of labour' (1966: 49). His solution of this riddle is to suggest that the transfer 'can only be to the public, to the whole local or regional or national community which has, through one agency or another, decided as a community to provide such services to itself' (1966: 49).

In my view, this is a very neat and unusual framing of what is at issue. In effect, he is suggesting that this is a form of socialization of labour that depends upon self-organization of the community, through the agency of government. Macpherson here gives succinct expression to Parsons' argument that the growth of the professions takes place alongside the growth of democracy and that democracy also transforms their operation. What is interesting is to consider what happens when that same agency – the government representing 'the community' – decides to privatize the services that higher education provides. It may do so in the name of the taxpayer, but notice that the class relation remains different from that of the private sector just insofar as universities remain not-for-profit. How do universities now relate to the wider inequalities of a liberal society based on private property when they no longer have the function of ameliorating those inequalities? Let's rewind a little. Macpherson was writing at a specific moment in the development of liberalism as a welfare state in which universities were increasingly incorporated, but universities had existed prior to the development of the welfare state, just as they now post-date it.

Taking the long view, universities have always adapted to their social and political circumstances and they carry the traces of their past. Higher education in the United States, for example, has been much more fragmented than that of the UK. There has been much less direction at the federal level and greater autonomy for individual states in the development of public higher education. The latter grew dramatically in the twentieth century, but that growth did not displace private, socially elite institutions. The early development of higher education was beset by *de facto* and by legal exclusions based on gender and race, as well as class (Smith, 2016; Wilder, 2013). The private colleges were frequently racially exclusive, while segregation in public institutions in the southern states of the United States did not end until the 1960s.

The situation in the UK was somewhat different. While a university system (mainly that of Scotland) was exported to the colonies, the expansion of higher education within Britain took place primarily in the post-war period and coincided with the end of empire. 'Race' was externalized, and the expansion of higher education after the Second World War created a single system in which the elite institutions of Oxford and Cambridge were also incorporated. The distinctive characteristics of Scottish universities were left in place, but the universities were funded similarly and performed similar functions.

The Robbins reforms after 1964 in the UK, then, produced a more complete approximation to a system of public higher education than was the case for the United States (with the possible exception of California and Clark Kerr's 'Master Plan' that was implemented at around the same time). The character of Britain as politically highly centralized has meant that not only the shift towards a public higher education system was more complete than that of its Anglophone fellows, but also that the retreat from it into a neoliberal knowledge regime has been more complete, too, enabling us to be clearer about its incipient social relations.

Two notes of caution: I will restrict my observations primarily to England because, since 2000, higher education is a devolved responsibility. Much of what is to be found in English universities is also found in Scotland, for example, but the shift from a system of public higher education to a fully marketized system is more extensive in England than in the other devolved jurisdictions. The new system began in the academic year 2012–13 for students in England (and in a modified form in Wales), but not in Scotland, where the devolved Assembly has powers over higher education policy and elected not to follow the UK government's determination of policy for England. Equally, while there are similarities between English higher education and that of the United States, the latter has a more mixed character; public higher education was not so dominant and financialization has taken on different forms (both with regard to for-profit education (Cottom, 2017) and the systems of student debt finance entered into by prestigious universities (Eaton, 2022)).

The publicly backed, income-contingent loans of the English student loans system have significant consequences for how students are addressed by the revenue-maximizing practices of English higher education, but student debt is less consequential in the future lives of graduates in the UK than it is in the United States. Here, I must post a word of caution – insofar as the government seeks to reduce the cost of underwriting the loans and it does so by extending the repayment period and by reducing the income repayment threshold, the debt burden on graduates will increase with those on lower incomes more disadvantaged than those on higher incomes.[1] At the same time, removing fees altogether would disproportionately benefit the better off. This is the neoliberal 'lock-in' achieved by the introduction of fees in circumstances of austerity, where redressing other social inequities will have a higher salience among voters.

In effect, the transfer that Macpherson identified is now taking place between employees in higher education and the wider public (represented by the government and its underwriting of loans) and between employees and students (as the consumers of education and the potential beneficiaries of the investment in their human capital, but also facing loan repayments).

What is at stake in the shift from a system of public higher education to a neoliberal knowledge regime? From the perspective of government, these changes represented a step towards a properly functioning market in higher education where student choices would determine the distribution of students across universities and programmes of study within them. At the same time, for-profit providers are allowed to compete for students, thereby opening up institutions with a broad set of purposes – teaching, research, cultural reproduction and debate – to competition by institutions (newly allowed the title, 'university') with a single purpose – teaching – under the imperative of profit.

This suggests an 'Americanization' of English higher education with several caveats. On the one hand, the fact of a publicly funded income contingent loan system has also created an incentive for government to maintain a cap on fees, which, in turn, has led Russell Group universities to lobby for the lifting of the cap (alongside arguing for no restrictions on student numbers). However, the fee cap has also undercut the ability of for-profit providers to compete since the future cost of a degree (in terms of debt repayments) to students does not depend on the nature of the institution at which someone has studied. On the other hand, while senior managers of universities had thought they would achieve political independence, they have found themselves no less subservient to political control. In fact, they are probably more subservient, given that government has shown itself more dirigiste as incomplete marketization has proceeded.

For students, this creates a somewhat paradoxical situation. They are confronted by revenue maximizing institutions seeking to secure as many students (and their loans) as possible. But the costs of their degrees to them are largely determined by a different political struggle. Their loan repayments are generally understood as a form of taxation on earnings above the income threshold for repayments and subject to attempts to reduce the threshold or extend the loan period to minimize the cost to the Exchequer. University management is complicit in that they seek higher fees, but that can only be traded off against lowering the cost to government. Students are 'enrolled' as future taxpayers with an interest in the reduction of the 'burden' of income contingent loans, especially if they anticipate being in that group whose level of earnings will entail the repayment of their loans. This dynamic has been analysed in the United States by Meister (2011) and Newfield (2016) and its relation to English higher education by Holmwood (2018).

Moreover, if the 'transfer' from university teachers is now to students, understood as private investors in their human capital, the incentive is to claim back that transfer in the form of higher salaries. The normal understanding of 'class' proposes an opposition between 'managers' and 'workers'. The former may seek to minimize costs, at the same time as they maximize revenue, but there is a deeper alignment between managers and academic workers which places them each with interests opposed to students. The greater the revenue generated by universities, the more there is to distribute – in the case of universities this is not to shareholders but to those who create value for the institution, namely academics (and, of course, in returns to senior managers). Just as there is an internal division among students between those anticipating to pay off their loans and contribute through taxation to the underwriting of the loans of those who do not, and the latter, so there is a potential division among academics (and associated staff). Casualization of employment covers two distinct positions – the entry position to secure employment and the precarious position of those who take on mass teaching and other roles that improve the conditions of those deemed by their institutions to be of high value through their contribution to 'rankings' (Holmwood and Marcuello-Servós, 2019).

We can assume that these are tensions that may lead to a shift closer to what the Browne Report had initially proposed when recommending reforms in 2010, where fees would be uncapped, and universities would negotiate their own loan systems (after all, the proportions of students at each institution that go on fully to repay their loans varies, reflecting the return of 'positional' social status factors in the determination of future incomes). This would also create the conditions for more effective competition from for-profit providers, but this would operate within a stratified system where fees were competed down for some institutions while others were able to bid them upwards, as situation similar to what obtains in the United States (Newfield, 2016).

Of course, once these developments are described as the application of neoliberal policy prescriptions to higher education, then, as with any trajectory, its 'moment' can be projected backwards to the 1980s and the introduction of 'cost-centre' budgeting, following the Jarratt Review (1985) along with an escalation of the techniques of new public management through audit measures and performance indicators applied to teaching and research activities, and the outsourcing of ancillary services. One of the consequences of this projection backwards, however, is to neutralize what is distinctive about the present moment as *a moment of recognition*; or, more specifically, a moment when we need to recognize that the university has undergone a transition *from serving democracy to serving the market*. A reduction in the public functions of the university follows from the reduction in its public support – this is an effect of the implicit 'class struggle' identifiable through Macpherson's succinct analysis.

One difficulty in making my argument stick is that democracy and the market need not be understood as opposed. Indeed, the relation between private benefit and public good has always been contentious in the context of higher education. Thus, the expansion of public higher education was not a simple extension of arguments that had been used to justify public secondary education and its compulsory nature. The latter was universal in character and, therefore, could be represented as a 'social right' that secures a public benefit, namely a common education for citizens, a benefit recognized even by Milton Friedman (1962), who also thought only directly vocational courses at university with high future returns (medicine, law, etc.) warranted fees. In the case of higher education, participation was not intended to be universal, merely to be expanded (in the UK case, closer to the level already attained in the United States).

In this context, then, there was always the latent issue that higher education secured a private benefit for its graduates, when compared with the circumstances of those without university degrees. Why would 'the community' support it through taxation? This was the question posed by Macpherson. This is especially pertinent once it is understood that, no matter how much participation might be widened, higher education would be likely to attract proportionally more of its participants from socially advantaged backgrounds. How could public investment in a private benefit be justified when it seemed to favour the already advantaged? This point is reinforced in Eaton's (2022) recent critique of debt-financing of US higher education and the difficulty of passing federal legislation to mitigate its impact on graduates.

We might note that those who make this argument in our current context are not otherwise advocates of redistributive measures to address inequality, nor are they hostile to the public support of private benefits in other domains (as in facilitating private landlords through 'buy to let', rather than support for social housing, for example – see, Boughton, 2018). Yet, it is precisely broader developments in the distribution of inequalities that explain both the earlier commitment to public funding (notwithstanding the private benefits that accrued) and present arguments that private benefits disqualify higher education as a legitimate or high-priority case for public investment. Thus, at the time of the expansion of higher education, there was a general expectation of a shift from an industrial to a post-industrial, knowledge-based economy, where there would be increased demand for educated labour and a general 'adaptive upgrading' of all jobs. Indeed, this was evident in the way in which a secular trend in the reduction of inequalities was regarded as 'institutionalized' across most Western societies, even if the level of inequalities was significantly greater in some (the United States, for example) than in others (Sweden, or the UK up until the 1980s for example). In effect, this was endorsed as 'fact' by Kuznets (1953) and his 'curve' demonstrating declining income inequality with economic growth.

Public spending on higher education, then, could be justified in terms of its wider benefits; even if an individual's educational attainments and preferences did not take him or her to university, there would be a benefit from the greater integration of higher education and the economy. In other words, higher education was part of a wider political economy underpinned by social rights (Holmwood, 2017; Holmwood and Bhambra, 2012). Nor was there perceived to be an insuperable conflict between the market and social rights. In this context, Robbins and Kerr were reflecting a general consensus (or at least consensus among political and policy elites) about the value of university education in a context where economic growth could itself be represented as an inclusive social benefit.

This all may strike some readers as somewhat passé and mainly of historical interest only. Indeed, Thomas Piketty's (2014) landmark book on inequality, *Capital in the twenty-first century*, makes explicit what was already becoming increasingly evident; namely, that the period of Kerr's *Master plan* and the *Robbins report* was a high-water mark in the commitment to public spending and the reduction of wider inequalities from which there has been a very considerable retreat in many countries. For Piketty, and most other commentators, this period of positive amelioration came to an end in the 1980s with widening inequality re-emerging such that its range has now returned to that of the late nineteenth century. Indeed, for Piketty, capitalism has once again taken a patrimonial form in which inherited wealth and inherited social position predominate, notwithstanding a continued emphasis in political rhetoric upon social mobility and equal opportunities.

Piketty, of course, is a critic of the wider patterns of growing inequality and argues for a return to progressive taxation, especially on wealth and high incomes. At the same time, he also sees education as a potential mitigating factor. In effect, this is a return to arguments that underpinned the expansion of public higher education, notwithstanding that it is now subject to the same pressures on public financing and the extolling of market-based policies that are associated with the very widening of inequality that is the object of his concern. Moreover, notwithstanding the emphasis on universities for stimulating local economic growth, they also can have disruptive effects on local communities through processes of gentrification (Baldwin, 2021). How can universities, and education more generally, be part of the solution to problems of inequality if, at the same time, they exemplify (and exacerbate) the very processes that are at issue?

Given that higher education continues to receive some 'community support' through taxation – albeit considerably reduced in both the UK and the United States – we can understand the invocation of the 'culture wars' as a means by which populist politicians in governing conservative parties seek to break the 'contract' that previously existed and align it with opposition to 'privileged' elites whose advantages are at the same time being enhanced rather than diminished. Indeed, rather than ameliorating inequalities, universities are now one of its engines and the university itself operates as a microcosm of wider inequalities in society, with increasingly wide differences in pay and conditions among different types of staff. Moreover, if the 'class(room) struggle' identified here is correct, then, academics themselves will be divided over whether to participate as beneficiaries in widening inequality, or act to allow transfers to 'private appropriators' temporarily as a step towards the restoration of public higher education.

What should be clear to us, however, is that while we may lament the changes and express deep concern at the politicization of knowledge claims involved in attacks upon experts and professional values, what we call 'politicization' is the shift in the politics of one knowledge regime and its replacement by the politics of another. We cannot invoke the professional ethics of disinterested knowledge developed under the social and political conditions of public higher education in the circumstances of the neoliberal knowledge regime. There are no transcendent professional values and to invoke the disinterested pursuit of knowledge in current circumstances is to participate in the instrumentalization of knowledge and the erosion of the university's functions for democracy. There are, however, powerful interests both within and outwith the university that secure its new role in the reproduction of social inequality.

Note

1 See, for example, the analysis by Paul Johnson, Director of the Institute for Fiscal Studies, 'Changes to university fees are set to penalise lower earning graduates' (22 February 2020). Available here: https://ifs.org.uk/publications/15955.

References

Boughton, J. (2018) *Municipal dreams: The rise and fall of council housing.* London: Verso.

Browne Report (2010) Securing a sustainable future for higher education: An independent review of higher education funding and student finance. Department for Business, Innovation and Skills. Available here: https://www.gov.uk/government/publications/the-browne-report-higher-education-funding-and-student-finance (accessed on 1 August 2022).

Baldwin, D. L. (2021) *In the shadow of the ivory tower: How universities are plundering our cities.* New York: Bold Type Books.

Cottom, T. M. (2017) *Lower Ed: The troubling rise of for-profit colleges in the new economy.* New York: The New Press.

Eaton, C. (2022) *Bankers in the ivory tower: The troubling rise of financiers in US higher education.* Chicago: University of Chicago Press.

Friedman, M. (1962) *Capitalism and freedom.* Chicago: University of Chicago Press.

Holmwood, J. (2017) The university, democracy and the public sphere. *British Journal of Sociology of Education*, 38(7): 927–42.

Holmwood, J. (2018) Inegalitarian populism and the university: British reflections on Newfield's the great mistake: How we wrecked public universities and how we can fix them. *British Journal of Sociology*, 69(2): 510–16.

Holmwood, J. and Bhambra, G. K. (2012) The attack on education as a social right. *South Atlantic Quarterly*, 111(2): 392–401.

Holmwood, J. and Marcuello-Servós, C. (2019) Challenges to public universities: Digitalisation, commodification and precarity. *Social Epistemology*, 33(4): 309–20.

Jarratt Report (1985) Report of the steering committee for efficiency studies in universities. Committee of Vice Chancellors and Principles. Available here: http://www.educationengland.org.uk/documents/jarratt1985/index.html (accessed on 01 August 2022).

Kuznets, S. (1953). *Shares of upper income groups in income and savings.* Cambridge, MA: National Bureau of Economic Research.

Macpherson, C. B. (1966) *The real world of democracy.* Oxford: Clarendon Press.

Meister, R. (2011) Debt and taxes: Can the financial industry save public universities? *Representations*, 116(1): 128–55.

Newfield, C. (2016) *The great mistake: How we wrecked public universities and how we can fix them.* Baltimore: Johns Hopkins University Press.

Parsons, T. (1971) *The system of modern societies.* Englewood Cliffs: Prentice Hall.

Parsons, T. and Platt, G. M. (1973) *The American university.* Cambridge: Harvard University Press.

Piketty, T. (2014) *Capital in the twenty-first century.* Cambridge, MA: Belknap Press.

Smith, C. M. (2016) *Reparation and reconciliation: The rise and fall of integrated higher education*. Chapel Hill: University of North Carolina Press.

Weber, M. (1948 [1918]). Science as vocation. In H. H. Gerth and C. Wright Mills (eds. and trans.) *From Max Weber: Essays in sociology*, pp. 129–58. London: Routledge and Kegan Paul.

Wilder, C. S. (2013) *Ebony and Ivy: Race, slavery, and the troubled history of America's universities*. New York: Bloomsbury.

Index

Abbott, A. 5, 159
academics
    alienated 101–5, 109, 111
    autonomous 99–104, 109–10
    community 10, 25, 34, 97, 108, 110, 164
    English 102–3, 108–11
    German 96–8, 102–3, 105, 108–9
    journal editors 47–9, 57–8, 60–2
    profession 3, 5–11, 15, 17–18, 23–5, 27–34, 38, 42, 66, 74, 86–8, 93, 101–2, 105, 108–11, 149, 159, 195–6
    situation 31
    subdued 104–6, 109
accountability 2, 6–7, 9–10, 24, 42, 83, 93, 95–6, 111, 149, 165, 171, 187
Adkins, L. 85
agents 123–5
Akram, S. 85
Americanization 199
Angermuller, J. 57, 64
Archer, L. 82
Archer, M. 85
audit culture 93
authority relations 95–6, 98, 100–1, 104–5, 109, 111

Baltaru, R. -D. 63–4
Bansel, P. 83, 87
Barcan, R. 81
Barnett, R. 16, 42–3
Baumfield, V. 17
Bhaskar, R. 30
Bolden, R. 46
Bourdieu, P. 12, 64, 143, 180–1
British Educational Research Association (BERA) 170–1
Browne Report 177, 200
Burrows, R. 80
Byrne, B. 78

capital 6, 12, 117, 124–5, 178–81, 184, 188–91, 199–200
capitalism 34, 192, 202
Castro-Ceacero, D. 49
Cathedrals Group 122
Chankseliani, M. 127
Choudry, S. 180
civilizing process 144–5
Clark, B. 106
Clarke, C. A. 82
Collini, S. 177–8, 186–7, 191
comparative research 10, 16, 95–7
complexity 4–5, 27–9, 134, 143, 146–7, 152, 162, 183, 185
compromising 56–7, 62
Council for at Risk Academics (CARA) 35
COVID-19 133, 190–1
criticality 36
Cropper, W. H. 63
culture ecosystem 31
curriculum vitae (CV) 82, 125

Daniels, I. M. 79
Davies, B. 83, 87
decoloniality 26
Deetz, S. 12
demanded professionalism 16, 44, 57
Department for Education (DfE) 165
Descartes, R. 29
disciplinary problem solving 178, 181–6, 188
discipline 5, 18, 74, 94, 96, 131, 181–7
Doig, B. A. 183
Donaldson, G. 170
dualism 30

Early Professional Development (EPD) 168
Eaton, C. 201
ecological professional 35–7
ecology 26, 36, 159, 184

economy ecosystem 30–2
eco-professionalism 32
ecosystem 23, 30–6
Elias, N. 6, 142–5, 147–8
embedded policy 169
Empowering Partnerships:
    Enabling Engagement (EPEE) 163
enacted professionalism 44
English for Academic Purposes (EAP) 120
English language 120, 126, 129–31
entanglement 30–2, 159, 183, 187
epistemic
    corruption 65
    justification 62–3
    worthiness 62–3, 67
Evans, L. 16
Evetts, J. 42, 160
excellence 24, 87–8, 170, 177

Faculties of Education 167–8
Fagan, C. 68 n.2
Farrugia, D. 85
Faustian transaction 65–6
Finkenstaedt, T. 52
Fisher, S. 66–7
Foucault, M. 12, 28, 143
French Revolution 17, 141–2
Friedman, M. 201

game model 143, 146–7
General Teaching Council Northern
    Ireland (GTCNI) 169–70
General Teaching Council Scotland 169
German mandarins 105–7, 109
Giaccardi, C. 13
Gibbons, M. 162
Giddens, A. 78
Gill, R. 84
Gläser, J. 12, 95
Gove, M. 169
Grant, J. 160–1
Gunn, A. 41
Gunter, H. 12

Hadley, G. 128, 132
Haglund, L. 78
Halsey, A. H. 24
Hardy, G. H. 186–7

Hernes, G. 57
higher education (HE) 1–3, 10–18, 25
    casualization in 74–6
    England 93–5, 97–8, 108–9
    English 108–9
    German 96–8, 102–3, 108–10
    international 119–20, 136
    processual sociology of 143–7
    public 198–9, 201–2
    UK 15, 73, 75, 77, 86, 129, 133, 171,
        197–8
Higher Education Academy (HEA) 165
Higher Education Institution (HEI) 121,
    123–4, 127, 130, 168–9
Higher Education Statistics Agency
    (HESA) 120, 128, 131
Hogan, A. 85
Holmwood, J. 18
Hope University 177–8
Huang, I. Y. 124
Hulme, M. 168
humanity 179, 187
hybrid professionalism 11, 16, 160, 167

imagination 37
inequality 78, 201–3
Initial Teacher Education (ITE) 165, 168,
    170–1
Initial Teacher Training (ITT) 165
interconnectivity 30
interdisciplinary problem solving 178,
    181–6, 191
international admissions standards 126–9
international higher education 119–20, 136
internationalization 117–19, 121–2,
    132–3, 135–7
international student recruitment 117–19
    agents 123–5
    inequity of 119–20
    institutional survival 121–3
    pedagogy 132–5
    pre-sessional courses 129–31
    private providers 131–2
Ion, G. 49

Jarratt Report 149, 200
jurisdiction 3–8, 10, 12, 15, 17, 163, 168, 198
justice 26, 28, 31, 191

Karseth, B. 43
Kenney, M. 76
Key Performance Indicators (KPIs) 150–1
Kidd, I. J. 65–6
Kimber, M. 73
Kitcher, P. 65
Knights, D. 82
knowledgeability 186
knowledge ecosystem 31
Knowledge Exchange Framework (KEF) 96
knowledge production 2–3, 8, 15–16, 41–2, 55, 58, 63–6
Knowles, C. 80
Kolsaker, A. 43
Kuznets, S. 202

learning ecosystem 31
Lomer, S. 17
Louis XIV, King 145, 147, 151
Louis XVI, King 141
Loveday, V. 16
Lucas, L. 41
luck 74, 78–81, 87–8
  and chance 78
  and power 78
  and success 77–81
Lukes, S. 78
Lund, R. 57
Lybeck, E. 17, 143
Lyotard, J. 35

Maclean, K. 82
Macpherson, C. B. 196–7, 199, 201
Magatti, M. 13
managerialism 36, 121, 161
mandarins. *See* German mandarins
marketization 73, 119–21, 123, 128, 142, 177, 196, 199
Maslow, A. H. 51
mathematics 183, 186–8
Maxwell, J. C. 63
Menter, I. 168
Mercer, J. 76
Merton, R. K. 108
metrics 107–11
  performance 96–107
  TEF 96
metrics-based evaluation systems 93–5, 97, 106, 111
Miller, N. 82

Mintrom, M. 41
monodisciplinary problem solving 183, 185
Moon, B. 164, 167
Morgan, D. 82
Müller, R. 76
multidisciplinary team 183, 186

natural environment ecosystem 31
Necker, J. 141
neoliberal/neoliberalism/neoliberalizing 12, 14, 34, 73–4, 84, 86–7, 88 n.1, 133, 149, 164–5
  governmentality 12, 83
  knowledge 196, 198–9, 203
Nerland, M. 43
networked complexity 42
New Power University 161
Nietzsche, F. 37
Nixon, J. 2
Noordegraaf, M. 43, 45, 160
Norbert Elias and the Sociology of Education (Lybeck) 143

organizational control 9, 15
O'Siochru, C. 16

Parsons, J. 195, 197
Pearson, W. S. 130
peer-to-peer interview 76
performance management 5, 33, 37, 149
performance metrics 96–107
persons ecosystem 31
Piketty, T. 202
politicization 203
polity ecosystem 31
post-critical approach 12–14
Postgraduate Certificate in Education (PGCE) 165
Postgraduate Diploma in Education (PGDE) 165
Postgraduate Taught (PGT) 127, 132
pre-sessional courses 129–32
private pathway providers 131–2
problem-solving approach 181–6
professional/professionalism 10, 34, 159–61
  demanded 44
  education 7, 17, 157–62, 164–5, 167, 171–2

enacted 44
entanglement 159
'ism' in 34
pressured 41, 44–5, 49–56, 58, 62, 64, 66
trends 8–11
workers 188–9
professor 46, 50–6
professorial academic leadership 45–7, 49–51, 54, 56, 63, 67
proletarianization 24, 190
pro-vice-chancellors (PVCs) 151
public good 11, 18, 25, 65, 177–9, 187–8, 190–1, 201
public spending 202
pure mathematics 186–7

Qualified Teacher Status (QTS) 165
qualitative and quantitative data analysis 49

radical relationality 23–4
reflective practitioner 160
Reith, G. 78, 81
Research Assessment Exercise (RAE) 149–50
Research Excellence Framework (REF) 6, 51, 56, 59, 68 n.4, 80, 96–7, 100, 108, 177
responsibility 34–5
Richardson, L. 142
Ringer, F. 105
Roth, W. -M. 182, 187
royal mechanism 144
Royal Society for the Encouragement of Arts, Manufacture and Commerce (RSA) 170–1
Russell Group 119, 122, 125, 128–9, 149, 199

Scanlon, L. 42
scholarship 5, 12, 15, 37, 42, 67, 122–3, 127, 132, 187–9
Scholasticism 36
Schon, D. A. 160
School University Partnership Initiative (SUPI) 162–3
Science, Technology, Engineering, Mathematics and Medicine (STEMM) 47, 51–3, 58–61, 66
scientific establishments 6

Šešelja, J. 62–3
Simard, S. 184
Smelser, N. J. 4, 143
Smith, M. 77
social contract 152–4
social existence 64, 144
social generativity (SG) 13–14
social institutions ecosystem 31
socially generative action (SGA) 13–14
Soysal, Y. N. 63–4
Stiegler, B. 37
Straßer, C. 62–3
Strübing, J. 76
structural accretion 4, 143
Sullivan, T. A. 67
supercomplexity 27–9
superstar individual 86–7
Švarc, J. 42–3
SWOT analysis 150

Tannock, S. 129
Taylor, C. 36
teacher education 158, 160, 162–72
Teacher Training Agency (TTA) 166
Teaching and Learning Research Programme (TLRP) 168
Teaching Excellence Framework (TEF) 96, 99, 108, 177
Teasdale, N. 68 n.2
third space professional 161
Tienari, J. 57
travelling policy 168–9

uncertainty 28–9, 42–3, 49–50, 74, 78, 84–5, 128, 130, 136, 144, 149, 162
The United Kingdom
    higher education 15, 73, 75, 77, 86, 129, 133, 171, 197–8
    teacher education in 163–71
Universities and Colleges Union (UCU) 190
Universities' Council for the Education of Teachers (UCET) 167
Universities Superannuation Scheme (USS) 4, 17, 141–2, 147, 152, 154 n.1
Universities UK (UUK) 142, 152–3, 154 n.1
university
    challenges 160–3
    functions of 179–81
    management 147–52

problem-solving approach 181–6
revolution 1, 5
University College Union (UCU) 141, 149, 154 n.1, 190
use value 177–8, 180–1, 185, 187–9, 191–2

van Houtum, H. 66
van Uden, A. 66
Veblen, T. 157–8
vice-chancellor's (VC) 149–53
vigilance 37

Wales 169–71
Weber, M. 195
Wellmon, C. 4
whistle-blower 33–5
Whitchurch, C. 161
Wilensky, H. L. 159
Williams, J. 18, 180, 182
Woodman, D. 85

young followers 98–100, 102–3, 109–10

www.ingramcontent.com/pod-product-compliance
Lightning Source LLC
Chambersburg PA
CBHW062224300426
44115CB00012BA/2209